YOUTH IN SOCIETY

Youth in Society

The Construction and Deconstruction of Youth in East and West Europe

Claire Wallace

Professor of Social Research
University of Derby
and
Researcher
Institute of Advanced Studies
Vienna

and

Sijka Kovatcheva

Assistant Professor of Sociology
University of Plovdiv
Bulgaria

First published in Great Britain 1998 by
MACMILLAN PRESS LTD
Houndmills, Basingstoke, Hampshire RG21 6XS and London
Companies and representatives throughout the world

A catalogue record for this book is available from the British Library.

ISBN 0–333–65225–8

 First published in the United States of America 1998 by
ST. MARTIN'S PRESS, INC.,
Scholarly and Reference Division,
175 Fifth Avenue, New York, N.Y. 10010

ISBN 0–312–21551–7

Library of Congress Cataloging-in-Publication Data
Wallace, Claire.
Youth in society : the construction and deconstruction of youth in
East and West Europe / Claire Wallace and Sijka Kovatcheva.
p.   cm.
Includes bibliographical references and index.
ISBN 0–312–21551–7 (cloth)
1. Youth—Europe—Social conditions.   I. Kovatcheva, Sijka.
II. Title.
HQ799.E9W35   1998
305.235'094—DC21   98–17285
                                                CIP

This book is printed on paper suitable for recycling and made from fully managed and sustained forest sources.

10   9   8   7   6   5   4   3   2   1
07   06   05   04   03   02   01   00   99   98

Printed and bound in Great Britain by
Antony Rowe Ltd, Chippenham, Wiltshire

Contents

List of Tables

List of Figures

All the world's a stage,
And all the men and women merely players:
They have their exits and their entrances;
And one man in his time plays many parts,
His acts being seven ages. . . .
And then the whining school-boy with his satchel,
And shining morning face, creeping like snail
Unwillingly to school. And then the lover,
Sighing like furnace, with a woeful ballad
Made to his mistress' eyebrow. Then a soldier,
Full of strange oaths, and bearded like the pard,
Jealous in honour, sudden and quick in quarrel,
Seeking the bubble reputation
Even in the cannon's mouth. . . .

William Shakespeare, *As You Like It*, II, vii

Generation X means a lot of things to a lot of people. We are a culture, a demographic, an outlook, a style, an economy, a scene, a political ideology, an aesthetic, an age, a decade and a literature.

(Rushkoff 1994: 3)

Preface

This book was produced by two people with very different experiences of growing up – one in 'communist' Bulgaria and one in 'capitalist' Britain – sharing their ideas. We first met at the Central European University in Prague, an institution funded by George Soros, and intended to bring together the new generation of young academics from Eastern and Western Europe to explore contemporary social issues and problems. We are grateful to Mr Soros's visionary initiatives and to the Central European University for making this endeavour possible.

The book began in 1987 as a text about youth, drawing mainly upon experiences of Britain but bringing in some European comparative material as was becoming increasingly desirable in a more 'Euro-conscious' contemporary world. However, the immediate problem was the lack of comparative materials upon which to draw. The Eurostat statistics indicate some very general trends but are often limited in scope and mainly cover Western Europe. The few books dealing with youth in Europe do so by juxtaposing different chapters on each country by different authors. Each author tends to give their own perspective and it is not always clear if this reflects only their preoccupations or real differences in the experiences of young people. In the meantime, some excellent general texts about youth in Britain were written (see for example the work of Bob Coles, Phil Cohen, Christine Griffin, Joanna Wyn and Rob White, Andy Furlong and Fred Cartmel) which made a further text about Britain redundant, but a text about youth in Europe even more important. However, Europe is a very diversified place and it is difficult to have the instinctive, in-depth knowledge or *verstehen* to make sense of what is happening in each country. Therefore, we have concentrated upon those countries which we know best from research and personal experience – Germany, Britain, Austria, Bulgaria, Poland, the Czech Republic and Ukraine – whilst trying to draw general comparisons with other countries where possible.

Then Europe itself changed. The European Community expanded from 12 to 15 countries and became the European Union. The developments in Eastern and Central Europe which surrounded us, expanded what we think of as 'Europe' still further and made whole new dimensions of comparison possible, drawing upon the rich reservoir of material gathered about youth in Communist countries. However, material of an appropriate kind was not always easy to find and involved considerable detective work. We wrote the book during visits to Prague, Vienna and Plovdiv, most of it whilst sitting in the seclusion of Sijka's parents' small flat in Plovdiv. We discussed chapters through faxes, and exchanging diskettes and later e-mail messages.

During some phases we were hampered by problems with the technology of communication (no up-to-date computers in Plovdiv, no cassettes for the printer). In addition, Sijka Kovatcheva had to struggle with the adverse conditions common to many academics in post-communist countries who are either unable to find academic posts in the newly slashed and cash-strapped universities and research institutes or are unable to live from their salaries when they do find a job. This means a constant search for additional jobs and grants to supplement income. However, one of the major obstacles was the disappearance of the Youth Institute in Bulgaria and other countries after 1990 (this had conducted most of the surveys to date) and, more importantly, the extensive library of the Institute which seems to have either disappeared or to be unavailable for public use. Reports had to be tracked down through personal contacts and this often proved time-consuming and difficult.

In order to achieve the publisher's target of 80 000 words, many things had to be cut. This book does not therefore aim to cover youth issues in any comprehensive way and we had to make some tough decisions about what had to be left out.

Many people have helped in the production of this book. Special thanks must go to Alexander, Sijka's spouse, who patiently drove us to the airport each time, took care of the technical and domestic infrastructure and endured endless conversations about the book in English. Next, we must thank all those people who read and commented upon early drafts – in particular, Peter Lentini, Ken Roberts, Roger Sapsford, Pamela Abbott, Mary Shaw, Jaroslava Stastna, Lynn Hayes, Paul White, John Bynner and others – especially the anonymous reader who made very detailed comments upon the earlier version of the text. Viktoras Radusis provided computing and technical support. In addition I must thank colleagues at the German Youth Institute for help which they provided and the DAAD (Deutsches Akademischer Austauschdienst) for funding. We would also like to thank Christian Haerpfer for his support.

The Institute for Advanced Studies in Vienna provided a research-friendly environment which made the completion of the book possible.

We would like to dedicate this book to Lore and Jordana whose youth was sacrificed to building brave new worlds in different parts of Europe and to Danny and Pepi who we hope will have a more unconstrained youth.

1 Introduction: Towards an Understanding of Youth in Europe

Europe is a very large and diverse region. There are about 350 million people in Western (European Union) Europe, of whom 14 per cent are aged 15–24 and a further 200 million people in Eastern (former communist) Europe (Eurostat 1993b). The collapse of the Iron Curtain in 1989 and the expanding role of the European Union in both Western and Eastern Europe has prompted some to ask: what is Europe? (Rose 1996). Although Europe is divided by politics, religion, culture, climate and a host of other factors, it is possible to identify some common trends in the construction of youth. Eastern and western European countries are characterized by highly developed industrial societies, with a generally high standard of living and extensively elaborated welfare states and this gives them common features in comparison with other parts of the world. The identification of youth as a social category and as a target for various kinds of interventions is also a product of the European experience, to the extent that 'youth' is not only a product of advanced industrial economies, but particular kinds of advanced societies. The project of writing a book about youth in Europe therefore makes some sense, especially when the Cold War division of Europe has gone and deepening of ties within the European Union, the harmonization of policies and common social trends make comparisons important. However, such a book cannot hope to do justice to the diversity of regional developments and state systems within Europe. Therefore, we have concentrated particularly upon certain countries where we have personal and research experience: Britain, Germany, Austria, Bulgaria, the Czech Republic, Poland and Ukraine.[1] We have referred to broad regions of Europe which these countries could be used to represent – whilst Eastern Europe usually refers to the former communist countries, it now represents the former Soviet Union, Central Europe spans the former Cold War divide in the middle and South Eastern Europe covers both former communist and non-communist Balkan countries. Where

1

possible we have drawn upon other studies and European-level data to show the more general trends and the contrasting experiences of other European regions.

The general argument which we develop in the book is about the way in which age relations in general and youth in particular are socially constructed as a phenomenon of modern European societies and this thesis could also be applied to other European societies which we have not covered to any extent here. The general tendency to *construct* youth as a social category can be found with modernization and is accompanied by a tendency to *deconstruct* youth in the process of postmodernization. However, these phases do not follow one another – rather, they interact. At the end of the twentieth century affluent and advanced European societies also contain a large and rising number of economically and socially excluded youth who suffer disproportionately from unemployment, homelessness and criminalization at the same time as they are one of the most privileged generations in history.

What other trends are common to European societies? Here we can list some general features which will be further developed later in the book:

- the fall in the number of young people following previous falls in the birth rate
- the expansion of education and training
- the increased participation of young women in education and in the labour market
- the contraction of the formal youth labour market (but increase in casual and informal jobs)
- the rise in youth unemployment
- the spread of youth cultures
- the postponement of marriage and childbearing
- new forms of household organization including living alone, co-habiting, single parenthood
- the over-representation of young people in crime, drug use and suicide
- increasing longevity

These themes are explored throughout the book. They mean that young people are more and more likely to be found in education or training rather than in work and that the period of transition – into families, into an independent household, into full time work – has been extended in the last three decades. A discussion has developed in most countries in recent years about what social policies are most appropriate for these large numbers of people who are not quite children and not quite adults but somewhere in limbo in between. Furthermore, it is not even very clear where childhood ends, as adult culture and behaviour extends to incorporate younger and younger age groups on the one hand; neither is it clear on the other hand where youth ends as the markers of adult citizenship in terms of a job and an independent household are postponed or remote for large numbers of young people. This blurring of the age boundaries is discernible not only in the case of young people – at the other end of the age spectrum there are arguments both for early retirement and for the postponement of the age of retirement as older people expect to live active lives for longer. This results in a new alignment in the relationship between generations, and a new 'generational contract' especially as contributors to and beneficiaries of hard pressed welfare budgets. The meanings of 'young' and 'old' become more relative and individual. A reassessment of age-relations in Europe is therefore required and here we begin by looking at young people, although 'young' is a relative concept and makes sense only in contrast to other age groups (Wyn and White 1997). We can therefore pose the question 'What is youth'? Our argument is that this needs to be seen in terms of a long historical perspective in order to understand how age-relations were first of all shaped by modern societies and then continually reshaped and at the same time de-structured.

This is then the general theme of the book. In the remainder of the introduction we shall develop our general argument further and then consider this in relation to sources of diversity and difference in Europe. Finally, we shall consider some of the other theories of 'youth' and generational relations in order to better delineate our own perspective.

MODERNITY AND POSTMODERNITY

The classical sociological theorists struggled to understand and explain the changes they witnessed in the nineteenth century as upheavals associated with the birth of modern society brought about a new social world, one which was different from the traditional, feudal or peasant societies which had existed in Europe previously. Whilst Marx emphasized the forces of the economy as the motor of change,

Weber and Durkheim stressed more culture, beliefs, society and
the growth of rationality as a principle of organization. Features
of this society which they (and those who followed later) described
were those of industrialization, urbanization and the creation of
mass society – large classes and interest groups based upon their
relationship to the means of production and their position in the
labour market. In this competitive world, universalistic and achievement oriented roles replaced those based upon kinship and tradition. The creation of universal education systems, compulsory up
to a given age, also tended to follow upon industrialization in most
parts of the world. Political parties, trades unions and formal associations represented these groups. Mass media and leisure industries entertained people, as time was divided between 'work' (normally
outside of the home) and 'leisure'. The growth of state systems
was reflected in the creation of large bureaucracies which increasingly intervened in society and the post-Second World War period
was characterized at first by the dominance of Keynesian models
of managing the economy, which provided the rationale for more
comprehensive welfare provision. These changes, their impacts and
the attempts by social theorists to account for them have been well
documented (see Giddens 1971). However, more recent social theorists have tended also to emphasize the 'enlightenment project'
of science and social improvement through the application of rational
principles of understanding leading to the creation of 'grand theories' which attempt to explain human life and 'grand ideologies'
which attempt to change it (Kumar 1995, Bauman 1992). One of
the most far reaching of these in terms of its consequences was
Communism, which attempted to self-consciously construct a better and more modern society, based upon the scientific shaping of
social and productive forces. The collapse of Communism in Europe since 1989 illustrates perhaps the limitation of that project
(Kumar 1995).

During the last few decades we can also discern alternative tendencies in European and industrialized societies, ones which have
been termed 'postmodern' (Harvey 1989, Jameson 1991). Daniel
Bell (1973) and others first identified the move towards a 'post-
industrial' society but these were followed in the 1990s by descriptions of a culture shift towards 'post-materialist' values, ones which
preferred self-fulfilment and a search for the quality of life to the
Protestant work ethic and a concern with survival (Inglehart 1990).
It was argued that culture and communications were supplanting

production as the motors of change (Lash 1990) leading to the study of consumption and taste as ways of defining social groups (Bourdieu 1986, Lury 1996, Featherstone 1991). Changes in the organization of production itself were also visible, beginning in the 1970s with the 'de-industrialization' of some Western European societies involving the closure of traditional manufacturing and extractive industries such as mining, steel production and ship-building or their transfer to developing countries and more recently to Eastern Europe. This leads to spatial realignments with the decline of the traditional industrial areas and disappearance of jobs in those areas, but also to the rise and expansion of new areas based upon information, communications and service sector employment (Lash and Urry 1987). Not all of these jobs are highly skilled – there is also a demand for a casual workforce, often young people and foreigners, to serve in the various service industries and the people who work in them (Sassen 1991). Mass production is being replaced by organizations linked by communications media, employing fewer people directly, and by more flexible patterns of work (Amin 1994). This is characterized by more extensive sub-contracting so that large hierarchies are broken up into specialized services and different functions, from accounting to cleaning, are franchised separately so that contracts can be swiftly terminated if the organization needs to rationalize. The corollary of this is that the old idea of training for one job for life has disappeared for ever larger numbers of people, and 'skill' becomes something provisional, in a constant state of change (Ainly 1993). Temporary and insecure employment, along with frequent redundancies or job change, once a hazard of the unskilled working class, is now more common at all social levels.

The continued expansion of the welfare state in Europe, a distinctive aspect of European capitalist societies in contrast to others in the world, also reached its end during the 1990s (earlier in some countries) as it consumed larger and larger shares of national budgets. Since the 1970s there has been a dismantling of European welfare states which includes creating 'quasi-market' systems (Le Grand and Bartlett 1993), through the privatization of selected services and through sub-contracting functions to the private or non-governmental sector (Burrows and Loader 1994). As in industry, contracting, outsourcing, privatization – or just neglect – have replaced a comprehensive model of welfare associated with Keynesian economic management and large bureaucracies (Flyn forthcoming). In post-Communist Europe the same changes have happened even more rapidly as states have been forced to retreat from the formerly comprehensive social coverage due to acute financial crisis compounded by rising unemployment and inflation. The fashion for privatization was introduced into these countries as well. The result is that citizens are increasingly left to find their own resources and organize their own paths through life in an 'individualized' way which is 'privatization' in another sense – removing the problem from public recognition and turning it into something outside of state intervention. Some have pointed to 'postmodern' tendencies as the delivery of benefits is targeted upon more and more specialized groups, in response to specialized campaigns, reflecting the increased recognition of 'difference' (Penna and O'Brien 1996).

Politics itself moved from the representation of mass interests to more specialized groups and the increasing disconnection of parties from their class bases (Haerpfer 1994). 'New social movements' based upon gender, race, sexuality and environment mobilized people and the postmodern discussion and recognition of 'difference' helped to create a new 'identity politics' (Anthias and Yuval-Davis 1993).

Modernity was associated with the need to divide people into strongly distinguished groups and with the elaboration of theories to sustain and justify this division. Hence, for example, Zygmunt Bauman (1989) argued that the scientific idea of 'race' was a product of modernization and the desire to classify people and to put them into hierarchies. Its consequences were the ordering of societies according to these classificatory principles and the forcible destruction or segregation of some people who were so classified: the holocaust and apartheid. The scale and rational efficiency of modern societies made it possible to carry out such large scale selection and destruction. Others have argued that there was likewise a tendency to create 'essentialist' categories of gender – that is, categories of men and women which are based upon 'natural' and necessary distinguishing features, which are rooted in biology, psychology, sex and from which a whole range of other characteristics follow which explain social differentiation as well (Abbott and Wallace 1997). We will argue here that within modernity 'youth' was similarly constructed as an essential category. Postmodern writers have generally challenged this view, arguing that the construction of such categories is a social process open to critical analysis and that it is not possible to fix age or sex or race so easily (Butler 1990). Many have argued for a postmodern ethic of recognizing and tolerating a variety of sources of 'difference' instead (Bauman 1992). Thus gender and age become uncertain and mutable divisions instead of fixed and taken for granted.

Other social theorists attempting to understand and analyse these changes taking place at the end of the twentieth century have insisted that they represent a continuation of the modernization process rather than a radical break (Beck 1986). This has been the dominant tradition in the German-speaking countries and Giddens (1991) terms this 'high modernity'. Beck (1986) in his analysis of what is termed 'late modernity' argues that the collective identification associated with class and other mass interests has dissolved or become weaker. Instead, there is a 'risk society': one in which roles and relations have become increasingly uncertain and one where people are threatened by science (from nuclear destruction to mad cows) rather than able to use science to control the world. He and others also identify a process of 'individualization' by which they mean that people are increasingly responsible for charting their own course through an uncertain world. It seems to us that 'late modernists' and 'post modernists' are often describing similar kinds of social changes but with a different emphasis.

A feature of late-twentieth century society which is underemphasized or ignored altogether in these accounts of social change is that the general changes in production and de-industrialization have created new categories of people who are losers. The former workforce and their offspring left behind by the changing tides of capitalist development form a majority in some parts of Europe where the prospect of regular work for many people has disappeared. They are no longer the working class as they are not working (at least not regularly) and have to manage in the informal economy to make ends meet. Others who lose out are women heading families, elderly people, young people unable to gain entry to the workforce or to housing markets, some ethnic groups and people without official citizenship. The dismantling of welfare states has left people additionally vulnerable as benefits are cut or increasingly narrowed in focus. Of course, the welfare states of Europe will not disappear. But they are unable to protect people from misfortunes in any comprehensive way and, being built upon outdated 'modern' principles of full employment, an insured workforce and stable nuclear families, they are increasingly incapable of coping with the changes described here. This means that problems have been 'individualized' and 'privatized' in the sense that it is for people to find their own solutions to the problems that confront them. This tendency was assisted by the influence of 'new right' ideologies in some countries in the 1980s (Abbott and Wallace 1992) but now the same strategies are introduced by more traditional conservative and even socialist or labour governments. It is difficult to know how to characterize these new and old forms of disadvantage and the term 'social exclusion', although rather imprecise, helps us to conceptualize multiple forms of disadvantage. 'Social exclusion' also helps us to include a range of forms of difference which *can* become disadvantages, including (dis)ability, ethnicity, homelessness, old age, sexuality and so on, but *need not* be so.

Eastern European societies were modernized rapidly and forcefully under communism.[2] Industrialization, urbanization and the creation of centralized state hierarchies followed, often with tremendous sacrifices in terms of hard working and living conditions, damage to the environment and the elimination of those who opposed it. G. Dimitrov (1995) argues that the 'catastrophe' of socialist modernization permanently crippled Bulgarian society to the extent that it is very difficult to construct a genuine civil society now. The collapse of communism was also the end of the experiment to scientifically shape society and the postmodern chaos which emerged has in turn had many impacts upon Western Europe. Tendencies towards de-industrialization, liberalization and the rationalization of industry in Western Europe have been accelerated by competition with cheaper eastern producers. Tendencies towards nationalism and racism are seen in both parts of Europe along with rising crime, rising drug use (using routes through Eastern Europe) and rising unemployment. On the other hand, trends discerned in Western Europe appeared in Eastern Europe in an almost exaggerated form. Eastern Europe became once more an experimental laboratory for prominent theories – this time theories of privatization, monetarism and rolling back the state.

Postmodernism is usually associated with social theories. These theories reject overarching and rationalistic explanations of society in favour of critical theories aiming to 'deconstruct' rather than construct explanations. These theories at their most extreme end in relativist positions which make social science itself (as a rational enlightenment philosophy) impossible (Gellner 1996). Whilst we would adopt a postmodernist 'scepticism of metanarratives' in the words of Lyotard (1984) we would not subscribe to theoretical postmodernism. Rather, we use the concept to describe aspects of social change which seem to us to be in contrast to the general tendencies within modernization described by classical social theory. However, we are not arguing that postmodernity followed modernity as an historical stage – modernity is still very much with us, we do not live in a 'postmodernity'. Rather, we are arguing that aspects of postmodernization are *tendencies* within contemporary European societies (Jameson 1991, Harvey 1989, Kumar 1995, Inglehart 1997). Nor do we argue that modernization (or postmodernization) are linear developments leading to convergence in societies as the earlier modernization theorists argued (see Bryant and Mockrzycki 1994). Quite the contrary, we illustrate the divergent models of modernization within Europe with often quite different consequences for family, gender roles and work and we assume that if one looks around the world one could find even more different examples.

Some general tendencies associated with late modernity and postmodernity are set out in Table 1.1. In the remainder of the chapter we turn to how these ideas can be applied to the study of youth.

YOUTH AND MODERNITY

As we grow through the life course our bodies and our minds change. However, age relations are a social construct, because the significance which this has in any society depends upon the social, economic and political order in that society. Any individual experience of growing up or growing old is therefore shaped by these beliefs and assumptions, and by the rights and duties which a society or a state expects of a person. There are also important variations *within* any society since, for example, someone may be seen as 'too old' to get married/have sex/smoke/vote etc. by one social group, but 'too young' by another. Heterosexual sex, for example, is allowed at an earlier age than homosexual sex in many countries. Thus notions of young and old – although they may seem self-evident and 'natural' – are socially relative.

Sociologists have argued, therefore, that youth is a social construct. But constructed of what? A broader look at Europe enables us to explore some of the different historical, social and political contexts from which youth has emerged. Ideas of 'youth' have had a long history and for many centuries there was speculation about

Table 1.1   Contrasts between modernity and late modernity/ postmodernity

Modernity	Late Modernity and Postmodernity
Industrialization	De-industrialization, growth of information and service industries
Urbanization	More flexible locations connected with communications networks
Achievement orientation and 'Protestant work ethic'	Post-materialist values of self-fulfilment and leisure ethic
Social groups based upon relation to means of production or labour market	Social groups based upon consumption and taste
	Also 'socially excluded' groups
Education systems tied to labour market	Extended education linked less to labour market
Mass consumption	Individualized consumption
Nuclear family	Fragmented family, negotiated roles
Political parties representing the interests of large social groups – workers, farmers, industry etc	New social movements addressing single issues such as the building of a motorway, also ecology, women's movement, gay and lesbian liberation etc.
Race as an essential, scientific category	Ethnic differentiation and post-colonialism
Essentially based male/female gender roles	Gender and sexual differentiation.
	Flexible roles
Welfare state protecting people from 'cradle to grave'	Fragmented and contracted welfare services, individualized self-help

the 'ages of man' (sic) as we see from the quotation from Shakespeare at the beginning of this book, but we also see that youth was a masculine concept. This meaning is still implicit in the term 'youth'. However, youth was associated with states of mind, of passion and love, rather than with precisely calibrated ages. 'Adolescence' or 'youth' as a social category in the sense in which we use it here is a product of modernity – that is of the development of the modern world associated with professional bureaucratic power, industrial society and enlightenment rationality. In the words of

Musgrove (1964), adolescence appeared at about the same time as the internal combustion engine. Individuals mature at different rates and in different ways, but modernity has imposed more uniform categories of life stage and attached these to chronological age. In fact, childhood, adolescence and 'youth', along with what is now termed 'post-adolescence' or 'young adulthood', have all emerged as separate life-stages in the course of modernization (Klein 1990). Life stages are therefore historically relative rather than universal in character and they also vary between different state regimes in different parts of Europe as we shall show in this book.

Why does 'youth' emerge from modernity? A number of factors seem relevant. First of all, the development of wage labour and a labour market, depending increasingly upon universalistic achievement-oriented principles, replaced the familial transmission of property as a source of subsistence. Then the development of universal education introduced a system for distinguishing unsocialized children from fully socialized adults able to compete in the labour market and societies with increasingly complex divisions of labour. At the intersection of these two institutions lies youth. The extension of the franchise also led to a definition of who should be accepted as a fully socialized citizen able to exercise a political choice – gradually this was defined by age. In the 'modern' family too, roles of age and sex are defined by the external relationship to the labour market and the education/state systems. Modernization therefore helped to define youth as a social category between education and work, between unsocialized childhood and fully socialized adulthood. Modernization also introduced a certain amount of self-determination in youth as an earned income introduced access to housing, consumer markets and an independent life-style. Partnerships leading to the nuclear conjugal family could be based upon 'choice' or 'romantic love' irrespective of property ownership. Social and cultural independence along with urbanization was made possible through the creation of space in urban areas where young people could congregate outside traditional forms of social control. The formation of peer groups as mediums for creating age-status groups helped young people to create their own communities of interest and, later on, consumer culture, popular music and youth sub-cultures spread these communities further and further afield.

However, most important has been the development of the modern state system with bureaucratic mechanisms, increasing rationalization and the capacity to grade, sort, control, punish, mobilize and put under surveillance those it defines as its population. One rational form of classification used by the state is that of numerical age. The systems of social support have been uneven in recognizing the self-determination of youth but in most advanced industrial societies there gradually evolved a system of social support for students, young unemployed and trainees, which allowed them to develop a measure of autonomy and independence. Youth came to be increasingly recognized as part of the development of welfare states. Thus, with the modern state 'citizenship' comes to determine membership and access to social goods such as income support, education, training and political participation – all determined increasingly according to numerical age (Jones and Wallace 1992). The date of birth becomes an essential item of information on all forms and documents as a way of locating a person.

This is linked to the sense of time which developed with modernity. Time seen as a progression, a linear march through history, created a sense of continuity. Time divided into parcels by which to measure the hours of the day, the days of the month and the months of the year has transformed notions of work and social life (Lash and Urry 1994). With modernity, social life was divided according to 'working time' and 'leisure time' and even these units were ever more discretely divided for the better control and utilization of time as a resource: time is ever more efficiently measured and used. Life regulated by the clock implies a different kind of living to one regulated by the seasons or by the weather. Similarly, the life course as measured by calibrated units of time becomes a different entity to one patterned by the rhythm of cycles of birth, inheritance and death. Thus the life course starts to be measured in chronological units of time rather than by natural phenomena or seasons. As people's lives are removed ever further from dependency upon natural events, so the life course becomes increasingly a subject of rational control. In this way people's lives can be sectioned and structured according to human institutions and accurately measurable units of time: at 6 a person starts school, at 16 they are allowed to have sex and at 18 they are able to vote (which has nothing to do with either their levels of maturity or their inclinations!). The life course becomes a progressional path punctuated by these discrete stages. Whether a person is 'young' or 'old' has less to do with the biological process of ageing so much as with their relation to these age-status transitions: 13 is 'too young' to have a baby (although women obviously do have babies at this age) because it is before the age of consent and marriage. Similarly, 70 is 'too old' to work because it is after the age of retirement (although people obviously do work at this age). People move from one stage to the other in seemingly purposeful movement and this constitutes their life. Zygmunt Bauman (1995) likens it to a 'pilgrimage'. However, we need to bear in mind that such age-phases are socially constructed and therefore relative to different societies at different points in time.

There were different roads towards modernity in different parts of Europe. These have implied different kinds of state development with different welfare systems forming an integral part. Britain, one of the first countries to be industrialized, evolved a modern state over the last three centuries. However, measures aimed explicitly at youth have been fairly recent (since the twentieth century and mostly since 1944), piecemeal and not greatly institutionalized. Germany modernized with more rapid intensity at the end of the nineteenth century and, following the unification of the country, there was a desire to build social cohesion through legislation. The result was that youth were targeted more specifically than in England. Universal education was introduced in the Austrian lands before either of these two countries, and prior to industrialization, by the 'enlightened' monarch, Maria Theresa, in the eighteenth century. In Southern Europe, many of the trends described as being associated with modernization and youth have only just started to happen and, until the last decades, gender and generational roles based upon traditional patriarchal authority were more the norm, with women and youth being subordinated, contained within the private sphere (Chisholm et al. 1995). In other parts of Europe, where modernization came later, such as Hungary, Slovakia, Poland and Bulgaria, it took place at a forced pace through communism after the Second World War. Women and youth were brought out of the home and installed in the public sphere of the workplace, education system and political organization. The effects of war, invasion and the imposition of totalizing ideologies such as fascism or communism have affected most European countries and some are still recovering from this experience, especially those in Eastern and Central Europe. The way in which modern states develop affects in turn the nature of their welfare legislation and therefore the way in which 'youth' is constructed.

We have used the term 'modernity' and 'modernization' because it encompasses all these developments and because it can be used to describe Eastern Europe under communist regimes as well as Western Europe under welfare capitalist ones. It is no longer possible to speak of 'capitalist industrial society' as if there was only one kind. Rather, modernization can include a range of processes with diverse results (Bryant and Mokrzycki 1994). Nor is modernization a one-way march of progress. In some regions of East-Central Europe, such as the Czech Republic, communist modernization arrested the development of a diversified economy, imposing nineteenth century styles of centralized, heavy industry. In Bulgaria, post-communist modernization in agriculture over the last eight years has replaced the collectively-owned tractor with the privately-owned horse and cart. Other developments follow the socio-cultural traditions of the region and therefore modernization is not a uniform phenomenon. New forms of social relations are continually thrown up and reshaped. Whilst we are mainly concerned with generational relations in this book through the perspective of youth, this inevitably draws upon other kinds of social relations such as gender, region, ethnicity and nation. What it means to be young and female in Greece, for example, can be very different to Denmark. Thus we need to simultaneously grasp processes of continuation and processes of change (Chisholm et al. 1995, CYRCE 1995).

In the study of youth, evidence of postmodernization can be found in the way age-status is becoming de-standardized or eroded. Youth is extended downwards into childhood through participation in consumer markets which introduce young people earlier into adult consumption and through communications technologies such as TV which destroy the innocence of childhood by giving children access to the adult media world (Postman 1983). The commercialization of popular culture means that children are encouraged to become consumers and to consume adult products as something exciting and sophisticated. Youth is also extended upwards into older age groups as periods in education and training are extended, encouraging people to experiment with life-styles, sub-cultures and identities for longer periods of time. Thus it is not clear where youth ends and adulthood begins, as standardized age transitions – such as getting qualified, starting work, getting married, starting a family – have all become diluted and unclear. They are more likely to happen in no particular order and are reversible at all stages (Olk 1988, Wallace 1987). The age-status transitions which were connected together under some conditions of modernity now start to become disconnected and our sense of time becomes more elastic.

This is reflected, for example, in the way in which we view the body. The use of fashion, styles, clothing, play and physical manipulation in the maintenance of the body (diet, exercise, plastic surgery) can all be used to defy biological processes of ageing (Featherstone and Hepworth 1991). Thus, the youthful body is as desirable as ever as the ideal, but unlike in Shakespeare's time, it no longer belongs only to the young! It is an aspiration for everyone. Youthful styles of behaviour such as falling in love, dancing, enjoying popular music and so on are also not necessarily confined to the young but can take place at any stage in life. Pop stars such as Tina Turner and Cher are more concerned to project a youthful, sexual body image than they were in their first incarnations 30 years ago.

'Postmodernist' and more recent social theories associated with the work of Bourdieu (1986) argue that, rather than inhabiting consistent and definable social strata, people are identified by their consumer tastes and interests. Diversification rather than mass consumption are emphasized. There has thus developed what some have termed a 'postmodern' trend in consumer styles based upon information culture and telecommunications, and here young people have been prominent. This has helped to create what Douglas Coupland termed 'Generation X', a generation of young people defined more by what they are not than by what they are, who are self-conscious and 'reflexive' about their manipulation of styles and tastes, who are sceptical towards metanarratives, being no longer able to believe in the certainties of previous generations of youth, who do not expect firm job prospects or life chances but who 'sample' different parts of the world and different periods of history in order to construct identities, as they would try on a new set of clothes. Young people who have grown up in a world of advertising signs are able to manipulate and reinvent them as part of their own culture (see Rushkoff 1994). They are the over-educated and under-employed. These sub-cultures are now not associated with working youth so much as with youth in an extended state of transition and with the opportunity to experiment with life-styles, ideas and identities. The spread of leisure styles throughout Europe has certainly been noticeable. For youth in Eastern Europe, popular Western music and styles (such as jeans) were influential even before the fall of communism and represented a subversive appeal. It is partly through these consumer styles that youth is defined and define themselves as a group. Other aspects of youth culture also link together different youth in Europe, including the spread of sub-cultures such as skinheads or punks which we consider in Chapter 5.

The diversification of life-styles is reflected in changing family relationships and transitions in and out of life-stages. The diversity of family forms and means of entering them is associated with the de-coupling of family from labour market transitions. It is no longer necessary for a man to have a job in order to start a family. It is no longer necessary for a woman to give up work in order to raise children. She does not even need to be married in order to do so. This in turn leads to the possibility of challenging normative standards such as the institution of heterosexuality, or conventional gender relations, which are strongly reinforced in many countries not just through cultural conservatism but also through social policies in access to housing, custody of children and so on. Young people have been significant in making such challenges and it is through such generational renewal that social relations can be transformed, as we explore in Chapters 4 and 6. However, this diversification also includes an increasing polarization in fortunes between ex-cluded youth and others as their incomes have declined and access to jobs and homes becomes ever more remote in many parts of Europe, creating groups of young people existing on the margins of society (Carlen 1996, Coffield et al. 1986).

In all countries the period of youth has been growing longer. In Western Europe the trend has been for youth to become a more and more extended condition over the post-war period. A combi-nation of educational reforms, increased demand for higher and further education, the introduction of increased vocational train-ing and rising unemployment have served to create an increasingly extended 'moratorium' period between ending compulsory school-ing and starting full time work. The extent and pace of this varies between different countries – in Germany it was a discernible trend many years ago, whereas in Portugal it has only just started. In Central and Eastern Europe, too, the trend was well established. The success of the education system under communism raised as-pirations so that more groups wanted to obtain higher education and this was seen as an important route to mobility. In Bulgaria, for example, education was introduced to semi-literate populations after 1945 and by the 1990s a sizeable slice of the age cohort was in tertiary education. However, housing shortages and low incomes ensured that young people were dependent upon parents for very long periods, even after marriage and the arrival of children – they were often co-resident into their 30s. Their full economic independence was therefore a very long term goal.

As a consequence, the earned income of young people becomes less important and they become increasingly dependent instead upon families or upon systems of grants and social security. Some might view this optimistically, seeing it as a progressive development – rather than being thrown 'prematurely' into the labour market to sink or swim unaided, young people are being granted a longer period of orientation and assistance (Hartmann 1985, 1987). From this perspective young people appear to be better off than ever before because they have more choices, more opportunities and more assistance from parents and the state. They are better educated, better trained and more 'liberated' from traditional patriarchal familial authority than any other generation in history. Others see this more pessimistically as creating a loss of income and a rise in the numbers of unsupported youth leading also to a rise in crime, unemployment, homelessness and poverty (Coles 1995). Young people are no longer independent, but rather segregated into their own age-ghetto, excluded from adult responsibility. This, according to Musgrove (1964) leads to a kind of infantilization: young people act irresponsibly because they have no responsibilities. Thus, in some ways this is the most privileged generation of youth seen in historical perspective, with the best material and cultural opportunities ever but at the same time large numbers are marginalized from what was assumed in the past to be normal integration into dominant society. We explore this paradox throughout the book.

There has been a growth in youth leisure and welfare services over the last hundred years staffed increasingly by professional as well as volunteer workers. Linked to this is a growth in programmes for young people within the criminal justice system, signalling them as a group requiring special treatment. The expansion of these different services, encompassing every aspect of young people's lives and behaviour, is justified in terms of the need to help young people assume their place in an increasingly complex society and to assist them to adjust where they are thought to be having difficulties. All manner of professional guidance services help to 'manage' the transition from one life phase to another. In communist countries youth organizations performed this role, ensuring the almost complete surveillance of young people in their movement through life. However, the retreat of the welfare state and the fragmentation of its services have undermined some of these bases of professionalism (Banks 1994, 1996), as we explore in Chapter 2.

Various new kinds of expertise have developed: different and not necessarily consistent ideas of youth are constructed through the market and commercial media, the education system, the training system, the criminal justice system, youth services and youth organizations. We need also to consider the role which academic 'youth' research has had in creating a basis for intervention. On the one hand there is the possibility for more self-determination as young people define their own peer groups, their own tastes and styles and chart their own courses through an increasingly complex and confusing set of transitions; on the other hand they are increasingly subject to professional surveillance. In addition, young people also impose their own meanings and ideas upon the institutional structures which surround them.

In some countries youth have been targeted more specifically as objects of political or social intervention. Although this has not been the case for the most part in Britain, in Germany youth have been the object of social policies since the nineteenth century as they were thought to be a group which needed integrating into the modern state. Youth have been increasingly recognized as a category within all European welfare states over the last century (Jones and Wallace 1992). Youth policies have been institutionalized through Ministries of Youth in a number of countries (although this is usually combined with other ministries). In Germany the state sponsored 'Youth Institute' for research and policy development has played an important role in identifying youth issues and assisting state responses. In all communist countries, youth were targeted very explicitly and official youth organizations set up which young people were under pressure to join and which all young people were obliged to use, because these were the only youth organizations existing, with a monopoly over leisure facilities. In many communist countries, Youth Institutes were formed to investigate the problems of youth and in Bulgaria, for example, this became an important and influential body. The monitoring and co-option of youth was felt to be important for the future of the regime. However, with the collapse of communism the youth institutes, youth organizations and many of the facilities which they owned, have disappeared (or gone into decline). At a supra-national level, the European Union targets youth explicitly in a variety of programmes aimed at academic and other exchanges but also in terms of regional aid which has filtered into a wide variety of programmes for youth. The European Union, by encouraging the modernization of the more backward and rural parts of Europe such as southern Italy, Greece and Portugal, has encouraged an accelerated 'modernization' of the youth phase in those countries, bringing women and young people more into education, the labour market and into public recognition (Chisholm et al. 1995). Thus, youth is identified and targeted in different ways in different parts of Europe.

All over Europe there have been attempts to recruit young people to various causes and to see them as vehicles for social reform. Indeed, much of the post-war youth research agenda has been guided by the need to ensure that young people are fully incorporated as democratic citizens (Stafseng 1994). There has therefore been monitoring of young people's political attitudes in the fear that they were more inclined to join extreme political organizations. However, in capitalist countries the majority of young people have followed mainstream political parties or been uninterested in politics. Nevertheless there are certain so-called 'new social movements' which are associated particularly with young people, including the movements against nuclear power and military bases, the green movement, animal rights and other such issues, which tend to be outside of mainstream politics. The student movement of the 1960s branded the consciousness of a whole generation of intellectuals. In communist countries it was the political activity of young people in joining the 'gentle revolutions' which helped to topple the old regimes and now it is young people who are joining the nationalist and quasi-fascist organizations, taking politics once more into the streets. For this and other reasons it is important to address the issue of why under some circumstances youth become politically active. This we consider in more detail in Chapter 6.

DIVERSITY AND DIFFERENCE IN EUROPE

Despite the general trends in common through European countries, there remain distinct forms of inequality and difference. Here we can enumerate sources of variation which are further elaborated through the book:

- social class backgrounds
- gender

- sexuality
- ethnicity and 'race'
- citizenship status
- disability
- special educational needs
- institutional care backgrounds
- involvement in the criminal justice system
- region
- religion

Access to education, jobs and life chances all depend upon where one lives in Europe, as do the relative positions of young men and women (Chisholm and Bergeret 1991). Marked differences between urban and rural areas still persist in many parts of Europe and between the Mediterranean countries and the affluent North. Religion can shape different models of social welfare, different family expectations and different gender expectations as Europe is divided between Greek and other Orthodox, Protestant and Catholic Churches in the Christian faith, then Muslim and other non-Christian faiths.

Furthermore, there are marked disparities between different groups with those at the bottom of the education system and some ethnic minorities being most vulnerable to high unemployment, likely to find the worst jobs, the least likely to travel or enjoy leisure opportunities (Roberts, Campbell and Furlong 1990). In general the lower one goes down the educational system, the more accelerated are the life transitions. These differences appear to be increasing rather than decreasing in today's Europe where educational advantage is increasingly important in determining other life chances. Educational advantages or disadvantages are affected by the factors listed above (see Chapter 3).

Gender has been studied as a fundamental division amongst young people in Western Europe over the last 20 years and studies have consistently highlighted the disadvantages faced by young women in terms of career opportunities. Despite the increasing numbers of women in the labour force, women's careers are still broken by responsibility for childcare and the segments of the labour market which they enter are the worst paid with the least prospects. Women are also most likely to be in poverty at some point in their lives. Many of these issues have been discussed due to pressure from feminist research and politics. In many European countries feminist ideas, which may previously have been revolutionary, are now accepted by a wide range of women who would not identify themselves with feminism (Wilkinson and Mulgan 1995). The younger generation of women take as given such things as the right to financial independence, an education or a job.

In communist Europe, women were obliged to work and there is still a far higher rate of female participation in the workforce than in Western Europe. Women also had the obligation to care for families, often under very difficult conditions, which involved hours of queuing and seeking comestibles with little in the way of domestic labour-saving equipment (Corrin 1992). Older women bear the brunt of the changes which have taken place in post-communist societies and still lead lives of hard manual labour caring for animals, growing food for the household in their gardens and managing the household budget – often for children and grandchildren as well (Wallace 1997). Meanwhile, a younger generation of women have rejected the serious, coarse, work-oriented images of the socialist woman and have turned towards more glamorous and playful role models. Childbearing and household formation is being postponed. New femininities are being constructed in such circumstances from different cultural materials. In the past, the token representation of women was ensured through quotas in formal political organizations. However, this was little valued in practice. The private sphere was in reality more valued and here women had an important role. Now women have lost even their token representation in the public sphere whilst the private sphere has been devalued in importance (Watson 1993). New problems have joined the old ones in affecting women, such as the lack of adequate contraceptive facilities, increasing restrictions on abortion in some countries and the privatization and individualization of welfare which hits women particularly hard as the main users of welfare services (Bridger and Kay 1996, Dimitrieva 1996).

Different state regimes emphasize masculinity in various ways too. Mac an Ghaill (1994) has described the way in which education systems can reproduce particular kinds of masculinity and this is also a way of interpreting youth cultures and criminal careers. However, probably the most important institution for classifying and distinguishing male youth is that of military service. Although in Britain it was abolished in 1950, military service continues for young men in most countries, with young men being obliged to serve between one and two years. It is an institution which deliberately

Youth in Society

maintains and strengthens an essentialist concept of gender roles and what it means to be a 'man'. In many countries it is possible to do voluntary service of some kind instead, but with the penalty that this takes longer. Military service is intended as an obligation of citizenship to defend the state and preserve peace by demonstrating military strength. It also serves another very important purpose of social control and discipline for young men and this traditionally marked the end of their 'youth'. When they returned, they were supposed to be grown men, hardened by their military service. In some countries there are even elaborate *rite de passage* rituals associated with going to and coming from military service. For modern states this is far more than just a form of self-defence: it helps to create a homogenized and disciplined group of people who can be appropriately socialized. This is sometimes also legitimized as a form of social service, whereby the cross-section of young men can be monitored for physical and social problems and helped, if necessary. In the former Soviet Union military service was supposed to be a form of ethnic levelling. This emphasis upon regulated 'modern' forms of masculinity is particularly important during times of war when young men are mobilized to fight, as has been the case in the Balkan countries and in some parts of the former Soviet Union.

However, there has been considerable resistance to military service in both Eastern and Western Europe through campaigns to get the period reduced or to substitute civilian service, and at an individual level by simply avoiding the draft. Since political reform in 1990, many aspects of communist society have been jettisoned, but military service was retained in Eastern and Central European countries (although in many countries the length of service was reduced and civilian service introduced as an alternative). The newly emerged states are trying to re-define their positions within the new military world order and a national defence force is still felt to be a necessary requirement. There has, however, been a transformation in young people's attitudes towards it. They have become increasingly critical of an institution which is now revealed to include violence, bullying and starvation. Far from being an ethnic leveller, it informally reinforced ethnic intolerance and hostility. Information about suicides and brutality against recruits to the army has been revealed. It seems that the disillusionment during the 1980s with the army increased with disillusionment with communism generally. Some people now exert all their wits to find ways of avoiding military service, which is seen at best as years lost from study or starting a business and at worst as a form of tribulation. Young men would continue studying until they had passed the age for being eligible for military service or spend a great deal of time and energy to find a doctor who was prepared to classify them as physically unfit (Roberts et al. 1995). Avoiding conscription was one very strong reason for emigration, especially from those countries experiencing war (Wallace and Palyanitsya 1995).

One possible explanation for this rejection of military service is that it represents an homogenized, standardized construction of masculine youth which is incompatible with young people's search for personal freedom and individuality. Military service was important in creating and constructing a category of (male) youth as a separate entity. However, the widespread individualized resistance to this institution may imply that it is no longer compatible with young people's own perception of age-status transitions.

Divisions of ethnicity and race are also factors which encourage diversity in Europe. Whilst in Britain and The Netherlands this takes the form of discrimination and disadvantage faced by black and Asian people from the former colonies, in France people from North Africa make up the main disadvantaged group, and in other countries it is those who lack citizenship status, often from the former Yugoslavia, Turkey, North Africa or Africa. The demand for labour in the post Second World War years was fulfilled in different ways by different countries. Whereas Britain recruited from the former colonies overseas, Germany, Austria and the Nordic countries imported workers from the South, initially on a temporary basis. The lack of full citizenship status of some of these workers – even those who have been resident more than one generation – means that they are not eligible for some rights and benefits in the same way as citizens. These earlier labour recruits have been followed by new waves of immigrants from Eastern Europe – for whom Germany and Austria have been the main target countries, but also from the south shores of the Mediterranean, for whom France, Spain and Italy have been the main destination countries. Many of these have no legal citizenship. Generally the children of these ethnic minorities leave school less well qualified than their indigenous neighbours, but this varies also between different ethnic groups. Whilst policies towards these migrant groups vary, policies of assimilation have generally been under pressure to give way to ones which recognize ethnic differences and this has coincided with the increasing demand for regional autonomy and the recognition of indigenous sub-groups such as Catalans, Welsh or Basques. One ethnic minority against whom there is continuing and even increasing persecution is that of the gypsies or Roma and Sinti, prevalent throughout eastern and southern European countries. Despite being present in Europe for centuries, their rights to citizenship and other benefits are still questioned. Institutionalized racism against Roma is compounded by the fact that they have generally resisted being controlled and regulated in the way required by many modern state systems, and have retained their own (mostly officially unrecognized) languages, cultures and, in some cases, styles of nomadism.

Despite the persecution of migrant Roma, the idea of nomadism and diaspora have been important in defining some new directions in social theory sometimes termed 'post-colonial'. These postmodernist tendencies have emphasized hybridity instead of ethnic homogeneity, the recognition of difference, but also the likelihood that people might hold a range of different ethnic affiliations of greater or lesser importance to them (Anthias and Yuval Davies 1993, Donald and Rattansi 1992). The backlash against this has come in the desire to form modern states which are ethnically pure and which are based upon an aggressively essentialist concept of race or ethnicity. This has resulted in a new wave of brutal ethnic differentiation in many former communist states, but this backlash is also evident in the increasing success of far right and explicitly racist movements in Western Europe (Gellner 1994).

Migration and youth have always been associated, but postmodernization has brought new forms of nomadism. The kind of white middle class and educated young people exemplified in 'Generation X', from core capitalist countries such as Sweden or the USA, are described as typically nomadic in their movement around the world, for example, but as privileged 'post-materialist' cultural travellers (Rushkoff 1994). For this group of 'postmodern migrants' travelling is a stage of life, perhaps lasting some years, as part of their education or an interlude between university courses or before starting a career. Although they may undertake casual jobs in other countries, this is not considered a permanent position for them. Such young, postmodern migrants form colonies in particular cultural centres such as Prague or Amsterdam (there are an estimated 20 000 young Americans in Prague (see Wallace 1998)). They are connected to one another and to 'home' through various communications media including telephone, fax and e-mail, which means they can be simultaneously abroad but in touch with things 'back home', able to return any time. Rather than sending money home, as classical migrants did, they have money sent from home through credit cards or electronic banking. These are the postmodern equivalent of the *Wanderjahr* youth of the pre-modern period. Having access to communications media, these young people are able to write about themselves and thus publicize their own problems.

Those leaving institutional state care or who have been involved with the criminal justice system represent the other end of the privilege spectrum because they are marginalized, often against their will. They are disproportionately over-represented in the numbers in poverty, homeless, or unemployed and for them this is not 'slumming' – they may well be trapped there. Coles (1995) has indicated the ways in which such young people can suffer multiple disadvantages in Britain and this pattern also occurs in other countries in an increasingly competitive world (see contributors to Hurrelmann 1994). However, even this group find their own way of forging a life-style which offers autonomy and some cultural freedom which may be preferable to institutional 'help' and control. Young people like those in *Trainspotting* are also searching for a cultural space outside of mainstream institutions, like 'Generation X', albeit with different resources.

Unfortunately, it is not possible for us to document in detail the forms of difference or disadvantage experienced by many young people in Europe. This is because we lack consistent comparative information about these factors as well as explanations for how they work in different contexts. They could be said instead to be the 'absent voices' in the words of Griffin (1993), the gaps in our explanations. Thus, for example, whilst educational participation is well documented, it is not always possible to find out the ethnic variations and non-citizens may not be counted at all in official statistics.

These factors raise issues as to the rights and benefits of young people. In all European societies young people are entitled to a package of rights and benefits which are allocated according to age. However, as welfare systems have faced fiscal pressure in the 1980s and 1990s due to rising unemployment, the need to care for an ageing population and increased global competition, the rights of young people have in some cases been threatened. In France and in Britain benefits for young people were cut in the 1980s and

1990s. However, in general the changes described here mean that their incomes have declined, making young people more dependent upon parents or others for assistance. The rights and benefits of young people differ between countries. The development of the European Union has meant an increasing importance of transnational organizations and one successful policy has been that of educational and youth exchange to encourage a better understanding of other countries and cultures. Most of the focus has been upon education and training, on getting young people into the labour market, although they have also been the beneficiaries of various structural aid programmes aimed at improving conditions in the more deprived parts of Europe. There is no sign as yet of any harmonization in social policies towards youth. Whilst some countries feel a need to recognize youth, even to have a Ministry of Youth, other countries such as Britain refuse to acknowledge young people as a social group for welfare purposes (Chisholm and Bergeret 1991, CYRCE 1995).

Thus far we have developed our argument about youth as a product of modernity and the changes associated with postmodernity. Now we shall consider how this differs from other arguments.

MODELS OF YOUTH

Although youth have been identified as troublesome for their elders since the time of Plato – and even in Shakespeare's time there was rumination about the 'ages of man' (sic) – our argument is that youth as a social category associated with a calibrated numerical age and particular defined features is a product of modern society. Social theories play some part in defining the characteristics of age groups and much social theorizing has been devoted to youth. We can read these theories as attempts to construct an 'essentialist' model of youth, one which was rooted in biological factors and psychological or 'necessary' social stages and which justified their separation and treatment by professional interests and bureaucracies in the modern period. Not only was there an attempt to construct an essential category of youth, but divisions between male and female youth as natural and functional categories were also created. Here we can distinguish distinct waves of studies which have identified youth in various ways.

The Construction of Youth as a Life Stage

The first main 'modern' theorist to provide a universal, scientific and precise definition of 'adolescence' was G. Stanley Hall (1907) in the USA, who tried to unite the disciplines of sociology, psychology, medicine and education to achieve a universal definition. He described adolescence as a problematical period of 'storm and stress'. Young people, it was suggested, were going through a difficult psychological phase as they adjusted to the biological changes in their bodies and they experience emotions and bodily changes over which they have no control and which they find difficult to understand. Each person goes through a process of development from early animal-like primitivism (childhood) to civilization (adulthood). In this social-Darwinist view of evolutionary development, adolescence was seen as an especially troublesome period, a period when young people were being pulled in two directions – backward towards the primitivism of childhood and forwards towards the rational and civilized state of adulthood.

Hall did not see female and male youth as maturing in the same ways. Female youth did not undergo the same stresses and strains as male youth because they did not mature to the same extent as male youth, being more child-like and closer to nature. Furthermore, he was greatly concerned with control of the adolescent body – with preventing boys from masturbating and with protecting the ripening bodies of young women. Rather than reading it as a scientific treatise, we can now read his work as a way of understanding how youth has been conceptualized (Cohen 1997). The idea of studying adolescence as a problematic life stage has continued. Coleman and Hendry (1990), for example, describe it as the period in which young people 'come to terms' with hormonal and physical changes of their bodies.

We would argue, however, that this is not simply a biological process. When a person is deemed 'mature' can vary considerably between different societies and within the same society over time. It can even vary within the same society as those lower down the social ladder tend to have accelerated transitions into adulthood, whereas those higher up have more protracted transitions, as we shall illustrate later on. 'Storm and stress' as a feature of adolescence can be related to transitions through major institutions. For example, the peak age of delinquency tends to follow the school leaving age – it is highest in the year before and after leaving school.

As the school leaving age has risen so has the age of peak delinquency (Corrigan 1979). In countries where there is military service, young men are supposed to 'settle down' by the time they come out (and this in itself can be quite variable). Therefore, factors which appear to be psychological or biological universals often turn out to be socially relative. This is even more evident when we consider the different ages associated with 'adolescence', 'youth', or young adulthood in different societies: in some places those up to 35 would count as 'youth' whereas in Britain we frequently think of it as ending after 18. Studies of youth are notoriously imprecise about this and it seems that they can be carried out on any group between the ages of 13 and 40. This lack of consistency in typification of adolescence and youth indicates not the lack of scientific precision, but the arbitrariness of the category itself.

Another well-known and influential psychological approach is to identify definite life stages in the development of the individual. Developmental psychologists such as Erikson (1968) have argued that individuals grow up through distinct stages through which they are integrated into society. The adolescent stage is associated with identity crisis and peer group associations. These peer group associations help the individual to come to terms with their identity and if successful, this leads eventually to the integrated person (O'Donnel 1985). For Erikson, youth represents a period of 'moratorium', of experimentation and self-discovery before taking on adult responsibilities. It is argued that the aim of research is to identify adolescence as a stage of development and (implicitly) to assist in turning out better socialized individuals. Hence, John Coleman and Leo Hendry (1990) argue that there are four 'developmental tasks' of adolescence:

1. Development of intellectual and social competence in order to acquire independently and responsibly scholastic and subsequently occupational qualifications with the purpose of taking up a job and thereby ensuring the economic and material basis for an independent existence as an adult.
2. Development of a gender role and building of heterosexual partnership which in the long term may form the basis for the upbringing of one's own children.
3. Development of a system of values and norms and of an ethical and political consciousness which provides the capacity to act responsibly in all areas of social participation.

4. Development of competence in the use of consumer goods and
   leisure activities available (including the media and luxury goods)
   for the purpose of developing an independent lifestyle.

   (Quoted in Hurrelmann 1994: 2–3)

Here we can see the attempt to construct an 'essential' model of
youth justified by the 'need' for biological reproduction and supposedly natural and necessary social roles. In constructing the idea
of adolescence, defined by the 'developmental tasks', a normative
heterosexual and universal model is used. The failure to develop
'normally' or the display of anti-social behaviour is attributed to
something going wrong in this developmental process, to hormonal
changes or to problems in the relationship with parents, to individual failures of adjustment. Other problems associated with this
life-phase include eating disorders, suicide and depression (Furlong
and Cartmel 1997). The psychological or social psychological model
was used extensively in the guidance and treatment of the young.
It was influential in the treatment of 'problem' groups such as
offenders in the 1960s and 1970s, whose development is deemed
to be incomplete or problematical, although social psychologists
themselves now take a less essentialist perspective and are more
sensitive to variations within youth as a social group (Archer 1994,
Heaven 1994).

In fact, the reality is often far from this model as many young
people are unable to find jobs, do not have useful qualifications
(or perhaps any qualifications) and may not have access to consumer goods – especially luxury ones. Young people may indeed
be *better* than their elders at handling consumer goods and the
media. Increasing numbers are rejecting the building of conventional gender roles and heterosexual families, deemed a necessary
task of adolescence – or at any rate postponing them. The construction of homosexuality as some kind of abnormal development,
or as a problem that will pass, is no longer acceptable in a world
where sexual differentiation is increasingly recognized for all age
groups (Griffin 1993).

We argue in contrast that the problems young people experience
need to be set in the context of not just their personal growth, but
also the social institutions within which they are situated – for example, the contradictory pressures exerted by media culture which
encourages participation in general youth consumer styles and cultural autonomy on the one hand and the increasing dependence

upon parents and institutions of education and training on the other hand. This tension between self-determination and dependency has psychological impacts too. This pressure affects not only deviant but 'ordinary' youth as well. Similarly the need to conform to dominant cultural models of masculinity or femininity can in itself create pressure upon an individual's search for 'identity' rather than being seen as the normal or 'natural' end product of the 'developmental task'. Finally, it is difficult to see what the final aims of these 'developmental tasks' are when the youth labour market for many young people has collapsed and large numbers of young people are permanently excluded from the model presented above.

As with the biological categorization of young people, the developmental model assumes that youth is a universal category which can be ascertained using objective principles – that it is an 'essential' category. However, very often the normative models being implicitly used represent those from dominant social and ethnic groups. Erikson's own model, like that of G Stanley Hall, is in some respects specific to a middle class white group in the USA and the problems which were associated with them at the time that they were writing. We shall argue that the individual development of young people is not universal, but depends upon their historical location and upon the way in which 'youth' is constructed in that society. It is no longer possible to have a universal concept of youth. 'Modern' institutional tendencies try to create such categories whilst 'postmodern' tendencies undermine them.

The Construction of Youth as a Social Category

Whilst there are undoubtedly biological and developmental components to what we understand by youth, it is also evident that these are related to the definition of youth as a social category. Anthropologists have argued that we can see youth in terms of a *rite de passage* from one state, 'childhood', to another, 'adulthood'. This is accomplished in different ways in different societies but the anthropologist who is best known for drawing inferences for Western society is Margaret Mead (1943). In her study of growing up in Samoa, she attempted to show that the American idea of troubled adolescence and the 'generation gap' was not universal: in Samoa young people were more successfully integrated into society as they did not have to endure confusing and conflicting moral standards. Although it has been claimed that she over-emphasized the degree of harmony in these societies and under-emphasized the degree of juvenile delinquency, Mead's work is nevertheless important in demonstrating the relativity of our ideas of youth. It is also evident from this debate that the categories and theories used for describing non-industrial societies are drawn from preoccupations in our own and this is why it is important to examine the different models of how youth is constructed. Despite the criticisms, we find this relative concept of 'youth' and adolescence a helpful way to understand how age-status are socially constructed in different contexts.

One of the first serious sociological attempts to develop a theoretical framework for age relations was that of Karl Mannheim writing in the 1930s. He analysed the issue of age and class as competing forms of stratification and argued that each generation developed a consciousness at a particular point in history and was formed by events at that time. Hence, we can talk about the 'generation of 68' as those who were particularly influenced by events at that time. In Germany this issue has been more obvious, as in Mannheim's day, the generation experiencing the First World War were indelibly stamped by that experience. Mannheim did not claim that all generations were created in the same way, because this would depend upon historical circumstances. We find this a helpful concept because, subsequently, those who had experienced fascism and the Second World War were similarly shaped by that experience. In post-communist countries such a generation gap is also emerging between those who were seen to be part of the system and those who came afterwards. Mannheim has been heavily criticized and has often marked a point of departure for more recent theories. First, it is claimed that it is not clear why 'generations' should be particularly identified with youth or formed by youth (Murdock and McCron 1976). In Mannheim's defence, however, it seems to us that he argues that forming an historical consciousness can take place in a dramatic way in the lives of young people as they become critically aware of their surroundings for the first time with no personal memory of what went before. Secondly, it is argued that the concept applies perhaps more in some contexts than in others: in Britain it is difficult to see such distinct generations (except perhaps those formed by youth culture: the 'Beatles generation' as distinct from the 'punk generation') whereas in other social contexts they are far more obvious. In our opinion the experience of having lived through great historical moments or changes creates a generational difference in the experiences and consciousness of people – between those who have been shaped by that experience and those who follow and were too young to have constructed their conscious lives in this way. This is often reflected in political movements and parties as we shall later show. Thirdly, Cohen (1997) criticizes Mannheim for failing to account for differentiation within the generations and the material bases of such differentiation. Mannheim's sociology of generations has enjoyed a recent rehabilitation as a way of understanding contemporary patterns of social change (Pilcher 1994). However, Pilcher makes the point that we need to distinguish between two meanings of generation: that of broad groups of young people or cohorts, and that between older and younger members of a family.

The most ambitious attempt to define youth in the context of modernity came from the structural-functionalist theories of the 1950s and early 1960s such as Parsons (1973), Parsons and Bales (1956), Eisenstadt (1956) and Musgrove (1964). These authors argued that youth is a period when people are between the particularistic values of the family and the universalistic values of the wider world. The separation of home and work means that young people cannot be socialized into the former by the latter and youth is the pivotal point of tension between the two systems. The peer group thus becomes the means by which young people learn the values of wider society. This work reflected concerns during the 1950s with the emergence of separate 'youth cultures' and the so-called 'generation gap' between the conformist elders brought up on wartime rationing and the hedonistic, consumer oriented youth. According to structural-functionalist theories, this is not evidence of a 'failure to adjust', but rather a form of adaptation, a 'normal' part of growing up. In the work of Musgrove (1964) and the influential work of the American sociologist James Coleman (1974) it was argued that youth was becoming a separate entity with their own forms of communication, subordinated to adult society – indeed, almost as a class in themselves. The problems faced by young people can be seen as a 'passing phase' before they are incorporated into dominant society. However, Musgrove was critical of this construction of youth, arguing that young people should be better integrated into society rather than kept apart. The functionalist view sees society as something stable and necessary, something into which youth should eventually be integrated, and this view is held also by many practitioners working with young people. This is once more an 'essentialist' construction of youth, one using normative assumptions and one which fixes people into a 'natural' and inevitable age-specific role.

De-constructing Youth as an Age Category

From the late 1960s onwards, more critical, Marxist perspectives developed, often stimulated by developments in the sociology of deviance where a body of work on 'sub-cultures' had been developed. The Marxists began by attacking structural-functionalists for their static view of society and for their neglect of the dynamics of class. For example, it was trenchantly criticized by Sheila Allen (1968) who argued that youth should not be seen as a universal category, but as a group divided by sex, race and class. Moreover, she argued that the idea of two generations was too simple; what was needed was a more complex account of the 'dialectics of structural change', a position which was taken up and developed in the critical perspectives which followed.

Particularly influential in this was a group of Marxist scholars at the Centre for Contemporary Cultural Studies (CCCS) at Birmingham University in the UK. They argued that youth as a concept was 'unthinkable'. It made no sense to talk about age as a form of stratification. Instead they argued that class was the most important social variable and youth cultures were simply the way in which different classes of young people expressed their opposition to the dominant order. The developments of this work by Willis (1977) and Corrigan (1979) situated sub-cultures in the transition from school to work in which working class boys developed responses to the dominant school order and in preparation for working life. The desire to relate cultural phenomena to 'real' material relations, however, meant that the way in which youth was constructed through legislation and professional interests was ignored. The more recent work of Bernard Davies (1986) provides a critical corrective to this by looking at the way in which social policy has responded to the phenomenon of 'threatening youth' – mostly through more social control, which he argued is reflected consistently in the different arms of the state which deal with young people – the criminal justice system, the training schemes, the education system and the Youth Service in Britain. Griffin (1993) argues that there has been a continuing tradition of this 'critical' discourse which has counterpointed mainstream youth theories and initiatives. Most recently, sexism, racism and the recognition of 'difference' have dominated this critical discourse, whereas previously it was class. These therefore tend towards anti-essentialist constructions of youth.

However, the model of class analysis used in the Marxist model is problematical, since the notion of class is reified and assumed rather than demonstrated (Connel, 1983). Jones (1987a) has attempted to develop a more empirically based model of the class locations of young people and Jenkins (1983), Brown (1987) and Wallace (1987) have shown that there are important cultural divisions within classes as well as between them and there are arguments that the more 'ordinary' youth should be studied in detail too (Brown 1987). The emphasis on class at the expense of other kinds of divisions is a feature of 'modernist' perspectives, whilst more recent perspectives have emphasized other kinds of social divisions based upon style, ethnicity, gender, dis(ability), sexuality and so on. The emphasis on 'style', for example, denies that there is any consistent or material basis for social divisions, although most youth researchers would retain the idea of socio-economic divisions, if in a weaker form (Furlong and Cartmel 1997).

More recently the volume of work produced by British researchers in the 1980s and 1990s has tended instead to focus upon 'career trajectories' – that is routes through education, training and work rather than straightforward class reproduction, perhaps because class reproduction is no longer straightforward. It is instead fragmented and channelled through a variety of new structures such as training schemes and college courses (see Banks et al. 1992). This work has helped to provide a large volume of empirical data about the changing experiences of young people during the 1980s based upon cross-sectional and longitudinal analysis (Raffe 1988). The implications of such studies are that we need to take account of the expanding structures of training and education in order to understand the fortunes of different groups of school leavers and this coincides with continental approaches to young people in which they are generally divided between different educational levels rather than in terms of social background. Although until the 1980s social class was seen as the dominant paradigm for analyzing youth in Britain, this recent empirical work would suggest that more complex forms of stratification are emerging, created through the interaction of training, education and the labour market. What used to define working class youth was that they went straight from school into jobs at the minimum age, whereas now this is not necessarily the case. Nevertheless, social background continues to play a role in the allocation of youth to different positions in society (Wyn and White 1997).

There is nevertheless a large and growing group of young people in Europe who are socially excluded from the labour market and from other parts of mainstream society. They may be homeless, jobless, without incomes, without qualifications and without prospects. Some social theorists define these as an 'underclass' (Murray 1986) and further identify them with crime, with drug taking, with fatherless children and with black people (Murray 1990). Many of these factors do not apply to European societies where the unemployed are mostly white and where fatherless children are increasingly *uncommon* among teenagers. However, we can also reject the 'underclass' thesis because we can see that different groups of young people find themselves disadvantaged for different reasons and at least some of the reasons are the regional changes in the structure of employment which we have already discussed (Coles 1995). They do not all form one homogenous group. For this reason the term 'social exclusion' has gained currency as a way of conceptualizing such disadvantages whilst avoiding the stigmatizing idea of an 'underclass' and the implication that it is a self-reproducing class of culturally deviant people as described by Murray (Abbott and Wallace 1992).

The Marxist and other perspectives have been criticized for neglect of gender. Feminists have developed their own perspective on youth, emphasizing the role of the gender typing, the family and sexuality in shaping the experience of young women and men (McRobbie 1991, Griffin 1985, Nava 1992, Lees 1986). Others have applied such ideas to exploring how young men acquire a gender identity and the idea of 'masculinity' under these circumstances (Wood 1984, Mac an Ghaill 1994). In Western sociology the idea of gender has become accepted as an important source of disadvantage, but as we have already indicated, ideas of gender relations need to be somewhat re-defined to fit the new expanded European reality and in Eastern Europe the gender perspective has not been so well developed.

A further critical perspective has emphasized the importance of 'race' and ethnicity in structuring the experience of youth generally but also in understanding the experiences of black and Asian youth in Britain. They have criticized white youth studies for assuming that the experiences of white youth are universal and have developed different theories, emphasizing 'race' as a fundamental

factor of division in society. Racism, like sexism, is seen as an en-
demic part of British institutions and not reducible to the preju-
dices of the population (Wrench, Cross and Barrett 1989, Solomos
1988). Youth researchers have emphasized the different experiences
of ethnic minority youth and have criticized the institutions which
tend to turn them into a 'problem' category rather than dealing
with their problems. Rather, we should see racism as helping to
construct race and some young people as the victims of the resur-
gence of racism throughout Europe since the 1980s. Many Afro-
Caribbean, Asian, Arab and Turkish youth in inner city areas
particularly have been hit hard by the recession and by state expenditure cuts creating groups of unemployed and socially excluded
youth who also suffer racial persecution and prejudice. It is possible
to read the various social policy recommendations and reports on
inner city rioting in the 1980s as attempts to deal with the 'problem'
of so-called 'black' youth and their perceived threat to white society
(Solomos 1988). However, when we consider the general European
context, these definitions of race and racism need to be broadened
to include ethnic and religious differentiation and persecution of
minorities more generally (to apply, for example, to Bosnia). The
construction of both race and racism should be seen as situationally
defined rather than consistent and homogenous (Back 1996).

In Britain the critical perspectives which began by emphasizing
class, race and gender in the study of youth started to develop into
post-structuralist and postmodern directions (Griffin 1993). These
theories tended to reject any overarching explanation of youth or
young people's problems and to emphasize instead the differences
and diversities in young people's experiences. Hence new divisions
of sexuality, disability and other factors were introduced which were
not reducible or even comparable to the classic social class divisions. There have therefore been rejections of 'essentialist' notions
of age, gender, 'race' in preference for looking at how these categories construct the people in them. This has led to a focus on
young people's media tastes and preferences, seeing consumerism
as a positive value rather than a form of capitalist oppression (see,
for example, McRobbie 1991). This represents then a postmodernist
tendency. However, this perspective in turn neglects the widening
inequalities between different groups of young people and the fact
that not all of them have equal access to consumption and leisure
styles (for further critique see Jones and Wallace 1992). We shall
develop this later in the book.

An important perspective originating in Germany is that of Beck (1986) who, deriving his analysis from theories of modernization, suggests that the loss of class solidarity and the traditional support networks of the family and community has led to an increased emphasis on the individual private world. However, 'new socio-cultural communalities' could emerge, based upon the interests, ambitions and commitments of individuals rather than upon class identity (see Jones and Wallace 1990, 1992 for a critique of this perspective). One expression of individualization processes is the increasing demand from all sectors of society for more individual control over one's life, and its corollary is increased risk and uncertainty. People need to choose their way between complex and competing alternatives with the risk of failure, if they make a wrong move: life thus becomes a 'biographical project'. Youth is a crucial moment in this biographical project because it is a period in which choices have to be defined and routes chosen (Bertram 1985, Hartmann 1985, Olk 1988). This affects young women in particular, it is argued, because they are no longer confined by the 'normal biography' of school-work-children-work. It is argued that they no longer perceive family-building as their only goal, but may be more likely to seek fulfilment in the labour market (Beck and Beck-Gernsheim 1995). Indeed, according to a review of current research by Wilkinson and Mulgan (1995), young women are becoming more ambitious than young men.

A number of studies of youth have reflected this 'individualization' perspective and provided evidence for it. For example, Hartmann (1987) argues that technology and housing developments mean that they have more choice: they can afford to buy their own leisure and have their own rooms in which to pursue these choices. Young people are able to seek their own pursuits regardless of parental direction and develop their own unique cultural styles, and adult authority is decreased (Zinnecker and Fuchs 1981). Parents have less control over their children: for example, the parents of young people who were questioned during riots in Stockholm often did not know where their children were at the time (Hartmann 1987). The increased emphasis on individual rights has been reflected in legislative changes which define children's rights as distinct from those of their parents, women's rights as distinct from those of men. Family relationships require negotiation and choice rather than blind acceptance of parental or patriarchal authority (du Bois-Reymond et al. 1995).

Most recently, Furlong and Cartmel (1997) tried to apply this concept of the 'risk society' to young people. They found that young people did suffer increased risk of unemployment, educational failure and homelessness and this was manifested in the increase in psychological disorders such as eating disorders, suicide and mental health problems. However, we find this concept of risk rather a weak one. Whilst it is evident that young people in Western Europe do suffer from anxiety, it is clear that their real risk from dangers such as starvation, political persecution, hunger and deprivation or destruction is less than it was for previous generations or for young people in other parts of the world. Risk is therefore relative. What we do find convincing, however, is the idea of individualization not just of risk but of problems previously tackled by employers, formal associations (such as trades unions and youth organisations) and the welfare state. This can be seen as one form of the 'privatization' of problems. Problems are thrown back out of the public realm and left for private solution.

Some have tried to account for the extension of youth by adding on new stages. The idea first raised by Keniston (1970) in the USA and applied to Germany by Zinnecker and Fuchs (1981) is that a period of what they call 'post adolescence' is being created based upon an extended period of preparation, free from responsibility. 'Post adolescence' is characterized by postponement of marriage and childbearing; by experimentation with ideologies, political beliefs and life-styles; by education and training rather than full-time work (Klein 1990).

Ideas about individualization and 'post adolescence' were developed in the 1970s and 1980s in Germany and the USA to account for more affluent young people who enjoy the most extended transitions. In Germany at least, the risk of unemployment for young people was very small until recently. The 'risk' was one of making the wrong decision rather than being excluded altogether from the labour market and individualization was developed in the context of a growing 'postmaterialist' orientation (Inglehart 1990). However, the situation where young people are in increasing risk of non-employment and where problems of failure are less and less cushioned by institutions, individualization takes on a different meaning – it becomes the way in which the problems are privatized.

In his description of the 'civilizing process' Norbert Elias (1976) argued that people were increasingly required to exercise self-discipline in the course of civilization, something which was also stressed as one of the 'developmental tasks' of growing up. For

Elias, civilization as a form of modernization was associated with more future security and longer term planning horizons anchored by the welfare state. Now, however, the contrary situation is emerging, one where there is less future security for the individual and shorter term planning horizons. We could say that market capitalist ideologies which have supplanted Keynesian models of social policy management in most European countries have led to a situation where it is impossible to plan in the long term – only short-term solutions are possible in a rapidly fluctuating market. The provisionality and ephemerality of the market enters other areas of social life. Many older skills are regarded as rapidly obsolete and people are encouraged to 'sell' themselves or their ideas on the labour market, like a product. Education systems increasingly resemble a 'supermarket' model of off-the-shelf courses. In such a system, individuals are left to manage their own educational and employment careers and are blamed for their own failures to do so. Although the individualization thesis did not originate in this climate, it fits very well the situation of young people having to find their own way, not guided by traditional paths into the labour market and unprotected by the welfare state. Social problems are privatized.

In Eastern and Central Europe individualization has not developed to the same extent as in Western Europe, because individual interests were subordinated to group ones and the scope for independent decision-making was less. Transition processes were planned and controlled to fit a centralized state-controlled economy. On the other hand there was no risk of unemployment as long as one conformed. Nevertheless, tendencies that have encouraged some measure of individualization, including the elaboration of the education and training systems and, since 1989, marketization, have helped to create choice of lifestyles so that more individualized identities could be constructed. At the same time unemployment and rising poverty for some families have been introduced. Young people are increasingly left to manage their own careers and prospects without much guidance from institutions and in a very uncertain economic climate. For young people in Eastern Europe too, problems are individualized and privatized.

PERSPECTIVES ON YOUTH IN EASTERN EUROPE

Under the former communist regimes no competing perspectives were allowed, so conceptions of youth were often implicit rather than explicit, although they also changed over time (Pilkington 1994). Youth was not considered a 'real' social category – only class was important in this respect. However, youth, heavily ideologized as being the future prospect of society, was an important tool of communist policy. Young people could also be potentially better indoctrinated since they carried with them less ideological baggage from previous regimes. In exchange for privileges they were expected to demonstrate loyalty and gratitude to the regime. Age and gender equality were proclaimed by the constitutions and supplemented with an elaborate system of protective legislation. Youth were also an important source of labour as both in the early days of communist reconstruction, and also later, volunteer or low paid labour from young people formed an important component of the workforce.

In practice youth were divided into three stages corresponding with the different youth organizations. At the basic level of schooling, young people joined a junior youth organization (given different names in different countries) and then from age 10 to 14 they joined the 'Young Pioneers'. From then to age 28 they joined the official youth organization, which was known in many countries as the 'Komsomol'. The youth organizations arranged excursions, cultural events and a whole range of educational and cultural activities, including mass rallies on significant occasions. Age-status transitions were therefore highly structured: everybody knew who youth were – they were those eligible to join the Komsomol (or equivalent organization)!

Youth research was one of the expanding fields of sociology in the communist dominated half of Europe. Although it was under the same ideological pressures as other research work, the generous support for empirical investigation which it enjoyed allowed the possibility to work out new concepts and methods, often as a reaction to the 'official' construction of youth. Many researchers, doing a variety of kinds of research, were able to hide under the mantle of legitimate youth research.

One of the early themes of this research in the 1970s was the specification of youth as a social group, especially whether youth was a biological or social category. Eventually a compromise description was reached – a socio-biological category. This was a tortured topic because both the biological and social definitions were inconsistent with the official Marxist philosophy of social groups being defined by their relation to the means of production. However, the new social and biological definition of youth did make it possible to begin empirical research with large-scale sample surveys to measure these characteristics. Thus, the obscurantist disputes about the specification of youth served as a legitimation for researchers to develop a sociology of youth and obtain state financing of this field.

The study of youth's integration into society and their life plans was developed through the more elaborate concept of socialization in Soviet sociology through the work of I. Kon and N. Andreyenkova. Although this was useful insofar as it enabled sociologists to study the development of personality in relation to specific institutions and social relations, it was heavily criticized by ideologists, who detected western influence (Kenkmann n.d.:1). Nevertheless, this paradigm persisted, strengthened in the 1970s by multi-national comparative surveys focusing on social reproduction, particularly in education.

An innovation of East European sociologists in this field was the idea of 'juventization'. First attributed to the Rumanian social scientist, Fred Mahler, but later developed by Bulgarian sociologists, they criticized the concept of socialization as representing merely the passive absorption of social norms through young people's conformist integration into society (Gospodinov 1981, Mitev 1982). Instead they argued that young people not only internalize and reproduce social norms, but also produce new ones. Using Marxist ideas of the relationship between people and their environment, they argued that society imposes norms on young people, but young people, through their active participation in social life, in turn change and 'juventicize' society. This was the basis for youth's highest form of social activity: their active role in transforming society (although in practice a very passive role was encouraged – see Chapter 2). In this way young people could become actors for real social change.

Among Baltic sociologists, the concept of 'self determination' was developed (Kenkmann n.d.). This was not self determination in a western sense, but rather it allowed the opportunity to look at young people's own attitudes and responses, something much neglected in communist-dominated sociology. Using this paradigm, it was argued that young people make choices with regard to education, occupations, work, marriage and so on, choices that needed to be explored through empirical investigation. Titma (n.d.) concluded from the results of these surveys that young people in fact controlled very few areas of their lives.

In Bulgarian sociology the same paradigm was interpreted as the 'self realization' of personality – the need for young people to realize potentialities in the various spheres of life. The entry into work attracted particular attention. The idea of 'career' was discouraged, being considered as unsocialist, but by considering the problem of professional realization, sociologists were able to detect some of the mismatch between qualifications and aspirations of young people and the jobs that were actually available to them.

The influential Institute for Youth Studies in Sofia helped to better elaborate theories of youth, and an early book by Peter Mitev in the 1960s claimed that youth – along with class struggle – formed an important element in the transformation of society. This afforded the possibility of legitimately studying the position of youth in society and their activities. At first in this discourse youth problems – such as vandalism, social apathy or sub-cultures – were regarded as deviations explained by the infiltration of the capitalist West. From the end of the 1970s, however, sociologists began to explain young people's problems in terms of the growing generational alienation revealed through their surveys.

Consequently, a range of surveys were conducted in the 1970s which detected increasing signs of young people's alienation. However, these were not allowed to be published and even now it is difficult to gain access to them. The growing consumer market from the 1970s onwards helped to fuel the idea of youth as a separate stage in life – but defined by themselves. The party hierarchy were powerless to prevent what they saw as this disastrous and decadent subversion of the communist ideal of youth (Riordan 1989a). In fact, Riordan concludes of the communist Soviet Union that the institutionalized structures containing youth were themselves so strong that youthful deviance was strictly limited. However, we argue that this limitation resulted in every action and every lack of compliance becoming politically charged. Passive resistance (termed 'apathy' or 'political and ideological deviance') was widespread, recognized as a problem by the authorities for whom anything short of wholehearted conformity was a problem of social control. There also seems to have been a growing questioning of the Soviet system from a generation too young to have experienced Stalinist terror or invading Warsaw pact armies restoring order (as happened in Hungary in 1956 and Czechoslovakia in 1968).

In the 1980s, the more grand theoretical concepts were left behind in favour of studying the new social reality. Thus, it was possible for the first time to study openly the range of youth cultures and what were called 'non-formal' groups in communist countries. Studies appeared showing the discontent of young people with working conditions, their participation in the informal economy, the formation of non-formal youth groups and their growing consumerism (Pilkington 1994). The youth sociologists were some of the first to detect and identify the changes taking place, but they were still not allowed to publish their results.

Many of the results referred to here are drawn from these surveys that at the time were not made public. However, even now access to them is difficult since many are held in private homes, by individuals. It is particularly difficult to find information about young people's own perceptions since this was seldom investigated, and when it was, the results remained confidential. For this reason we have had some difficulty in finding information which gives any accurate picture of the experiences of young people in communist regimes.

After 1990 the Youth Institute in Bulgaria closed. The extensive library moved and is still not open to the public. Many of the researchers who conducted youth research as a way of concealing the subjects in which they were really interested were now able to openly study these subjects. Other researchers went off to join public opinion and market research organizations, currently a growth industry. Some of the key members of the research teams took up places or scholarships in Western Europe and the USA or became involved in politics. The Youth Institute in Moscow has suffered from slow death rather than execution, as its resources were cut off, and many of its personnel have left. In other countries the youth research teams and Youth Institutes vanished almost immediately. In East Germany the substantial staff of the Youth Institute in Leipzig were laid off and only a skeleton staff remained, run from the West German Youth Institute in Munich. Now, youth is no longer seen as an interesting or relevant topic of research: it disappeared along with the official youth organisations such as Komsomol. Youth studies are treated with some distaste, as a relic from the old regime.

CONCLUSIONS

In the preceding pages we have reviewed a number of contemporary and past theories of youth arguing that they have themselves been used to construct youth as a social category. Whilst some theories were attempting to construct an 'essential' view of youth – one based upon 'natural' or normative biological, social and psychological imperatives and marked differences between the sexes – others were arguing for a more non-essentialist view of youth. We have not given a definition of youth and do not intend to offer one because our argument is that youth – and life-stage transitions associated with it – are social constructs. We aim instead to look at some of the ways in which youth is constructed in different social and historical contexts. A view across both East and Western Europe is helpful in this respect as it helps to see our own theories of youth, in whatever culture they were developed, in more relative terms. A comparative perspective enables us to grasp general tendencies in modernization and post-modernization regardless of whether these occurred in welfare capitalist, communist or postcommunist contexts and to look at their implications for age-status transitions. We argue that generations are relevant to an understanding of youth in Europe, not because we hold an essentialist concept of age, but because historical events and regimes do serve to shape the consciousness of those who spent most of their lives within them. Such historical experiences are more easily forgotten by those who did not experience them directly and not forgotten by those who did. We hope to demonstrate in the following pages how youth can be constructed in 'weak' or 'strong' ways: in some places and points in time, they are an important social category and at others less so. Inevitably our analysis of the construction and re-construction of age relations leads us back to the modern state system, its different political regimes and the role it plays in classifying and monitoring its populations. The tendency of modern state systems over the last 100 years to classify, monitor and construct a category of 'youth' in different ways is undermined by increasing marketization, the withdrawal of the state and the increasing influence of media communications and culture which all undermine such tendencies, deconstructing youth in a way which is more postmodern in character. We have confined ourselves to descriptions of Europe because in this sense 'youth' is a western concept associated with the development of welfare states characteristic of European societies. In many non-western countries children are supporting their families through work from a relatively early age and do not have the luxury of an extended youth.

In the remainder of the book we take up some of these themes in more detail. Chapter 2 considers the construction of youth in Europe through modernization and the expansion of the state; Chapter 3 looks in more detail at changes in employment, training and education for the construction of youth. Chapter 4 looks more closely at family transitions for the way in which the relationship between different generations is changing, and in Chapter 5 we consider the role of youth cultures and consumerism in creating a distinctive idea of 'youth'. In Chapter 6 we look at young people's involvement in politics as a way of understanding in what circumstances, if at all, youth could be said to mobilize as a social category.

NOTES

1. Information is drawn from the following research projects: 16–19 Initiative (ESRC); Anglo-German Foundation comparison of young people in labour markets in Germany and Britain; East-West Initiative (ESRC) study of young people in Poland (with Ken Roberts); ACE-Phare and INTAS programmes, studies of young people in Poland, Ukraine, Georgia and Armenia; McArthur Fund and Soros Open Society Institute, study of student activists in Plovdiv. We would like to gratefully acknowledge the support of all these organizations.
2. We have referred throughout this book to 'communism'. The word is a convenient label for the Soviet-style socialist regimes which existed behind the iron curtain. These states did not consider themselves 'communist' (they had yet to evolve to this stage in official socialist theory). Nor would they be considered communist by many western socialists. Many western analysts would not even regard them as true 'socialist' states and few socialist parties in the West saw them as role models. They were states built on a version of Marxist theory and had many similar features – although even communism took many different forms. Communist domination through the former Soviet Union imposed some kind of uniformity on otherwise very disparate countries and so we feel justified in classifying them all together as 'communist' as a convenient label.

2 Modernization and the Construction of Youth

The idea of youth emerged as a chronologically defined category with modernization, but in different ways in different parts of Europe. In this chapter we will consider how this happened. The periodization used here reflects the process of industrial change and the development of the state. In the second part of the chapter we look at the way in which youth services became incorporated into state provision for youth and the way in which modern and post-modern tendencies are reflected in them.

YOUTH IN THE PRE-INDUSTRIAL PERIOD

Youth was a distinctive phase in North-Western Europe even before industrialization but its duration depended upon factors other than numerical age (Rosenmayr 1992). The North-West European marriage pattern was one whereby people lived in small nuclear families based upon neolocal monogamy. A new household could be set up once the means – in terms of property or a craft – were acquired: 'youth' was thus the long period between leaving childhood and setting up as an independent household (Mitterauer 1993). Childhood ended at some time between the ages of 8 and 15 when offspring were sent away to live in other people's houses either as servants or as apprentices (Gillis 1981, Wall 1987). Adulthood began when they married and inherited property or obtained access to a livelihood of some kind, which was usually around their mid to late 20s: the rather long stage in between was 'youth'. Marriage and the inheritance of property were therefore connected as forms of transition and the age of marriage depended upon when property or a means of livelihood became available – although there were also ante-mortem transfers in the form of dowries or gifts and there was a great deal of variability in this pattern depending upon the area of Europe and the circumstances of individual households. Thus, the determination of youth was not so much *age*, as marriage, gender, inheritance and access to a livelihood. The age at which young men left home, went to college, went to work and so on was fairly loose and depended upon the demand for their labour by the household, funds available and a variety of other factors. Young men would move in and out of various activities depending upon their circumstances and young men of a variety of ages could be found in the same classrooms (Kett 1977). 'Youth' was not therefore a precise, age-graded category.

Youth was also associated with a period of apprenticeship to a craft or trade, which often involved living in the household of the master. Apprentices developed their own sub-cultures, to judge by the anxiety this provoked in some of their elders and the laws which forbade them to gamble, go out at night, wear extravagant clothing or grow their hair long, although this applied more to male youth. The long period which young people spent outside the family encouraged some autonomous social life. In Germany social control was more formalized through a tradition of strong fraternities and sororities which further regulated behaviour by encouraging celibacy and controlling courtship (Gillis 1981). These also acted as a form of social support for itinerant and apprenticed youth or journeymen. However, young people generally were subject to the patriarchal authority of the household in which they lived and where they worked for their keep. Although youth meant male youth, Mitterauer (1993) suggests that there may also have been cultural life for young women based upon sex-segregated employment and activities such as spinning. Youth at this period was therefore a stage of life wherein young people were semi-dependent upon other households.

In South Eastern Europe a different family form prevailed, one based upon the extended co-resident household, and this meant that youth was not such an extended period, but rather the period between childhood and getting married at some time between age 12 and 18. Only women left home on marriage and youth was seen as a brief carefree period before hard agricultural and domestic labour started to wear people down. The needs of the group took priority over those of the individual and parents chose the marriage partners of their children (Bobchev 1906, Khadzijski 1974). Hajnal (1965) has suggested that the European style of nuclear families with small numbers of children, late or no marriage and relative independence for women can be distinguished from the more communal styles of household which existed further east in such countries as Bulgaria where children and women were strictly subordinated, expected to show proper obedience and modesty, and youth was very brief or non-existent (Grekova 1991).

Disruption and Change: The Consequences of Industrialization

These age-relations broke down with the advent of industrialized urbanization. In North-West Europe this occurred mainly during the nineteenth century and even earlier in some regions. In other areas of Europe similar changes followed much later – in Bulgaria not until the twentieth century. The growing predominance of wage labour and the migration from rural to urban areas meant that the traditional link between marriage and inheritance was severed. The physical concentration of the population and the regulation of work by time and wage labour which was brought about by industrial capitalism meant that young people became a more conspicuous unregulated group in the cities. In many parts of Europe, 'youth' are still considered to be an urban phenomenon for these reasons until quite recently, because in rural areas they were simply absorbed into the unwaged household economy (Pavelka and Stefanov 1985). With the concentration of young people with 'free' time and not necessarily holding regular jobs, came the concomitant problems of social control and Pearson (1983) documents the various 'moral panics' and street crime which escalated at this time in Britain as a result.

It is usually the case that younger people are the ones to migrate, and this may have helped to break down traditional patterns of authority and dependency. However, to begin with, the authority of the family may have actually been strengthened, as chain migration and early industrial conditions, including 'out work' and the employment of the entire family in the same factory under the authority of the father, provided an inducement for working families to keep their children at home. In general though, industrialization led to the growing independence of young people; for the first time they were able to earn a wage and wage labour also meant that young people could set up families independently at an earlier age.

Modernization brought with it mass education, but at first there was only education for the elite. The reform of middle-class education, particularly in the public schools of England between 1827 and 1839, was accompanied by the development of pedagogic theories which held that schooling was supposed to provide a moral, physical and intellectual training for young men as a preparation for later life. Indeed, for Gillis (1981), it was here that the whole concept of 'adolescence' was born. Education also became important for access to middle-class careers. As competition for professional places increased, with an increasingly complex division of labour, so the period of training and study was prolonged and access regulated through examinations (Gillis 1981). The professions themselves began to develop their own theories of practice and identities which led to them demanding longer periods of preparation and later ages of entry (Kett 1977). Hence preparation in schools and universities had be taken more seriously.

The influence of Protestant Christianity, particularly in America, led to a concern with the moral development of the individual, particularly with their 'conversion' as a developmental stage in life, and thus a focus on youth (Kett 1977). However, perhaps more important was the idea of the male 'individual' which was nurtured within capitalist society and deriving from the Enlightenment concept of the individual as a moral agent – as a free standing person capable of exercising choices, making decisions and forming contracts. If such an individual was necessary in an industrial, capitalist economy, at what stage were they capable of becoming free agents? How much preparation did they need for this?

Hence, for bourgeois social groups, adolescence became a period of preparation for adult life with seclusion from the outside world through sexual and age segregation. Furthermore, the fact that these sectors could afford to segregate their offspring in special institutions was also a source of status and privilege – as indeed, in England it still is – even though the standard of instruction in many of these institutions was low or non-existent. The discourse of education as a reform movement, a way of training and socializing the young had yet to gain wide currency. Preparation was achieved through the kinds of academic and physical training which the public schools sought to promote. At this time, the idea of adolescence was not thought to apply equally to working class youth or to women. For middle-class young women, the separation of work and home meant that the 'respectability' of the household could be demonstrated through cloistered femininity. Marriage and domestic pursuits became the main focus of women's and girls' lives and the adolescent middle-class girl was the ideal embodiment of Victorian femininity: dependent, child-like and innocent (Gorham 1982).

For the working class, youth was far more brutal. For them, the pre-industrial notion of extended youth had disappeared. Far from being cloistered from the adult world of employment, they were forced into long, hard hours of labour from the time they were small children. Indeed, Gillis estimated that in the first decade of the ninteenth century, 80 per cent of workers in English cotton mills were children. Children carried out a variety of services or joined a form of 'apprenticeship' which was often used to exploit them as unpaid workers. These conditions shocked middle-class reformers because by mid-century they had grown up with a different, more 'cloistered' and 'innocent' idea of adolescence (Gillis 1981, Muncie 1984). Gillis goes on to argue that the concept of 'adolescence', which the middle-class had developed, was gradually imposed upon the working class through the course of the nineteenth century. The ideal of seclusion, sexual segregation and innocence meant that they were continually concerned about the 'unnatural' precocity and worldliness of working class youngsters, which they saw as evidence of delinquency.

Hence, with industrialization, social changes served to radically alter the way in which work and the family were organized. Moreover, the advent of urbanization and wage labour significantly affected the social construction of youth. For the working class, youth was a shorter period as they were absorbed into the production process from childhood onwards, whilst for the middle-class it was longer as they were removed from work until later. Natural and 'essentialised' age and sex differences were inscribed into modern institutions which also segregated social classes.

In South Eastern Europe industrialization also brought with it changes in the concept of youth and in youth transitions, but delayed industrialization and economic backwardness under authoritarian states meant that there was little room for the kind of civil society which would have encouraged social reform movements and the small middle-class were involved mainly in nationalist struggles (Schöpflin 1992). Even by 1939, for example, Bulgarian industry accounted for only 15 per cent of national income and the average enterprise employed only 26 people. The labour of young people between 9 and 25 was important in early industrialization in this region, as they made up 50–70 per cent of the labour force, mainly in textile, tobacco and coal production. Young women and girls were a particularly important source of labour because they were cheaper to employ (Mitchev 1987). Although protective legislation restricting child and female labour was some of the first welfare

legislation passed in 1907 in Bulgaria it was never properly implemented and children and young people continued to work very long
hours in hazardous conditions. Those working in factories were usually
migrants from the countryside with nowhere to sleep but on the
factory floor. As in Britain, the early industrialization may have
upset traditional hierarchies of sex and age but in the next phase
of modernization these were institutionalized in different ways.

THE BEGINNING OF STATE INTERVENTION

From the late nineteenth century adult male labour increasingly
replaced that of child and female labour in the workplace in North-
Western Europe as the idea of 'the family' as a domestic haven
spread. With the ideal of domesticity came that of childhood as a
period requiring nurture and intensive care with women as the carers.
However, most working families could not afford to fit this model
and brought work home as well as going out to work (Allen and
Walkowitz 1987). The trade unions defended this division between
home and work, campaigning for better working conditions and
helping to construct a 'respectable' working class (Stedman Jones
1971). For some, an apprenticeship became the respectable route
into skilled working class jobs, although it was a system much abused
by some trainers. For this section of the working class, 'youth' was
also a period of tutelage and dependency, and this was in contrast
to both the more extended dependency of the middle-class or the
rapid independence of the casualized working class. However, the
extent of this 'apprenticeship' system was limited in England; in
Germany the medieval system of crafts and trades absorbed the
range of new trades and divisions of labour. There was a deliberate attempt to develop a strong 'respectable' and conformist working class rather than an unskilled and unreliable one. This idea of
skill and training became more and more identified with masculine
trades.

   In Britain and Germany from the late nineteenth century, ideologies of interventionism began to replace *laissez faire* economics.
The centralization of the nation state and the rationalization of its
functions as it came to regulate more and more areas of social life
made the intervention in youth possible. The impetus for reforms
came at first from individual middle-class reformers and from philanthropic and religious institutions, from campaigns and organiza-

tions. Very often it was exposure of the horrors of some of the effects of early capitalism and the brutal exploitation of children described by novelists such as Charles Dickens and Charles Kingsley which helped to promote such reforms.

In Germany it was the work of the 'youth savers' from late nineteenth century period onwards which helped to shape a distinct 'youth politics' in Germany. The unification of Germany under Prussian domination from 1870 led to a strategy for social legislation designed to unite the different communities, including the Protestant and Catholic churches. The tradition of loyalty to the supreme state, combined with rapid industrialization, meant that in Germany social intervention took place in a more self-conscious and far reaching way. The social insurance legislation for health, old age and other contingencies along with universal education introduced at this time was designed to create a loyal, conforming and respectable working class with a stake in the system. Of particular concern were young males between the ages of 14 when they left school and 20 when they joined the army and so this was the age range which were defined as 'youth' and a locus of intervention.

Industrialization also caused major disruptions to traditional life. In Central Europe it was characterized by migration from the rural areas to the cities and from the eastern agricultural regions to the western industrial ones. The migration was mostly undertaken by young people who often left their families behind them, leading to problems of under-employment and homelessness in cities. The old craft apprenticeship system based upon small family workshops was replaced by large factories employing unskilled workers and the lines of patriarchal authority which had existed in the family, and in the craft industry regulating young people, broke down. Consequently, there was a fear of unregulated young people who might have become morally degenerate or turned towards subversive political movements, especially after the Paris Commune of 1870. Hostels were set up to house young people and a number of youth organizations tried to create new forms of association in this industrial setting to compensate for the lack of social support for youth. The churches were particularly active in providing hostels, but municipalities also helped to house the in-coming young people. Thus in Leipzig the number of places provided in hostels rose from 9604 to 22 897 between 1880 and 1900 and in Berlin there were 100 000 beds provided for young people (Linton 1991). In Germany and Central Europe voluntary associations and churches played an important role in providing for the needs of young people and youth associations also played a role in this. For example, the Weimar Republic laid down some very comprehensive legislation for young people, who were by that time recognized as an important target of intervention.

Social intervention took a number of forms: intervention in working conditions, through education and through the criminal justice system. Here we consider each of these in turn.

Constructing Youth through the Regulation of Working Conditions

Industrialization brought concentrations of workers in mass production living and working in appalling conditions. In Britain, reforms of working conditions took place with the introduction of the Factory Acts from 1833 onwards and these were reinforced by campaigns by reformers to protect orphans and avoid the economic exploitation of children. This employment legislation served to gradually reassert the male head of household's authority and was supported by male trade unionist campaigns for a 'family wage' (Humphries 1981, Muncie 1984). However, in Britain youth were not identified explicitly in such laws and the youth debate was not so clearly articulated as in Germany.

With the shift of young people's jobs towards the distributive trades from the turn of the century in Britain, the main problem identified was that of 'Boy Labour'. This was where young men were employed until they became entitled to adult wages at which point they were replaced by someone younger. Hence, it was feared that young men were too ready to enter 'dead end' jobs with no future. However, despite discussion of the problem, no legislation followed. Intervention in the youth labour market was prompted only by rising youth unemployment during the inter-war period when youth were targeted for special temporary employment measures, some of which involved additional training and forcing them to take the jobs which were available (Rees and Rees 1982). These schemes were only temporary, since with the coming of the Second World War unemployment disappeared and new priorities emerged. Apprenticeship training was subject to sporadic reform in Britain, the most comprehensive attempt to regulate it being in the 1960s (Roberts 1984). However, it was never comprehensive and even those crafts and industries which were covered by formal training declined in the later decades of the twentieth century. It is evident that in Britain intervention in youth took place only when there was some crisis; comprehensive protective legislation for this age group, as existed in Germany, was lacking.

In Germany, by contrast, a number of Imperial Laws at the end of the nineteenth century and early twentieth century identified youth in particular as a category to be protected. Laws in 1871 and 1896 regulated youth wages, their hours of work, holidays, conditions of employment and their health and this was already building upon an established tradition of regulating conditions for young workers. Great emphasis was placed upon vocational training and the model was of the young apprentice as a disciplined and diligent young worker, who would accept authority and become a good, conforming citizen, who would later draw a pension. Hence, apprenticeships were introduced within a number of new industrial trades. It was argued that young people should receive vocational counselling and the Chambers of Commerce and the various craft guilds took a keen interest in the inculcation of appropriate work discipline in young workers. Most important in these reforms was the role of the 'continuation schools', begun on a part-time, voluntary basis for young people after they had left compulsory full-time education at 14, but later made a formal part of the education/ training system which continued to the age of 17 or 18. Legislation passed in the early 1920s also regulated the conditions of work for young people and standardized apprenticeship training (Linton 1991).

In much of Eastern Europe full industrialization took place under communism where it was prioritized as the 'most important political task'. After the Second World War, East-Central Europe (between western Ukraine and Bratislava) consisted of backward, mainly rural countries, in which industrial production constituted only a small share of the national product. Furthermore, these countries had faced terrible devastation from war. Industrialization was introduced under communism following the Soviet model, with the nationalization of the means of production and co-ordination according to a centralized national economic plan. Youth played a particularly important part in this socialist reconstruction and were mobilized in the Youth Brigade movement, being brought in as 'volunteers' to work on the construction of roads, railways, factories and dams – the creation of an industrial infrastructure. As industry developed, so this unskilled volunteer labour force became unnecessary, but the Brigade movement continued, usually through sending young people to work in agriculture because this was thought of as an important component of a socialist education during summer (Daskalov 1991). For example, in the period 1957–1962, two and a half million young people from schools, colleges and administrative jobs worked as volunteer labour for two months of the year in Bulgaria.

Young people also formed an important part of the normal labour force, being heavily represented in industry. Women participated in this socialist industrialization as well as men so that by the 1960s they were nearly half the labour force (Semov et al. 1986). Industrialization continued to draw young people from the countryside to the towns under socialism, with three quarters of migrants being below 30 years old and nearly two-thirds of these being women (Beltcheva and Bozhikov 1981). This was welcomed as 'a revolutionary change – thousands of young people changed their class affiliations' from peasants to the more progressive working class (Semov 1972:50), but from the 1970s there was growing anxiety about the de-population of the villages. The urbanization and industrialization of Eastern Europe represented a major social change achieved through centralized control over a very short period of time, but it created a new situation of large concentrations of young people who had to be regulated in new ways, as we shall see later.

Hence young people formed an important part of the industrial labour force in all parts of Europe. In Western Europe intervention to regulate their working conditions was prompted by a fear of social disorder which young people could cause and a desire to produce a conforming citizen, whilst in communist countries there was a more deliberate attempt to mould young people into the ideal socialist citizen in order to build a new society.

Constructing Youth through Education Reforms

Modernization was associated in all countries with the introduction of mass education as a compulsory duty up to a minimum age. From the nineteenth century onwards (earlier in the Austrian Empire), full-time compulsory education was introduced in many countries of Western Europe for all people. It thus extended the period of 'childhood' dependency, often in opposition to the needs of working class families who needed the extra income from these children. However, oral histories indicate that resistance took the form of working whilst truanting, which was common, and that young people continued to work before and after school (Humphries 1981). Bells, timetables and regimentation were all modelled on the factory system and intended to produce docile and employable workers (Johnson 1976). These reforms were not universally welcomed, especially amongst the unskilled working class, and resistance included riots, truanting and school strikes.

For the middle-class, however, education became increasingly important for granting access to jobs and maintaining social status. Hence, the grammar schools and boarding schools were increasingly put under pressure to provide the correct type of socialization for these class positions. An extended period of schooling beyond the minimum age was thought necessary to provide this for male youth. From the end of the nineteenth century the role of education as a civilizing mission for the working classes, to socialize young people into their proper stations in life and to compensate for the inadequate instruction it was supposed that they had received in their own homes, became more widespread and accepted. Furthermore, the pedagogic discourse became more influential with the development of the teaching profession and influential in this was the work of the US author, John Dewey, who argued that education was crucial for the development of the individual.

In Germany, the work of Georg Kerschensteiner helped to spread a model of 'civic education' combined with vocational education for working youth (Linton 1991). Kerschensteiner in an influential essay argued that, to become new model citizens, young people needed to be taught civic duty and to be encouraged to work for the common good instead of selfish goals. These ideas were instituted through 'continuation schools' which were part-time post-compulsory educational institutions absorbing about 9 hours per week of the young person's time up to the age of 17. Building on an already established tradition of voluntary schooling, these became widespread after 1900 and were later instituted in law. They were divided according to craft guilds and large firms took an interest in these continuation schools, seeing them as vehicles for education of the model young worker. They also learned about the laws governing the employment of young people, business and booking-keeping skills, history and knowledge of their trade.

For young women in the early part of the nineteenth century there was little formal education (Dyhouse 1981). Middle-class women mostly were taught the feminine arts to prepare them for marriage such as embroidery, playing the piano and a little conversation to make them good companions for their husbands. However, they were also expected to know the skills of housewifery, since most middle-class families could not afford sufficient servants to keep them in genteel leisure. Too much learning, it was feared, would lead to sickness. In the late nineteenth century, however, a number of reforms of women's education took place with special schools for girls offering more formal education and women's colleges were established in Oxford and Cambridge (although women were not allowed to obtain a degree) (Dyhouse 1981). For working class girls there was an explicit emphasis on training for domestic service, a subject of particular interest for the middle- and upper-class patrons of these schools. Youth work and compulsory education for girls were directed towards producing good mothers and to addressing the problem of poor health and nutrition resulting in high mortality amongst the working class (Linton 1991).

Many of these interventions can be traced to the changing ideology of the family – that it was a cosy domestic unit, separated from the fierce world of the market place, a place of comfort and leisure maintained by women (Davidoff, L'Esperance and Newby 1976). This cloistered view of domesticity was reflected in principles of town planning and building design and reinforced through philanthropic charities and through legislation which assumed that women and children belonged at home. This vision of domesticity helped to create the idea of children and women as weak and helpless dependents and the adolescent girl was part of this world, whereas the adolescent boy needed to be encouraged to venture out. Magazines for Victorian young men and women reflected these different gender stereotypes and the *Boys' Own* magazine – full of adventure stories – began its life in the 1850s in Britain.

In general, the spread of universal education marked an important moment in the standardization and institutionalization of age-grading. But this happened in different ways for young men and women, for different social classes and in different countries. Thus divisions of sex and class were likewise institutionalized.

In South Eastern Europe modernization in education had an additional meaning – it served as a means for national self-determination. Intellectuals valued education as the means for inculcating a national consciousness and therefore it always held a special and revered place. Although the first law making education compulsory from ages 7 to 11 (raised to 14 in 1921) was issued in 1892 in Bulgaria, in practice non-attendance was high, reaching 75 per cent among village girls (Yoncheva 1943). Whilst the early pedagogical ideas emphasized equal access to education by girls (Karavelov 1876) and although women teachers and writers practised and propagated this idea, female education still lagged behind that for boys and was focused mainly on agriculture, cooking and sewing. Secondary and higher education was almost non-existent and those who wanted to extend their education usually had to do so in one of the main centres of learning, often in a different country and usually in a different language. Illiteracy was widespread before the communist takeovers.

From the time of the communist rule, however, mass education was seen as a priority and there were rapid changes. General education was made compulsory for everyone and access to higher education was offered to everyone for the first time, with full state support until a person had finished his or her education. This resulted in a dramatic changes in the education of the population which went from being semi-literate to full participation rates and Higher Educational participation of similar levels to Western Europe. This will be discussed in more detail in Chapter 3, but at this stage we should note that rapid mass education helped in the further classification and age-grading of youth and and its segregation in society. From being the subordinated household workers of the pre-industrial period youth became a privileged group whose main duty was to study. The youth phase became general for the first time in this region.

Constructing Youth through the Criminal Justice System

Another source of anxiety in industrializing and urbanizing countries was that unregulated, unskilled young people in cities would turn to crime, and through this period various attempts were made to deal with the problem of youth crime. Reforms of the criminal justice system likewise imposed a more 'sheltered' concept of adolescence upon working-class young people. In Britain, up until the mid-nineteenth century children were traditionally treated not much differently to adults in the eyes of the law after the age of 7 (Muncie 1984). Campaigns by Mary Carpenter and others fought for a definition of children and young people as less criminally responsible than adults. Rather than being subject to hanging, imprisonment or deportation, they should be 'improved' though training and assistance in separate institutions removed from the contaminating influence of their families. The Youthful Offenders Act of 1854 and later the 1908 Children's Act introduced reformatories for young people and, later on, the first Borstal. It is doubtful whether in practice this 'treatment' model, which served to pathologize working-class behaviour and legitimize intervention in their lives, was ultimately more humane. However, it did introduce the idea of childhood and adolescence as periods in which young people could be 'cured' of delinquency and therefore helped to legitimate them as a target for intervention.

A further form of intervention which served to define young people during the nineteenth century was that surrounding sexuality and the age of consent. Much of the middle-class campaigning had involved going into the slums and 'saving' 'fallen' women and working-class children from a life of vice. The very high rates of prostitution, and particularly child prostitution, reflected the sexual vulnerability of girls and women at the time, this being one of the main careers open to working-class women after they had been pushed out of the factories by 'protective' legislation (Walkowitz 1980). Whilst for boys it was their street life and gang life which caused concern (Pearson 1983), for girls it was their sexual misdemeanours which needed reforming. Hence, legislation aimed to control sexual contact and these campaigns involved the redefinition of women and young children as innocent victims of male abuse and sought to protect them from this in the law (Jeffreys 1985). As young people came to be defined as a special group, so the regulation and control of adolescent sexuality came to be a major preoccupation in textbooks on youth, health and education during this period. Masturbation in young men was thought to cause particularly severe problems including physical weakness and mental ill-health. It was believed that girls needed to be protected from their own bodies, particularly after the onset of menstruation, otherwise they would become subject to illnesses such as hysteria or 'chlorosis' which described a wide range of symptoms (Gorham 1982). Hence, this too had the effect of raising the age of sexual responsibility, extending childhood and formalizing age-status transitions through state intervention.

From the late nineteenth century, concern with moral purity, as evinced in a variety of campaigns, meant that children were on the one hand treated as victims in need of protection and on the other were also guilty of immorality themselves. This ambiguous status justified their segregation in special institutions. This was linked to the rise of the institution more generally as an instrument of 'scientific' reform (Scull 1977, Foucault 1975). Hence orphanages, prisons, schools and reformatories all had much in common in their organization and their custodians developed into professional specialists for the care and treatment of differentially classified social problems. In the twentieth century, such 'treatment' was elevated to the status of a 'science'. Working-class delinquents were defined as having personality disorders which were in need of correction and treatment. This work, claiming a 'scientific' legitimacy, was influential in the creation and training of the teaching and probation professions. The treatment took the form of correcting the supposed inadequate socialization and parenting which the young delinquent had received at home.

In Germany children and youth were also treated differently in the law and from 1876 a law made it possible to take children away from parents where they were in danger of 'complete moral collapse' (Linton 1991). Young delinquents were dealt with in separate juvenile courts and instead of punishment they could opt for welfare education and reform. Young people under 18 were not thought to be criminally responsible in any case, although in England this was and still is set at the age of 10. Thus in Germany, the juvenile justice system, as other areas of state intervention, served to single out youth as a special category for protection to a much greater extent than in England.

In Bulgaria the age of criminal responsibility was not defined until 1896 when it was set at age 10 and the first correctional home was built in 1917 funded by voluntary donations (Khinova 1969). The first specialized law for juvenile offenders was issued in 1943 – nearly one century after that in Britain – and although the age of criminal responsibility was raised to 12 it was still possible to execute a child from age 10 onwards. The legal code of the communist state raised the minimum age of criminal responsibility to age 13 in 1951 and 14 in 1956. Since 1968 the death penalty was made applicable only to young people from age of 20 – except for those serving in the army. Until 1944 the only penalty available for young people was incarceration, but after that new measures for improvement and re-socialization were introduced.

Thus there has been a tendency towards treating young people more leniently in the criminal justice system and as a category separate from adults. The duration of this category in terms of chronological age has generally been extended since the legislation was first introduced. Broadly those defined as junior in the law are thought less responsible for their actions and more capable of being reformed. This was associated with modernization as is clear from the different times that similar legislation was introduced in the more advanced North-Western European countries and the more backward South-Eastern ones.

THE CONSTRUCTORS OF YOUTH: THE YOUTH MOVEMENTS

Many of these reforms took place as a result of campaigns at the end of the nineteenth and beginning of the twentieth centuries urging more state legislation to regulate social life after the disruptions caused by industrialization. Of particular importance were the various youth movements which occurred all over Europe. These were mostly led by middle-class people who sought to impose a disciplined and dutiful middle-class model of youth not just upon the youth from their own class, but particularly upon the working-class youth, whose discipline and morality were seen as a major problem. Working-class youth worked long hours in poor conditions and, in places which urbanized rapidly, they often lived away from home. They had access to a street life, they had little education and they eagerly absorbed popular culture in the form of cheap novels, music halls and pubs. Middle-class reformers were concerned that they could easily drift into a life of crime, casual sex and drink. Unlike in the pre-industrial period, they were not subject to patriarchal authority or the traditional youth associations and so their behaviour was not regulated. Through these campaigns, a middle-class view of youth was imposed upon the working class (Springhall 1977, Gillis 1981).

The development of the youth saving campaign in the late nineteenth and early twentieth century in North-West Europe was linked with scientific ideas about eugenics which were gaining currency at this time – the idea that the race of the nation was deteriorating on account of immorally and indiscriminate breeding and the 'stock' needed to be improved and saved. This also linked the youth movements to nationalism: youth were seen as the seed corn of the future. Therefore by winning and improving the youth a more glorious national future seemed assured. Thus, youth movements in both

Britain and Germany embodied a number of racist assumptions. In Bulgaria youth movements were linked with national revival and their main focus was on nationalism. Therefore, the construction of 'youth' was linked with ideologies of nationalism and the nation state. Religion also played an important role. Let us now look at some examples.

The first movement to be set up in Britain was that of the Boys Brigade organized by William Smith in 1883, which sought to replace the earlier settlement and improvement schemes in working-class neighbourhoods with military-style drill and regimentation, although its main membership was lower-middle-class rather than working-class (Blanch 1979). The Boy Scouts were set up by General Baden-Powell in 1908, inspired by his experiences in the Boer War. This was reflected in the militarism of its aims and organization which were to inculcate ideals of Empire and nationalism. Others, however, set up less militaristic alternatives: Leslie Paul's Woodcraft Folk and John Hargreaves' Kibbo Kift Kindred were examples of these. Although the movements was supposed to be classless, the bare knees and extended boyishness that it involved as well as the secret rituals and sexual segregation were characteristic of upper-class conceptions of adolescence (Gillis 1981). Other youth movements included the Church Lads Brigade, the YMCA, the Jewish Lads Brigade, the Catholic Lads Brigade amongst others, with varying mixtures of militarism and religion.

For girls the ideals of militarism and preparedness were not thought to be appropriate. Although they still needed to be educated and reformed, it was to different ends. Youth work with girls was originally stimulated by a desire to protect girls from the corrupting effects of factory language and morals and this was the basis upon which the 'Snow Drop Bands', popular around 1889–1890, were formed. For the working-class girls, there was also a fear that financial independence would encourage sexual precocity and so these childhood-extending movements were all the more important. Other clubs for girls were designed to preserve the morals of working-class girls and help them in turn to improve the morality of men. The Girls Friendly Society was set up by the Anglican church in 1885 and boasted 821 branches within a few years. It existed on upper-class patronage, and like many of the schools were intended to improve the quality of domestic servants and to purify women with notions of chastity and subservient femininity. As Dyhouse (1981) points out, it is paradoxical that organized leisure for middle-class girls was concerned to protect their delicate constitutions and not cause undue intellectual strain, whereas for working-class girls it was thought necessary in order to channel off their surplus energy! Sport and exercise was not supposed to encourage girls to become rough and uncouth 'hoydens' (Gorham 1982).

In Germany there developed a group of what Linton (1991) calls 'youth savers' from the end of the nineteenth century. These helped to develop the discourse of 'youth' which later became the legitimation for intervention through pamphlets, booklets, books and conferences. These conferences were often attended by several thousand people including teachers, businessmen, people from the municipalities and others who had an interest in youth. These recommended a progressive pedagogic approach to looking after the interests of young people during what was defined as their 'storm and stress' period. On account of what was thought to be the delicate and unstable condition of adolescence, they argued, associations were needed to provide moral support and guidance for young people. Like the reformers in England, the German youth savers were middle-class and were dismayed at the condition of urban working-class youth. However, they were more systematic in analysing the situation of youth and in targeting them explicitly than was the case in Britain. These youth savers of the nineteenth century tried to grapple with what they saw as the problems of modernity – the disruption of traditional community relations and the problems of working with mass production in alienating conditions. As in England, it was the working-class youth in urban areas which were the targets of reform.

In Germany, the tradition of youth fraternities continued into the nineteenth century although now they were romantic and somewhat nostalgic evocations of the 'brotherhood' of the earlier period by young men at universities. From the end of the nineteenth century a number of more general youth organizations were founded leading to the creation of a general council for federated youth. These were founded around a range of issues – churches and professions began their own youth groups and others were issue-oriented, concerned with nudism or against alcohol. These had a mainly middle-class constituency. The best known of these early youth movements was the 'Wandervogel' promoting an outdoor life during leisure hours. They relied upon a romantic rejection of industrial development and encouraged trips to the countryside, summer camps and their own uniforms, songs and rituals (Becker 1946). Such early organizations may have served to sustain the idea of youth as a singular and rather idealistic stage of personal development and certainly youth appear to have had a high profile as an issue of public concern in Central Europe.

From the late nineteenth century more mass organizations developed. The Evangelical Church in Germany was instrumental in setting up hostels for the young people in cities but also in providing youth clubs, lectures, songs and libraries. By 1912 they had 143 000 members (Linton 1991). The Catholic Church, too, provided Catholic education for the members of its youth club as well as encouraging self-control, budgeting and personal hygiene. These religious movements were more or less anti-socialist in orientation but despite the repressive laws against them the socialist youth organizations were amongst the most successful for urban working youth. They operated under the guise of 'Worker Gymnast' associations before 1904 and also formed bicycle and singing clubs. There were a variety of sports groups and from 1911 a more explicitly military Young Germany League was founded with the aim of providing nationalistic training and military exercises. With significant state assistance, this became the largest youth organization with 750 000 members by the outbreak of the First World War. Its orientation was also explicitly anti-socialist and it used the continuation schools as its recruiting ground. Youth sports organizations also formed part of the Czech national revival as represented through the Sokol organizations to be found in every town and creating the prototype of mass synchronized exercises in sports stadiums which was later adopted by the communist and National Socialist governments. From the twentieth century onwards, youth groups began to be more and more state supported in Central Europe and were seen as an element of nation-state-building.

During the late nineteenth century, much of the non-institutional work with young people was undertaken by volunteers in North-Western Europe, but during the early twentieth century they increasingly began to develop as specialist professionals: what Kett (1977) calls the 'architects of adolescence'. A discourse of helping and 'cultivating' youth began to emerge along with a more formalized idea of age-status transitions based upon eligibility for membership. We return to this topic later in the chapter.

Organized youth movements in Eastern European countries such as Bulgaria mostly took the form of recruitment by adult organizations or directly by the state. Both spontaneous protest and formal organizations were highly politicized covering the whole range of the political spectrum: nationalistic and fascist; communist and agrarian. There were youth sections of the numerous liberal, conservative, Christian and Catholic parties. Even youth tourist, gymnastics, educational and abstainers' organizations were politically polarized. The state made many attempts to form a mass youth organization under its control and in 1934 a youth movement was established on the model of the Hitler Youth. During the War in 1943 the state renewed its efforts to impose this organization on all youth and many autonomous youth organizations were proclaimed members. Although youth movements raised general political issues rather than presenting youth interests on the political scene, they encouraged public discussion about this 'problem' group.

Through this politicization of youth associations, youth came to be seen not just as people who were troubled or troubling, in need of help and protection, but also as the bearers of the future, the transformers of society. Therefore they were selected as a group with a particularly important role to play. This reached its apotheosis in the communist and fascist movements which emerged in central and eastern Europe.

YOUTH AS TRANSFORMERS OF SOCIETY: FASCISM AND COMMUNISM

We have already described the way in which youth came to be seen as important instruments of nationalist movements. However, it was under totalitarian regimes of communism and fascism that youth were identified most fully as agents of change for the whole of society. It was in societies where these regimes held power that youth were targeted most fully as objects of intervention. In Germany, from the early 1920s youth movements started to become more political in character as the main political parties founded their own youth wings and an element in youth politics came to be aligned with either the extreme right or the extreme left, who fought pitched battles in the street. National Socialists started to organize a youth wing (later called the 'Hitler Youth') which carried on the youth movement tradition of organization by and for the young, set up a national organizational structure and organized national rallies as a way of collecting funds (Becker 1946). After Hitler finally assumed power in 1933 and consolidated the Third Reich based on an ideology of anti-Semitism, racial superiority and aggressive nationalism, the Hitler Youth included all youth aged 10 to 21 and women were organized into the 'Bund Deutscher Mädchen' (BDM). After that young people were recruited into the SS or the army. Since the National Socialist party held absolute power, the Hitler Youth could absorb all the other youth organizations, whose leaders were forced to conform or terrorized into submission or even sent away to concentration camps if they refused to comply. The membership swelled from 107 956 in 1932 to 3 577 565 in 1938 (Koch 1975).

This creation and consolidation of the Hitler Youth happened because youth were seen as an important and essential part of the fascist mission. They were the rising new generation of the future and inculcating the right ideals was a priority through both education and indoctrination (Koch 1975). The Hitler Youth was institutionalized with its own full-time officers – there was strong moral pressure for everyone to join and a programme of activities was constructed, designed to weaken parental influence and inculcate total commitment to the National Socialist state. At the same time, young people were given great powers, encouraged to inform on their parents and teachers and to effect a fascist transformation in schools and universities from below (Koch 1975). German youth were elevated as a privileged group and protective legislation in the workplace was passed, although in fact much of the new legislation to protect and promote youth was never enacted because of the continuing pressures of war. Instead, young men were supposed to sacrifice themselves for the Fatherland: younger and younger people were used in the war effort, first of all in welfare and social campaigns and later in active service. The result was that those too young to smoke, but deemed old enough to fight, were allocated a sweet instead of a cigarette ration (Koch 1975). Despite the great efforts to indoctrinate young people and to make the organization replace other influences on their lives such as school or family, much of the propaganda material was ignored and there was even some resistance to it. Some youth retreated into youth sub-cultures based upon swing or jazz music, even though these were condemned as 'subversive' in much the same way as was to happen in communist systems later (Polster 1989) (see Chapter 5).

Hence, through the Hitler Youth, young people were identified strongly as a group and as agents of transformation to a new era. The same trend can be observed in communist countries where youth organizations were supposed to help create the 'new socialist person' (Pilkington 1994). Young people were to be nurtured, controlled, cared for and brought into the Communist Party. In return they were to show their gratitude with loyalty and obedience. Political activity was channelled through the only authorized channel – the Young Communist League, sometimes known as Komsomol.

The so-called 'Komsomol' was first established in revolutionary Russia. Although the Bolsheviks had no youth organization before the revolution, the Komsomol was created in 1918 with the intention of recruiting only the select 'vanguard' of youth (Riordan 1989a). It was supposed to be independent from the Party, but under civil war conditions it was taken over and controlled by the Party and was unable to ever again become independent. The leaders were nominated by the Party and were Party members. Until the mid 1920s Komsomol was small and had to compete with other youth groups such as the scouts or the YMCA, but from then on other organizations were proscribed and Komsomol became the only organization for youth. It then started to have a mass membership and aimed to represent all youth – at its height it had 40 million members in the Soviet Union. It served to define age-status, because 'youth' were all those who belonged to the Young Communist League (14–28 in Bulgaria, but up to age 30 elsewhere). The Komsomol was therefore a key institution in understanding the social construction of youth under communism.

YOUTH UNDER COMMUNISM: CONSTRUCTING THE NEW SOCIALIST PERSON

The creation of youth as a category under communism followed a different ideological pattern than in Western Europe. Rather than identifying youth as a problematic life-stage, the communist state ideology interpreted 'youth' as collective agent of social transformation. From the time of the 'socialist revolutions' in Eastern Europe, youth were officially constructed as 'the builders of the bright communist society' and this served to legitimize party intervention in adolescent life. Therefore, the purpose of control over young people was not on account of their deviation from 'normal' life, as in Western Europe, but in their responsibility for the realization of the communist ideal. At the same time the Party was the supreme power and the 'leading force of communist construction'. Since the

Party had the benefit of being armed with the knowledge of how social development should take place, it could offer the best strategies which youth would be called upon to put into practice. This attitude explains the peculiarities of the Communist Party youth policy – monitoring young people rather than meeting their needs. The policies were aimed at the incorporation of young people into society and were subject to conflicting pressures, between protection on the one side and indoctrination on the other. The main goal of Communist Party youth policy was ideological education, and welfare provision was only a secondary consideration, intended to bolster this goal. Thus, young people were provided with free education and guaranteed jobs, cheap leisure and social security in return for submitting to the study of school programmes designed by the Party and to work which carried out the plan of the Party. The principle – Party care for faithful youth – embodied the paternalistic nature of authority in which youth were presented as being in the forefront of social change but were, in fact, completely subordinated to this authority.

From the beginning of the establishment of the communist regimes in countries such as Bulgaria after the Second World War, Komsomol was the only official youth organization (Kitanov 1981). Its aim was to incorporate youth into communism through enlightenment and instruction. The new Soviet Party rules in 1986 stated that the Komsomol was 'the active assistant and reserve of the Party. It is to help the Party educate young people in a communist spirit, involve them in the practical building of the new society, and shape a generation of all-round developed people ready to work and defend the homeland' (quoted in Riordan 1989a). The Komsomol was the last stage of a hierarchy of organizations which sorted and graded young people according to age. The first organization – called 'Octobrists' in the Soviet Union but given other names elsewhere – were for children 6–10 and this was followed by the 'Young Pioneers' for those aged 10–14 and then the Komsomol up to age 28 (or 30 in some countries). In the Soviet Union 65 per cent of young people were members by 1987, whilst in Bulgaria between 80 and 90 per cent of the young population joined. However, many joined for instrumental reasons – because they needed a Komsomol reference in order to get into higher education for example – or because Komsomol provided leisure and sports facilities. Therefore, membership was much higher among students than among young workers (Pilkington 1994).

Later on, following the spread of youth cultural activities in the 1960s and 1970s (described in Chapter 5), there were fears among the leadership in Bulgaria that young people had different tastes and interests to those of the older generation who had fought in the Second World War. There were calls for organizational reform of the Komsomol with attempts to better represent young people's interests through more youth representatives in public organizations (Mitev 1988). One result was a building programme for stadiums, swimming pools and so on, all ostensibly for the benefit of young people. This material aid deflected attention from the lack of real autonomy of the youth organization. By the end of the 1970s, however, there was a reversal of this trend once more and rights, resources and power were taken over by different state organizations, although this was followed by further instructions from General Secretary Zhivkov for reforms (Peneva 1982). However, Komsomol activists continued to operate in their established way, which meant obedience to the hierarchy. Although the Party called for more trust in youth, in practice they considered suspicious every gathering of young people outside secondary education without parents or teachers present even when Komsomol activists were there. For example, students were seen as potential dissidents and all their meetings had to be supervised. Therefore, although there were repeated calls for greater autonomy of the Komsomol, none was very successful.

The Komsomol had a number of explicit functions. First, the 'socio-economic function of Komsomol' was to help the schools in the educational process and to help enterprises in the fulfilment of the national economic plan. Secondly, there was the political function of Komsomol. However, the definition of this function – to incorporate youth into the realization of the Party's decisions – presupposed that the right conclusion had already been reached and, therefore, that further discussion by young people within the organization was unnecessary. Thirdly, the Komsomol also had an ideological function, to educate young people in socialist principles, and this was carried out through a system of lectures. The measurement of success was purely quantitative and was counted in terms of the numbers of organized lectures and the numbers of young people attending them. Despite these pretensions, most of the Komsomol activities in which young people really participated were things such as organizing courses for learning to drive, amateur arts or organizing dances – what were in fact fairly 'light' lei-

sure activities. Since the Komsomol had a monopoly on such facilities for young people, most people participated.

The Komsomol proved unable to reform itself radically to reflect the changing interests of young people. It remained primarily
a 'transmission belt' for Party policy rather than a vehicle for representing young people's interests, and so by the 1980s it was growing
increasingly out of touch with young people's real interests and
aspirations. However, the institutionalized hypocrisy whereby people
learned to pretend to conform concealed much of this disconnection between real aspirations and the Komsomol representation of
youth. From the 1970s and 1980s the growth of 'non formal' groups
described in Chapter 5 posed a challenge to the Komsomol. These
ranged from sub-cultures to semi-organized groups for ecology or
music which eschewed formal organization but nevertheless had
informal leaders who enjoyed more credibility than the Komsomol
leadership. One response in the 1980s was to attempt to absorb
such groups by offering official space, but in general the Komsomol
was unable to accommodate the changing aspirations of young people
to the extent that in 1980s Mikhail Gorbachev was able to describe
it as 'marching down one side of the street while young people are
walking down the other in the opposite direction' (quoted in Riordan
1989a: 16).

THE JOB OF CONSTRUCTING YOUTH: THE GROWTH OF YOUTH PROFESSIONS

The different issues associated with youth have resulted in the growth
of different kinds of agencies – and with the professional agents
defined through them. These different professional groups then define
their own 'knowledge base' or area of expertise – that is, the treatment of the social problem which has been identified. Whilst many
of these may share models of youth which we explored in Chapter 1,
they also interpret them according to ideas developed within their
own organizational structures. Many of the theories outlined in
Chapter 1 also form the basis for professional intervention, forming part of the 'expertise' of the profession. The relationship between ideas or theories of youth and ways in which they are dealt
with by professionals is close.

Professional work with young people (outside of education) takes
a number of forms. For example, youth work usually involves

intervention in the 'free time' or 'leisure time' of young people outside of school, training or work but also social work and work with young people suffering various social and physical problems. In communist countries this was heavily politicized, although in both parts of Europe participation in these kinds of youth services was usually voluntary and such services depended to a large extent upon voluntary staff as well (in communist societies participation was not compulsory but, unlike in the West, was near universal because of the more extensive control and surveillance of the young population). The second main form of intervention is in dealing with youth who deviate in some way from the accepted norm, either by breaking the law or through various kinds of disruptive or anti-social behaviour, which means that they could not be accommodated within normal schools and institutions or because they are victims of some sort – as orphans, or having been removed from their families. These are more likely to fall under the aegis of social work, probation work or the criminal justice system for minors, which is mostly distinct from that designed for adults. Whilst lower-class young people are likely to find themselves the objects of intervention by such agencies, middle-class young people find themselves objects of a different kind of professional gaze: their parents are likely to turn to the help of a range of professional counsellors and experts – psychologists, doctors, psychiatrists, psychotherapists and so on – for help in regulating and understanding young people's problems (Aggleton 1987). This means that there is also an array of professionals in the private or semi-private sector who specialize in the problems of people in this age category. In diverse parts of Europe we can see the problems of youth being allocated rather differently between professional groups. In the communist half of Europe, youth professionals did not claim to be neutral or detached in their approaches, but rather were committed to politically mobilizing youth as an element of their professional purpose.

Whilst in Western European societies the purpose of intervention was to bring 'deviant' youth back to the 'norm', in communist societies the emphasis was quite a different one: the purpose of intervention was to assist youth in the realization of the norm. The project of youth in social transformation and building a 'bright new future' meant that, rather than being saved and normalized, youth had to be educated and monitored to achieve this goal. Deviation did not officially exist in any case, although there were very large numbers of children and young people in institutions and a view of how they should be dealt with existed based upon official ideology. No strong discourse of professionalism developed around it. In Britain and Germany we can see the contrast between 'weak' and 'strong' models of youth intervention and in communist societies, the strongest models of all.

Who were the youth professionals under communism? The professionalism and professional training of youth workers was a field of discussion in the East just as it was in the West. However, the main tension was between the need for a necessary knowledge base and the requirements for the so-called autonomy of the organization. Youth workers were synonymous with Komsomol officers and this was a politically as well as professionally charged role. By the 1980s Komsomol was numerically a mighty organization with 40 million members in the Soviet Union, 350 000 full time officers, 49 colleges, 33 museums, 7 propaganda trains and 3 publishing houses among other assets (Riordan 1989a). In Moscow alone there were 2700 professional Komsomol workers, more than in any of the Ministries. These could be characterized as the 'youth professionals' of the former system. Whilst Komsomol workers sought to safeguard their professional status by erecting entrance barriers, this contradicted the idea that Komsomol should be an organization run by and for young people themselves. Thus Komsomol workers aspired to professional status not so much through qualifications but by emphasizing the 'organizational abilities' of officers, but this was concealed by the politicized nature of appointments and by the widespread practice of nepotism. Because the Komsomol could be an important stepping stone to a political career and therefore social mobility, the people who aspired to be youth professionals were seldom motivated by any concern for young people. Indeed, many of them had little interest either in their members (as long as members attended appropriate meetings) or in the slogans they were promulgating. However, a high Komsomol position was also a *nomenklatura* position which brought with it access to special hospitals, shops, holiday facilities, tax-free additional income and chauffeur driven limousines which were not available to ordinary people. The organizational abilities and ambitions of these youth leaders is evidenced in the fact that many of them are now senior political leaders under the reformed post-communist governments.

Although posts in the Komsomol were elected, in practice all positions had a nominee and there were no more candidates than there were positions (Riordan 1989a). This undermined faith in the democratic potential of the Komsomol. One survey about attitudes towards elections for Komsomol posts gives an indication of the alienation of most members from their organization and the lack of real autonomy which it represented saying 'The election results have been decided beforehand by the director of the school so we only have to vote (to confirm them)' (Mitev 1979: 60). Since the Party had the decisive say over all levels of the organization – from the election of the lowest unpaid secretary in the local unit to the highest officers – the workers in the organization directed their attention upwards. They developed an attitude of arrogance and social distance towards ordinary Komsomol members since these had little relevance to the real priorities of the Komsomol. This meant that Komsomol officers were increasingly out of touch with the mood and preoccupations of young people on the ground (ibid.).

Young people in turn became alienated from the youth professionals and from the organization itself. A survey by the Bulgarian Youth Institute in 1978 of 10 000 Komsomol members aged 14–28 found that members thought the organization ought to be providing leisure facilities rather than having any broader political or representational goals (Mitev 1979). The growing polarization between the Komsomol membership and the leaders of the organization meant that for many young people participating in the survey, the Komsomol leadership and the organization itself were synonymous and they did not feel that it represented their interests at all. When criticism was invited of the Komsomol in the Soviet Union under *glasnost*, the letters of protest were harsh and uncompromising. One writer complained of the 'Komsomol leader in his black limousine and three-piece suit who turns up at subbotniks (voluntary work days) just to declaim about the public spiritedness of youth ... It is time to speak the unpalatable truth to Komsomol bureaucrats, lackeys and time-servers, all those for whom the Komsomol is a step on life's self-propelled escalator ... you can't carry on like that!' (quoted in Riordan 1989a: 29).

The Party elite paid special attention to the recruitment of women among Komsomol cadres but, in practice, women tended to be found amongst the lower ranks of the organization whilst the higher offices were dominated by men. At the lower levels of the organization women were the majority. For example, in the junior 'Pioneer' organizations, 90 per cent of all paid staff were women, but there were few among the higher ranking political cadres and even within these cadres women were more over-represented in the lower posts rather than in the Central Committee (Ivanov 1981).

It is easy in hindsight to see the progressive organizational failures and creeping sclerosis of the Komsomol organization. The policies it enacted – whatever its official organization – tended to be based upon prohibitions rather than stimuli, on sanctions rather than encouragement. The Komsomol suffered from over-centralization, sometimes resulting in absurd regulations being passed down to the local units. As Mitev (1988) has pointed out, they played the role of the persecutors of young people rather than their defenders. As a result it lost the real support of young people who increasingly only pretended to conform to its requirements.

Thus the Komsomol had constructed a pervasive mechanism of surveillance and control over young people which was intended to supervise their activities outside of formal institutions of work, training or school. This was based upon theories of transformation to communism including the reconstruction of personality. The Komsomol had an important position in the construction of the New Socialist Person, but it was clear that by the 1980s it had become rigid and insensitive to the real needs and aspirations of young people. Nonconformity and criticism were expressed in social surveys but also through espousal of new youth cultures and later sub-cultures (which we explore in Chapter 5).

With the fall of communism many youth organizations disappeared. The 'modern' idea of youth as missionaries for a brave new world evaporated. The majority of young people, tired of compulsory activism, refused to join any organizations. In some regions the Komsomol continues to exist as an organization, although in places like the Czech Republic, Poland or Hungary, the continuation of the Young Communist League would be unthinkable and the new youth organisations – de-centralized and far more modest in scope – are groping for a new role (Stafseng 1992). In Bulgaria the youth organization has been reconstituted as the 'Bulgarian Democratic Youth'. This came one month after the transformation of the Communist Party into the Bulgarian Socialist Party in January 1990. Although they had a representative in Parliament and have been active in the 1990 elections in support of the Socialists, the new leaders claimed that this was a 'purely social' organization and had nothing in common with the dissolved Komsomol. During the course of her research in 1992, one of the authors (Sijka Kovatcheva) found that in one of the universities in Plovdiv no section of the Bulgarian

Democratic Youth existed and in other universities where it did supposedly exist, no member of the organization could be found apart from its leader. However, some students regretted the passing of some of the activities of Komsomol which had actually helped students in their studies. In the absence of the official youth organization there has been the reintroduction of west European youth organizations, including Boy Scouts, YMCA and various religious movements which have been active in recruiting young people. In Russia 40 000 new youth associations were founded in 1991 which included ecological, patriotic, historical and charitable activities. It is claimed that 30–40 per cent of youth took part in such organizations and 13 per cent are members (Sviridon 1994). However, in many places nothing equivalent has replaced the Communist Youth Leagues. The collapse of the official youth organization is indicative of the disappearance of youth as a category for official intervention in the new post-communist reality. At present there is mainly a vacuum which is being filled by commercial youth culture (no longer condemned) or economic activities. The highly ordered and controlled progression through age-status and transitions which the Communist Youth organizations supervised has been replaced by a diversity of different groups and in many places by nothing at all.

The collapse of the formal youth organization has meant the disappearance of much of the provision for young people in Eastern Europe. What were youth camps are now private hotels; what were recreational facilities for young people now charge admission and run for profit (if they have not simply closed down). Whilst in Western Europe new connections between youth work and other aspects of welfare for young people are being developed, in post-communist countries these links disappeared along with the official youth organizations. Post-communist modernization has not necessarily been always progressive and it will take some time to rebuild a conception of youth which allows for any kind of humane intervention or provision. At present, due to the crisis of youth research, this seems unlikely to happen. The mass modern concept of youth under communism is replaced by privatized and fragmented alternatives.

In Western Europe, the statutory youth service, like other 'caring professions', developed out of nineteenth century philanthropy and the movement by reformers to re-mould and remoralize the working class (especially the rough working class) in an image of middle class, imperial efficiency. The concern was to turn out good soldiers and conforming citizens and to create and sustain appropriate gender roles for the two sexes. In some countries youth work was more concerned with moral education, most likely undertaken by one of the religious organizations or denominations. Through extended education during leisure time it was hoped to guide young people – particularly those in working class and industrial areas where social control was believed to be weaker – into more conforming roles. In the twentieth century this developed into a concern with 'character building', 'leadership' and 'service' and later into models of education or welfare for young people. However, the changes which took place in the post Second World War period, which we have described in previous chapters, with the development of commercial entertainment, along with youth culture and sub-cultures, meant that many youth services were no longer in touch with young people's preoccupations. Young people preferred to join unorganized groups.

Here it is interesting to compare Britain and Germany as Western European countries because in Britain the youth service had some difficulty in establishing itself professionally, whereas Germany is an example of a country with an organized youth provision (Stafseng 1992). This was on account of the 'strong' model of youth developed there as discussed in Chapter 1.

In Britain, there was an attempt to put youth work on a professional footing in the 1944 Education Act, which included provision for a youth service, but this was never fully implemented. The Albermarle Report in 1960 argued for a large scale investment in youth services as a way of tempting young people away from commercial entertainment and into what were perceived to be more educationally improving pursuits. In the wake of 'moral panics' about deviant youth sub-cultures, the youth and education services were envisaged as instruments for imposing what were seen as 'better quality' leisure interests. However, given the 'weak' model of youth intervention, there was a real shortage of trained personnel to run the Youth Centres and most of the staff remain volunteers. For every full-time youth worker there were 1000 part-time or volunteer workers working in a variety of voluntary organizations such as the YMCA, the Guides and Scouts and the uniformed junior branches of the Armed Forces (Jeffs and Smith 1987, 1990, Smith 1988).

Just as youth services were supposed to integrate working-class youth into dominant middle-class culture, so there were attempts to integrate ethnic minority youth into dominant white culture (Davies

1986). The Hunt Committee Report 'Immigrants and the Youth Service' in 1967 argued for the integration of young ethnic people into mainstream youth service in order to promote racial harmony and a 'national culture'. 'Integration' therefore meant creating a class-less, race-less and gender-less youth through the absorption of working-class into middle-class culture, and black into white culture, and so separate provision for girls was swept away. From the Albermarle Report onwards there were attempts to create a neutral professional language based upon principles of education and developmental psychology; Carl Rogers' notion of counselling to achieve 'self actualization' was influential in the 1960s. The youth worker was to be a counsellor helping young people through the 'storm and stress' of adolescence. By the late 1960s youth work had become attached to more community-oriented 'social education' and was seen as a branch of the local education services with 'unattached' youth workers working away from institutions.

During the 1970s the impetus towards expansion continued with attempts to set up a more independent and professionalised youth service but these were largely unsuccessful (Tucker 1994). New directions within youth work had developed, including the recognition of the separate needs of different groups of youth – Afro-Caribbean and Asian, girls and disabled youth (Imam, Khan, Lashley and Montgomery 1995). More radical paradigms of feminist and anti-racist philosophies began to gain currency within the youth service which rejected the orthodox 'middle-class' norm which had been criticized in earlier youth work. This reflected the influence of 'critical discourses' of youth described by Christine Griffin (1993) and in Chapter 1. Instead of 'saving' youth for dominant society, they were to be 'empowered' (Banks 1996). This reflected more post and late modern tendencies towards individualization a recognition of difference rather than a standardized model of youth and an attempt to 'lead from behind' rather than impose solutions from above (Morely 1995). However, this postmodern direction also fitted conveniently with the 'market model' of youth which started to prevail, one whereby problems were individualized and privatized (Barry 1996). By the 1980s, the political atmosphere of the New Right tended to militate against the further development of a youth work profession. Cuts in services and the dismantling of Local Educational Authorities, which had been the home of the Youth Services, eroded the resource base and resulted in many projects being cut or jeopardized. The contracting-out and privatization of services, along with the fragmentation of the welfare state generally, led to increasing specialization of different youth workers and their division through a range of different projects which would come and go. Nevertheless, Jeffs and Smith (1994) detected an 'authoritarian drift' as projects associated with young people became more and more coercive and intended for their surveillance and control at the same time as they became more decentralized and fragmented. One example of this was the proposals for 'curfews' for young people to keep them off the streets in Britain, following the US model (Jeffs and Smith 1996).

Some, nevertheless, argued for a continuation of 'modern' styles of youth intervention. David Marsland (1993) argues that in the absence of clear paths to adulthood, young people are faced with a set of conflicting demands from a range of institutions and that the youth services should provide a framework to help them through life transitions. He argues that this should be based upon a clear concept of youth as a knowledge base rather than a range of critical perspectives.

Girls were traditionally perceived as posing less of a threat to the social order, being less likely to get into trouble on the streets, less involved in crime and more controlled by the family and home. Consequently, the majority of provision was male oriented. Over the post-war period the liberal model of youth provision favoured promoting 'equality' and integration of the sexes by providing a service for girls and boys together. However, these co-educational principles conceal the inequality still lurking behind youth provisions. Indeed, feminist youth workers have argued that inequality has actually increased as a result since girls are subordinated underneath the apparently neutral idea of 'youth'. Within youth clubs activities such as pool, darts, and team games often marginalize girls as boys take over and dominate. Most of the staff are men. It was estimated that five times as much in resources was spent on boys as on girls (Nava 1984). Feminist youth workers nevertheless tried to create the space to work with working-class girls separately and explore issues of sexuality, gender and so on, often with rewarding results (Spence 1996).

In Germany, youth work is better established and provisioned than in Britain. The Ministry of Education, Health, Women, Family and Youth organizes reports every two years which bring together experts in the field to explain the latest social trends and theories and which put forward recommendations for new directions in the Youth Services. This is partly a product of the range of well established youth organizations or associations which have existed since the early twentieth century and are now incorporated as partners in welfare provision. There are several categories of youth associations: firstly, the Protestant and Catholic churches' youth organizations; secondly, the youth wings of the political parties; thirdly, those of some of the trades unions and professional associations and finally the 'independent' youth organizations such as the 'Pathfinders' (rather like Boy Scouts), the Red Cross, sports organizations and so on. These organizations and the local community departments mean that youth welfare is targeted as a special issue, rather than being spread around different departments within the local authority such as social work and education.

Following the post-war reconstruction, youth services were reconstituted in the new German Republic. During the 1950s and particularly the 1960s a new conception of youth began to emerge – 'teenagers' were discovered as a 'problem' as the new youth cultures and mass media made it possible for young people to conspicuously assert their own priorities and develop their own distinctive styles. Political security and growing affluence encouraged this new generational experience. As a result, youth work began to change from the mid-1960s. It was identified in the 1960s educational reforms as a 'fourth learning field' alongside the family, education and training and therefore had a central place within policies for young people. In the Structure Plan of 1970 and the Educational Plan of 1973, youth work was identified as an important area of education. This meant a new remit for youth workers. They were no longer providers of leisure space working within one of the associations; they now needed a new knowledge-base and training in education. Youth work became something more generalized, based upon general models of adolescence. Youth work also had an important place in regional plans in dealing with 'problem groups' such as those taking drugs, those who were homeless, the children of foreign workers and so on. Increasingly, they were seen as serving not just the needs of organized youth, but those of the community more generally and were required to work more and more outside of established youth centres.

In response to the new cultural autonomy of young people, youth work had to adapt or find itself ignored by young people. Consequently, youth centres started to develop an 'open door' policy with unstructured use of space by young people for their own ends. An

additional role taken on by youth workers was to provide relaxa-
tion and counselling for young people, who are seen in Germany
to be increasingly pressured by the education and training system
into performing and passing examinations. In addition to these pressures came the fear of unemployment in the 1970s and so youth
workers saw themselves as providing support to young people suffering from increasing stress and unable to bring their problems home
to parents who also put them under pressure to achieve and improve themselves (Bönisch and Schefeld 1985, Bundesministier für
Jugend, Familie, Frauen und Geshundheit, 1980).

   In both countries, about one third of young people join youth
clubs or some other organization, whilst the most popular form of
membership is of sports clubs in all countries (Biorcio et al. 1995).
Many more may attend the discotheques and activities provided in
youth centres. As in Britain there has been an increasing recognition that most youth work is male oriented and separate facilities
and times need to be arranged around young women in order to
meet their needs. Following feminist campaigning, the need for
gender-specific organizations began to be recognized in Germany
from the 1970s and was complemented by the provision of women-
only cafés, bookshops and so on, all inspired by feminist campaigns.
Anti-racist youth work or that dealing with ethnic minorities is not
well developed in Central European countries where 'integration'
remains the main model. This is because citizenship is based upon
ethnicity – therefore it was necessary only to integrate the ethnic
Germans arriving from the East – and the rest were considered
temporary visitors. This division is changing somewhat now with
greater civil and political recognition of the guest workers and their
children.

   During the 1980s the youth services have debated many similar
issues to those in Britain with marxist, feminist and anti-racist critical
discourses becoming more important. Sociological analysis of 'individualization' and 'de-standardized biographies' (see Chapter 1)
has led to a move away from the further professionalization of
youth work and the institutionalization of youth services and towards more flexible services reflecting more flexible life-styles. It is
now argued that services should be de-centralized and more open
to participation from the community with statutory youth services
working in partnership with other community groups and even the
private sector. There has been in particular a reaction against psychiatric and therapeutic intervention and recommendations instead

for 'social pedagogics' which opens up critical discussion rather than recommending technocratic solutions. In the 1980s and 1990s there is greater recognition of the position of girls and ethnic minority youth and concern about how best to meet their needs. The idea of empowerment or giving young people more responsibility and opportunities for participation is also raised (see Bundesministier für Jugend, Familie, Frauen und Gesundheit 1980, 1990). In 1991 a new Youth Welfare Law was passed which emphasized an integral approach to youth problems and in particular the all-round support for youth including such things as housing (Gaiser and Munchmeier 1994). The statutory position of youth work with the voluntary and local authority sectors mean that youth workers are recognized and established as a professional group to a much greater extent than in Britain.

Ideas of postmodern diversity, the recognition of 'individualization' and the increasing rights of young people in society have required new approaches to youth work. The provision of a range of facilities to recognize the needs of different groups – girls, ethnic minorities and so on – has led to the breakdown of the idea of a 'national' youth with homogenous interests and means the recognition of work with individuals and communities towards 'empowerment'.

It would seem that services for young people on both sides of Europe are groping towards new definitions, ones that will encompass the increasingly complex and reversible nature of age-status transitions, ones that could take into account their new roles within the family, within education and training and within the labour market. The increasingly amorphous nature of youth makes it difficult to build any comprehensive model of intervention and those states which tried have patently failed to succeed in the 1990s.

CONCLUSION

We have illustrated how the process of modernization created a category of 'youth' as a mass phenomenon and various institutions and professions associated with it. Historians and sociologists such as Muncie (1984) and Gillis (1981) have tended to stress the 'invention of adolescence' as a universal phenomenon through the nineteenth century, particularly the imposition of middle-class adolescence upon other social classes (Muncie 1984:41). It is evident that this model cannot be applied without some modification to young women. By contrast, we have tried to show that youth was not a new phenomenon – it was a product of the North-Western European family pattern. What changed during the course of industrialization and modernization was the construction of youth as a more precisely age-graded social category and their incorporation into expanding state and nation state-building systems. This corresponds with the development of theories intended to explain the idea of 'youth' or 'adolescence' explored in Chapter 1.

However, our argument is that youth was a product of 'modernity', in particular of the creation of state systems through which age became bureaucratically calibrated. Without a comprehensive state, such precise definitions of age would not have been possible. With the creation of a nation-state it became necessary to order and regulate the lives of its citizens through age. In this way, youth was constructed as a social category, one destined for educational, legislative and other interventions. In addition, new scientific studies were developed to analyze this new category and this provided the professional ideology for the new youth professionals. In those capitalist societies which developed earlier, this was done through pressure from voluntary organizations and individuals who constituted an active 'civil society'. In states which developed later under authoritarian control, this construction of youth took place more obviously as a product of state policy. Under both fascist and communist states, youth held a key position as agents of the transformation of society and in these societies they were strongly identified as a social and political category.

Just as youth were constructed as a social group and a mass phenomenon, through modernization, so sex differences were also institutionalized as were differences of class. The politicization of youth organizations at various points in history made them into a national cause, bearers of the new future. Even in societies where this was not so strongly the case, such as Britain, the improvement of youth services was often carried out along nationalist and eugenic principles. However, the post-modernizing tendencies of the last few decades have tended to erode the differences between the sexes, replaced classes with more complex, often non-material sources of differentiation (such sexuality, (dis) ability etc.) and blurred the stages of youth so that it is not clear where it begins or ends.

By the 1990s, institutions and organizations in all countries of Europe were facing the consequences of the social changes affecting youth which we have described in this book: increasing differentiation amongst young people, the extension of youth to both younger and older age groups and the individualization of young people. There have been various responses, but the rights of young people have been more generally recognized along with the need to negotiate with them rather than only impose solutions. New paradigms of intervention involving the facilitation of self organized groups and the attempt to 'empower' young people have emerged as a result. However, the privatization and fragmentation of the welfare state means that it is even less likely that any consistent idea of youth or youth policies will emerge, except perhaps at the pan-European level.

3 Transitions in Education, Training and Work

One of the most significant institutions to structure age in modern societies is that of education. Universal education systems, evolving with modernization since the nineteenth century, have absorbed widening groups of young people and sorted them according to pedagogically defined stages. In the early schools, classes could contain a range of children of different ages, but the systematization of education in the twentieth century was associated with age differentiation and the development of pedagogical theories to explain and legitimize age grading. This helped to construct standardized age status transitions associated first with different levels of the school system, then with finishing school and entering work and following that with different layers of training and higher education. However, whilst the initial tendencies were towards standardizing age-status transitions, a combination of educational reforms, rising unemployment and extended training since the 1970s has tended to remove young people from full-time employment and turn them into trainees or students instead. To put it at its most stark: whilst in 1945 80 per cent of 14 year olds in Europe went straight into employment from school, at present 80 per cent of 14–17 year olds are still in education (Coleman and Husen 1985). This has had the effect of lengthening and then de-standardizing age-status transitions. It is no longer so clear at what age a person finishes education or training or at what age they begin work.

The increasingly complex division of labour in modern industrial societies and the need for ever-changing skills have necessitated longer periods of preparation for work and retraining or re-education throughout life. The changing needs of the economy pose constant challenges for education systems which in turn interact with selection processes to filter young people into the occupational hierarchy. Comparisons between welfare capitalist countries, where education is generally state controlled or at least managed but employment is allocated through a competitive market mechanism, and communist countries where 'central planning' was intended to ensure the close functional fit between labour demand and labour supply are particularly interesting in this context. In neither system are the consequences of planning completely predictable, and the aspirations and actions of the recipients of the system do not always fit the models imposed.

Modernization brought with it an increasingly complex division of labour with positions filled (at least in principle) through universalistic, achievement oriented criteria. Education was supposed to furnish these criteria and since the Second World War education throughout Europe has been informed by a discourse built upon the principle of meritocracy: that those with ability should be able to benefit from education to rise to the highest levels and with this form of selection (as opposed to one of privilege or wealth) better and more efficient societies could be built. This provides legitimation for social systems in both communist and capitalist societies. However, in all systems, education operates as a form of social selection which advantages those who are already privileged, who already have an educational advantage, or have the means to buy or manipulate access to it. This has been an impetus for reforming education systems through which there have been attempts in different countries to make the selection process appear to be meritocratic and to give access to those from working-class or minority backgrounds who might otherwise be disadvantaged. A further discourse developed around how to compensate for social disadvantages and tap the pool of talent which was believed to be lying undiscovered amongst the educationally disadvantaged (Griffin 1993). As a result, credentials have become increasingly important as a method of selection and competition for educational places increased. These are seen not so much as ends in themselves but as means to ends – as a way of acquiring access to the right job and the right social strata. Thus studying is often undertaken less to acquire knowledge than to secure the qualification at the end of it. This causes stress and anxiety for young people as well as the so called 'diploma disease' whereby higher and higher qualifications are required to do the same job. This increased credentialism also creates higher expectations. Once qualified, the graduate may be unwilling to undertake more menial work – they want a good job which they feel they deserve after their studies. The achievement orientation translated into educational certification therefore creates long term tensions and unfulfilled expectations.

Competitive meritocratic systems create losers as well as winners. What about those with no possibility of acquiring a good qualification? Some are prepared for positions in the labour market with lower qualifications (some education systems foster considerable correspondence with labour market positions whereas others do not). However, those at the bottom of the educational ladder tend to drop out before the race has started. In a credentialist labour market they are increasingly disadvantaged. Furthermore, knowing that they have little to gain from education (apart from being branded as 'failures') they tend to have the most dissatisfied attitude towards it, to be reluctant to conform to school disciplines and to leave at the earliest possible opportunity. This group may not even accept the value of the skills and values institutionalized through education. The young people in this educational 'subclass', forming about 10–20 per cent of all educational systems, are usually disadvantaged in other ways too, and are more likely to find themselves unemployed or on training schemes when they leave.

Educational systems also reflect other forms of inequality. Because they reinforce the dominant hegemonic ideology associated with any given national culture, this tends to disadvantage those minority groups which are not members of the dominant culture (Gellner 1983). Thus, for example, migrant groups and minorities who do not speak the majority language are likely to be disadvantaged, particularly if prevailing ideologies present them as less educationally able or more deviant than other children. Young people from minority groups suffering educational disadvantage, and coming from families which are themselves from the lower levels of the labour market, are further disadvantaged by the lack of relevant cultural capital necessary for educational success and by negative educational 'labelling' by teachers and others (Stocke 1995, Bhattacharyya and Gabriel 1997). However, it is also the case that some ethnic groups do better in school than the host population and so we have to be careful to distinguish between different groups. Increasingly there is pressure towards having separate educational provision for minorities in their own language and with their own religion. Additionally, schooling systems tend to reinforce the gender divisions existing in any given society through either an overt or a 'hidden' curriculum (Deem 1978, 1980). Communist countries even tried to counter this by explicitly encouraging sex equality. Indeed, women have been some of the main beneficiaries of educational expansion in the post-war period, a paradox which we address later in the chapter.

The effect of progressive educational reforms has been to extend the period of youth. Most reforms have extended the number of years of schooling or training: the tendency is to prolong these further with each set of reforms. The length of education and training varies between different countries, although the trend is the same in both Western and Eastern Europe: longer periods in schooling and a variety of training and vocational schemes have prolonged the transition from school to work. In Eastern and Central Europe this trend, already existing under communism, has been reinforced further by the transition towards a more market-oriented economy because of rising youth unemployment. In Southern Europe, such reforms have taken place somewhat later, but the trend is in the same direction (Chisholm and Bergeret 1991). In the late twentieth century such developments have produced a situation where there is more vocational rhetoric and more training courses, but education is also linked *less* directly to the labour market. The outcome of education and training is uncertain, unemployment is a risk and the proliferation of routes and opportunities through education and training has resulted in a very complex and rather open-ended situation for young people. Being a young person in Europe at the close of the twentieth century increasingly means being a student or a trainee of some description. It also means facing the risk of unemployment, underemployment and possibly having to change one's occupation – or certainly one's job – a number of times throughout a career. It means having to organize one's own pension and sickness payments. One consequence has been the individualization of biographies as young people are forced to make decisions about their lives at each juncture, to choose between different options and to take responsibility for their decisions. Even constructing a life through a curriculum vitae becomes a skill taught on youth training schemes and professional agencies even offer such services. Failure appears, therefore, to be a consequence of lack of sufficient training or individual diligence rather than structural inequality (Evans and Heinz 1994, Roberts 1995).

In the remainder of this chapter we begin by considering in more detail some of the developments in education in different European contexts, comparing East and West Europe. We then consider the way in which the relationship between education and the labour market is managed and the extent and nature of state involvement in this process. Education systems are specific to national cultures and we are not able to describe all of them here, so we shall point to some general features with examples from particular countries. Finally we consider the implications for stratification.

SECONDARY EDUCATION: THE CONTINUED
EXPANSION

In all industrial countries, educational expansion was seen as important both for creating an internationally competitive industry through a better socialized and trained labour force. It was also regarded as important for creating a unified national culture and well-disciplined citizens, aware of the importance of punctuality and of respect for authority, who would accept their position within a complex division of labour (Bowles and Gintis 1976, Johnson 1976, Gellner 1983). However, the process was uneven. In Southern European countries there remain high rates of illiteracy and considerable educational disadvantage in rural areas (Pavelka and Stefanov 1985). After the Second World War, education was expanded still further in most industrialized countries, since it was seen as important for the post-war reconstruction: the new world order would be built with a more highly educated and technologically sophisticated population – one chosen through rational means of educational selection. This period, therefore, saw the passing of important legislation. The discourse of 'youth', developing out of the discourses of preparatory education and training, was an important development in this because it created a period during which children were prepared for work and for later life through their education, their leisure and sometimes through their work-based induction: it was an 'apprenticeship' to life (Cohen 1997).

In many Eastern and Central European countries it was only under communism that rapid industrial development took place, and with it the expansion of universal compulsory education. The elimination of illiteracy was one of the first tasks of the communist regime. Thus, in some countries there was an educational transformation inside one generation (although the statistics are not always reliable as they do not very accurately represent the educational disadvantages of minority groups and tend to exaggerate the 'success' of the system). This was accompanied by a dramatic shift in the population from rural to industrial and urban areas and from a largely non-educated to a mainly educated population. For example, in Bulgaria, the numbers of students in secondary education grew fourfold between 1939 and 1969 (Semov 1972). In Poland, there was a similar dramatic transformation: in 1960 45.2 per cent of the population had not completed elementary education, but by 1984 this had fallen to 8.7 per cent (Kurzynowski 1990). Such rapid improvements in education, however, led to dramatically rising expectations, which the socialist labour allocation mechanisms were not able to meet, as we shall see later. However, the patterns of educational mobility in the former communist countries reflected less the communist system of education than the way in which each country industrialized. Studies carried out during the period found more similarities with western countries such as the Netherlands than might be expected and considerable variation within Socialist states (Peschar et al. 1990). Czechoslovakia and the former East Germany, for example, already had developed educational systems before communists took over.

Educational selection also affects patterns of labour market recruitment. In many parts of Europe the secondary school system is itself selective, with different tiers. This is used to sort young people into clear tracks with differentiation according to ability, leading to different kinds of schools and different kinds of examinations. The top layer prepares people exclusively for university entrance through some kind of nationally recognized qualification. In England, universal access to grammar schools was granted with the 1944 Education Act, based upon academic ability rather than ability to pay, and attempts were made to put such selection at age 11 on a 'scientific' basis through IQ testing (which was later dropped). In Germany, France and much of Central Europe, the grammar schools, gymnasiums or lyceums provide such an academic education for an elite. In England, those who were selected as less academically able went to 'secondary moderns', left at the minimum age and went into employment in some more practical trade or job. Elsewhere, a layer of more specialized, higher level school existed between the elite grammar and lower level basic schools which offered certificates for starting training or work in clerical or technical trades (for example the 'Realschule' in Germany or the 'Secondary professional' schools in the Czech Republic, Hungary and Poland). These different school systems grade young people in terms of age-status transitions and points of entry into the labour market.

From the 1970s non-selective comprehensive schools came to predominate over the selective system of education in many regions, but these tended to also reflect rather than abolish educational selection which was also perpetuated through the use of different examinations. In Britain at any rate there was a return to selective education once more in the 1980s and de-centralization of budgets and powers to schools as part of a sub-contracted welfare state. From the 1980s Britain followed much of continental

Europe in introducing more standardized educational attainment targets associated with specific age groups. State control of the curriculum was, of course, most highly developed in the communist countries where subjects and examinations were centrally prescribed.

Private or non-state alternatives exist only in some countries. In Britain, for example, private and independent schools were always an important element in elite education and enjoyed something of a revival in the 1980s under encouragement from a Conservative government. In other countries, such as Germany, they are almost non-existent. In the Netherlands, however, private schooling was far more common as a way of incorporating different denominational schools. Even where there is a private sector, it is usually state subsidized through grants, scholarships or tax relief, and private schools tend to prepare students for the nationally recognized, state controlled examinations just as public sector schools do. Hence, in these respects private schools are extensions of the state schooling system.

Some countries – such as Germany, Austria and Switzerland – have evolved elaborate inter-connections between school and the labour market at the post-secondary level through continuing part-time education once a young person has begun work and nearly universal apprenticeships which involve some extended education. Sometimes called the 'dual system' this extends the acheivement-oriented, credentialist system into training after school as well and can be seen following from the 'continuation schools' discussed in Chapter 2. We could term this indeed the 'Central European model' of education and training because similar systems exist in Poland, Hungary, Slovakia and the Czech Republic as well.

The communist countries of Central and Eastern Europe favoured comprehensive 'polytechnical' schools up to the age of 14 or 15 after which pupils were selected into a three tier system. These schools encouraged links between young people and workplace teams and pupils were encouraged to spend days at agricultural collectives or industries from an early age. From there they could go to a general secondary school where a broad curriculum was pursued and could lead towards a university entrance exam. Others would go to a specialist secondary professional school which would prepare them for some profession – such as health care or library work. These courses could last 2 to 4 years and could also prepare people for university entrance. The remainder of the age cohort would attend vocational schools linked more directly to work for an additional 2 years. They would normally work some days of the week in the workplace and some days at school with their work placement time increasing throughout the course. Such arrangements were very often linked to enterprises who would provide money and resources for the school along with work placements. For the enterprises this was a source of cheap labour and generally speaking there were more jobs offered than people to fill them.

People were not expected to change jobs very much and were trained for one main profession. However, there were some variations in this throughout Eastern and Central Europe, and the role of general secondary schools could be very different in different countries and regions. In Bulgaria the general secondary schools were the route into higher education and accepted the majority of pupils. In the more under-developed Asiatic regions they were the least privileged educational streams (professional and vocational secondary schools were more expensive to develop and in some regions were simply neglected) whereas in the Northern regions of the former Soviet Union these were more elite schools seen as preparing people for higher education. In practice therefore, the quality and length of schooling varied widely across the territories of the former Soviet block. In the Central European countries, following Germanic traditions, the main divisions were between the schools preparing people for universities (sometimes called gymnasium or lyceums) taking only about one quarter of pupils, the middle level technical schools taking roughly another quarter and the more common vocational schools which were the lowest tier of the educational system and absorbed about half of the school pupils, training them directly for the predominant manual jobs in heavy industries.

Schools were linked directly to the needs of a centrally planned economy and this was more strongly emphasized in the early years of communism, where, in Poland for example, the labour office put out labour contracts for each school leaver and their destination was controlled. By the 1980s, however, the labour contract system had been abolished and young people were more free to choose their own training (Roberts et al. 1995). The jobs for which people were prepared were those of an economy based upon heavy industry, armaments and collectivized agriculture. In Russia, since unemployment was illegal, young people had to find a job within 3 months of leaving school and the majority were simply allocated employment rather than choosing it. However, a growing minority were able to choose their own work placement, a trend that occurred during the 1980s and which continues now.

These patterns of transition were associated with the fact that young people in the eastern bloc countries completed all their transitions at an earlier stage than people in many western countries and this was linked to earlier family transitions which we discuss in the next chapter (Dennis 1985, Bertram 1992, Schober 1992). However, there was also great variation within welfare capitalist countries of Western Europe. On account of the lack of development of the training system and the relatively short duration of the first degree (the three or four year 'Bachelor' degree), the age-status transitions of young people in Britain tended to be relatively accelerated compared with those elsewhere in Europe – they could be through with their education and training and potentially into the labour market by 16 or, in the case of higher education graduates, by the time they were 21. Under the Central European model, education and training continues until at least 17 or 18, albeit part-time and in most parts of Europe higher degrees take a minimum of five years. Therefore, age-status transitions tend to be more protracted. There are also differences between social groups with those lower down the social ladder making more accelerated transitions than those higher up because of the length of time before entering the labour market and earning sufficient income to become economically independent. This was also the case in communist systems.

In addition to the expansion of basic compulsory and secondary schooling, there was also an expansion of further and supplementary education throughout Europe, particularly after the Second World War. In Britain, the further educational colleges, designed initially to provide off-the-job training for apprentices and other vocational qualifications, expanded and started to broaden their range of options to include general vocational courses and studying for academic qualifications (Gleeson 1987). The pace of change in this respect has been very rapid with a marked rise in the number of young western Europeans staying beyond compulsory education in school or training in the 1980s. Thus, whereas in 1987 35 per cent had pursued some post-compulsory education or training, by 1990 this had risen to 42 per cent (Chisholm and Bergeret 1991:44). There were considerable variations between countries with about one third of students in the UK and one quarter of students in Italy still being found in vocational training a year after leaving school, as against 90 per cent in Ireland and over 80 per cent in Denmark (Eurostat 1992:97). In Germany, too, the variety of part-time and full-time vocational schools became increasingly popular over the post-war period, also offering a vocational as well as an academic path to university, and in Bulgaria various kinds of extension schools were provided by the communist regime so that people could combine work and study to improve their qualifications. In most Soviet-style socialist societies, young people could study at weekend and evening courses to improve their qualifications, and post-secondary professional schooling became more common up to the end of the 1980s. Indeed, this was a very important part of the communist education system. In Bulgaria more specialist evening courses were offered in subjects such as engineering and economics and one third of those doing extended study in Hungary and Poland were studying in this way (Adamski and Grootings 1989). Educational expansion had the effect of stratifying young people by age within different stages and levels of the education system. However, at a later stage, age distinctions were more eroded because people could move in and out of education, they could do it part-time or full-time at different points of their career.

In the communist half of Europe attempts to introduce equal opportunities in education were far more extensive and could be rigorously imposed from the top down. Based upon an egalitarian ideology, these regimes explicitly tried to widen the access of working class and disadvantaged children through giving those from worker's and peasant backgrounds greater opportunities through positive discrimination. In some countries there was also a quota for women. However, despite the official ideology of egalitarianism, a parallel system of privileges evolved which tended to undermine this. For example, in Bulgaria, a small elite set of foreign language and other specialized schools were founded which offered better education for a small number. The system of giving greater access to the sons and daughters of workers or to the children and grand-children of 'active participants in the anti-fascist struggle' or the 'heroes of socialist labour' could be manipulated to give privileged access to the children of the political elite. This had a demoralizing effect on other children who had to work harder to gain a place in such a system and emphasized the lack of rights of teachers in the selection process. Parents in the political elite *nomenklatura* families were able to pull strings and to exert additional influence to secure their children a place in higher education. In addition, a system of bribery developed which further unofficially undermined the official egalitarian goals of communist education.

The problem in these former communist countries was that the educational expansion also raised the aspirations of pupils, so that an education and a professional job were much more highly prized than a manual job: this was exactly the opposite value to that promulgated in official propaganda in which workers were seen as the most important people. The economy, which was geared towards heavy industrial rather than service work, could not accommodate so many educated professionals, and so the problem became one of 'mismatch' between the needs of the economy and the aspirations of individuals. This phenomenon was noted as early as the 1960s by the Russian sociologist Shubkin and reinforced by others studying this field since (Adamski and Grootings 1989). Surveys in Poland, for example, found that the highest status profession was that of university professor, followed by a director of a large industrial enterprise and then a physician (Worotynska 1985). These were all professions from the educational-administrative elite, a rather small strata in these countries. Furthermore, by the 1980s the 'baby boom' created a new wave of young people seeking jobs. In conditions of full employment the only alternative was to 'over-employ' people or to put them in trades which they did not want. Since the inefficiencies of the planned economy resulted in a permanent labour shortage, this was not difficult to do. A further factor was that the lyceums, gymnasiums and general secondary schools which prepared people for higher education did not prepare them very well for other levels of the occupational hierarchy. There were pressures to further vocationalize this academic level of education, especially since in countries such as Romania and Bulgaria and many parts of the Soviet Union most people attended the general secondary 'grammar' school and the more vocational schools were much less developed than in Poland, Hungary and Czechoslovakia.

As new technologies were introduced into employment, so new forms of education were required. The response was to try to organize more vocationally oriented education and to extend the length of schooling. However, this did not work as well as the reformers had hoped and the vocational stages of education were in practice greatly limited and not well targeted. One reason why the reforms did not work was that the planners failed to take into account young people's own preferences so that only one third of young people training in a given profession had any desire to work in that profession and only one fifth of those who had left school were happy with the preparation they had received there (Kutev 1983). In socialist societies, graduates expected to find a job which matched both their educational level and their professional training: sociology graduates expected to become sociologists and librarianship graduates to work in libraries. This precipitated a 'legitimation crisis' which was more serious in communist countries where the ultimate fulfilment was supposed to be through participation in work, than in capitalist countries where 'mismatch' could be more easily blamed upon the vagaries of the labour market.

In Western European countries there was a range of further reforms in an attempt to modernize the educational systems from the 1960s onwards. A discourse developed around the fear that young people would enter 'dead end' jobs with no training and prospects. Furthermore, it was believed that earning a wage and enjoying a youth consumer culture would tempt young people away from education and training duties with their deferred gratification (Roberts 1984, 1985, Griffin 1993). Educational reforms aimed to raise the educational aspirations of pupils and thus to encourage them to seek better jobs with training and long-term prospects. This discourse was also prevalent in Germany (Gaiser et al. 1985). The result was that access to university was widened and the training and apprenticeship system in Germany expanded still further with a 'second educational route' created to enable people to work their way up to higher education through vocational and other routes as well as the conventional academic school one (Wallace 1994). In Britain 'Access' and other courses offering alternative entrance to higher education had the same effect.

In both Western and Eastern Europe, educational expansion has been accompanied by rising aspirations. A combination of economic recession and the decreasing supply of training and work places, along with educational expansion, meant there was more demand for education and increased competition for each place. This can be exemplified in Germany where there was an increasing tendency for young people to go into the higher tiers of the school system rather than the lower and more vocational tiers. Hence the numbers in grammar school (*Gymnasien*) increased from 20.5 per cent to 31.1 per cent between 1960 and 1991 whereas those in the lowest tier schools fell from 64 per cent to 33 per cent in the same period (Bundesministier für Bildung und Wissenschaft 1992/3). One consequence of such trends in all countries has been that of 'certificate inflation' with larger numbers getting more qualifications. Thus, in Britain between 90 per cent and 93 per cent of young people left school with a qualification in 1988/9 as compared with 44 per cent in 1970/1 (Social Trends 1992). The number and type of qualifications proliferated to such an extent that in more *laissez faire* Britain there was some confusion as to what they meant and an attempt was made to consolidate them into different bands or levels through a general national qualification system.

The situation in post-communist societies reflects these trends in a more extreme form. Whereas previously, people were trained for specific professions in accordance with centrally determined needs, they are no longer guaranteed jobs after their training and many of the links between education and enterprises have collapsed, especially at a local level. The response has been an increased demand for new skills – languages, computing, business studies – which schools have sought to provide, even though they have great difficulty attracting teachers with these competencies on low state salaries. Schools which have done this successfully are in great demand and in Poland some even work shifts to accommodate all the pupils. There is also an increased demand for longer and more general education so that 2 year courses have extended to 3 years and so on. More people want to attend the grammar schools rather than the vocational and apprenticeship schools as in the past and more want to go to universities. Local education authorities in Poland, Czech and Slovak Republics have responded by trying to cut back vocational education and expand the more general education, especially at the higher levels. In Gdansk, for example, in 1992 grammar schools have increased their intake from 18 per cent to 28 per cent of young people over the previous three years, technical schools have increased from 20 per cent to 24 per cent whilst apprenticeship schools declined from 62 per cent to 48 per cent (Roberts et al. 1995).

Some of this demand cannot be met by state provision and is met instead by a developing private sector. Private schools provide training in business, languages, information technology but there are also private grammar schools. Parental donations are also needed to keep state schools going and it was common even under communism for schools to accept 'voluntary contributions' from parents. This helped to pay for equipment and it meant that schools where parents were relatively wealthy could be very well equipped. However, those with poorer parents could become demoralized and shabby, especially when schools have also lost sponsorship from enterprises. The system of bribes, private tuition and voluntary donations continues in a more formalized way through the introduction of fees. Thus, the 'market model' of education includes encouragement towards privatization which is seen as one way of meeting demands which the state cannot fulfil.

However, the education system was not changed in its main features. With little money to implement widespread reforms, the post-communist governments were forced to work within existing parameters. The first priority was seen as the need to change the orientation of education towards the needs of the pupil rather than towards the needs of the planned economy and this was done by decentralizing responsibility to the local level, trying to offer greater choice in schooling and schools and to give the directors of schools more scope to introduce their own initiatives and respond to market demand (Roberts et al. 1995). Extra funds were found through schemes such as opening the school canteen as a facility for the general public. However, this also created tensions with teachers' salaries falling still further behind that of other workers (from an already low level) and teachers being forced to take additional jobs to supplement them. These jobs often take the form of private tuition – a practice already prevalent before the fall of communism. There have been several waves of teachers' strikes in Bulgaria and Poland to protest against this situation.

Hence secondary education throughout Europe was expanded following the Second World War and started to assume a more important place in the filtering and selection of young people for the labour market. However, this also had other consequences including the extension of youth, raised aspirations and the increasing competition for places. Next we consider the implications for other levels of the educational system.

THE INCREASING DEMAND FOR HIGHER EDUCATION

One major impact of these reforms in Western Europe was on higher education, which expanded substantially from the 1960s. In general, the numbers in higher education in Europe rose by 30 per cent between 1983 and 1993 and this continues a longer term trend (Eurostat 1995). In Britain, for example, the ratio of those in uni-

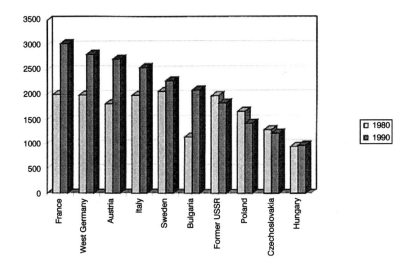

Figure 3.1   Higher education per 100 000 inhabitants in 1980 and 1989/90

Source: UNESCO Statistical Yearbook, 1992

versity went from 1 in 20 in 1955, to 1 in 10 in 1967 and is now closer to 1 in 3 (Halsey et al. 1988, Social Trends 1996) and in Germany, where all those who pass the relevant school leaving examination are eligible to go to university, the numbers going into higher education increased sixfold between 1960 and 1994 (Bundesministier für Bildung und Wissenschaft, Forschung und Technologie 1995/6). There has also been an increased number of people taking secondary degrees and post-tertiary professional training, thus extending the time taken in education.

Figure 3.1 illustrates the numbers of people in higher education as a ratio of the population generally. In all countries there has been quite a dramatic climb even over 10 years, although in Western Europe, this climb has been steeper than in Eastern Europe (in Poland there was even a slight drop during the period of martial law). Differences between Eastern and Western Europe had therefore widened during the 1980s.

In most educational systems in Europe, the basic degree takes five rather than three years as in Britain, but students can take even longer to finish their degree so that they have to fit other aspects of their life around higher education. For example, they may take a paid job either part-time or full-time for a while to make ends meet. In Britain too, young people frequently have to take paid employment in order to finance their studies as the value of student grants has been eroded. As the many routes through education and training have proliferated, so it becomes possible to take indirect paths through higher education, for example by people undertaking an apprenticeship before going to college or by working their way up through vocational courses until they are able to enter higher education. In a world where the outcome of education is uncertain, this can be a form of insurance against possible future unemployment (Bynner and Roberts 1991). Students take longer to complete their education and the average age of finishing a degree in Germany is now 28, whilst in Denmark many do not even begin their degrees until they are in their thirties, preferring to work for a few years first. This means that people can be in their thirties before they finish higher education and this has been the trend throughout the countries of Northern Europe. The educational reforms of the 1960s and 1970s in Britain and Germany helped to set up alternative higher education institutions where professional training could be combined with higher education studies. In this way the distinction between finishing education and starting working life is blurred. In Britain, although education has been extended, most people still finish their degrees in their early twenties. Yet even in Britain the increasing numbers of 'mature' students being admitted to higher education has started to erode these age-status transitions at least for some groups of the population.

These trends have turned higher education from being an elite pursuit into a form of mass education. In many continental universities there are up to 50 000 students, although universities in the UK tend to be much smaller. In many countries it is up to the students themselves to ensure that they attend the necessary seminars and have the right number of courses, and drop out rates can be very high – for example in Spain they are estimated at 80 per cent (Planas 1985). As more people obtain degrees, so these are used increasingly as a filtering mechanism for the labour market and class of degree, subject of degree, which institution the degree was obtained from and so on, become more important (Ainly 1994). It is less the content of the degree which is therefore important so much as the access this provides to other opportunities.

In the communist-dominated half of Europe, the very success of the schooling system meant that there was an increasing demand for higher education from all social groups. However, the numbers wanting to enter higher education were far higher than those who actually able to get in – in Russia for example, one survey estimated that between 60 per cent and 85 per cent of young people aspired to higher education (Babushinka 1985). Higher education became one of the routes to mobility and a career in the Communist Party, although people also valued education for its own sake (Stefanov 1983). A university level education did not lead to the highest paid jobs, which were manual ones, but parents in the 'intelligentsia' nevertheless put a very high value on university education and would go to great efforts to secure their children a place there either formally or informally through manipulating connections or by offering bribes.

In the communist-dominated half of Europe, the education system was designed explicitly to equalize opportunities for young people from different social strata. One way in which this was carried out was by offering more points to the children from workers' or peasants' families. In Czechoslovakia the sons and daughters of the middle class were so effectively discriminated against that a generation was almost missing from universities from these classes (Mateju and Rohakova 1993). In Bulgaria 'workers' faculties' were introduced which were intended to compensate those from more disadvantaged backgrounds by offering a 'short cut' into higher education without passing the normal entrance examinations. These were intended as transitional devices to compensate for the disadvantages 'that fascism put over talented boys and girls from poor backgrounds' (Znepolski 1959: 127), but they continued in a modified form until 1989 as a means by which *nomenklatura* children could obtain a higher degree without going through the normal competition.

The numbers of those in higher education grew not only in full-time but also in part-time courses. In Bulgaria, as in other countries, this was particularly important for women who accounted for 58 per cent of young people in this category in 1990/1 and also helped those who were married or from poorer families. In Britain the inception of the Open University, providing opportunities for part-time study at home, opened similar opportunities for working people and for women. From its foundation in 1972 it has swelled to become the largest university in Britain. The former polytechnics and colleges also offered a variety of evening degrees which could be taken part-time or as part of in-service training (Ainly 1994).

In Western Europe this rising popularity of higher education has been matched by a rising demand for young graduates on the labour market, although not all of them are able to get jobs commensurate with their qualifications: the degree holding taxi-driver is as much a feature of late capitalist Europe as the executive or the politician with a doctorate. A degree became a requirement for entry into many professions although the subject of the degree did not matter and few expected to continue working in the subject of their degree. In Eastern European countries where full employment was guaranteed, everybody had a job, but not necessarily the job they wanted. Many had to go into jobs which were a lower-grade than that for which they were qualified, producing a frustrated and disgruntled layer of people who later helped to fuel the transformations of 1989 and afterwards.

In the post-communist situation the status of a higher education degree has changed. Initially, higher education graduates were particularly vulnerable to unemployment and many were forced to take low status jobs – such as waitress or cleaner – in order to make ends meet (Kovatcheva 1995). At first, therefore, there was a decline in applications for higher education in some countries. The declining status of university and research personnel *vis-à-vis* the new rising economic elites make obtaining a degree a less attractive option and the lack of economic rewards associated with higher education continued in the post-communist era. Hence, in Kovatcheva's (1995) study one graduate expressed her disappointment with the fact that as a journalist she was still earning less money than a cleaning lady. In Bulgaria the number of applicants to higher education has declined by 15 per cent between 1992 and 1989/90 with growth only in applications for economics or medical schools (Ministry of Education and Science, Bulgaria, 1992). One important reason for this is the decline in student living standards. Whereas before 1989, 50 per cent of students received state grants and the rest were sponsored by a state organization in return for work after their graduation, with the changes all such contracts were cancelled (World Bank 1991). Student grants no longer kept up with the high inflation and it became more difficult to buy books as price liberalization put these out of the reach of most students. The main problem was the very large difference between what was needed to maintain higher education and what the state budget granted. One way of compensating for this shortfall was to charge fees for courses.

The post-communist labour market does not offer opportunities for specialized graduates – for example in Ecology or English Literature – because many of the research academies and institutes have closed down or been reduced in personnel. However, in the longer term the prospects for the more educated are better than those for the less educated. Evidence suggests that the situation of university graduates in the employment market is improving – in Bulgaria they constituted 41 per cent of the unemployed in 1990 but by June 1992 they had declined to 22 per cent (Sapio Research Centre 1992). As in Western Europe, undertaking a degree was a way of postponing entry into an uncertain labour market and increasing one's human capital, even though it was not clear how valuable an asset this might be in the future. The result was that from the mid 1990s there was an increased demand for places in higher education and the numbers of students expanded (Roberts et al. 1995).

Some of the newer disciplines such as Business Studies and Economics are very popular and new business schools and colleges have opened. Graduates with foreign languages, computing or survey skills (from such disciplines as Sociology) are able to get jobs in marketing where these are available and opinion polling has become a growth industry benefiting low paid, moonlighting professors. Private enterprise is meeting some of these demands with commercially funded schools opening and ordinary universities are compensating for the cuts in state financing by charging fees to students who do not receive scholarships as the competition for places increases and new part-time degrees have been introduced to meet this demand. In all post-communist countries more of the costs have been passed back to the consumers of education with astonishing speed. However, as the number of places in higher education has risen, the quality has not always risen correspondingly, with some qualifications granted on a rather dubious basis and educational standards have become generally lower, with less selection.

RISING UNEMPLOYMENT AND THE EXPANSION OF TRAINING

Rising unemployment from the 1970s onwards at first caused shock and disbelief in the prosperous North-Western European countries which had enjoyed a long period of growth and full employment, although it was a more familiar situation for the poorer southern

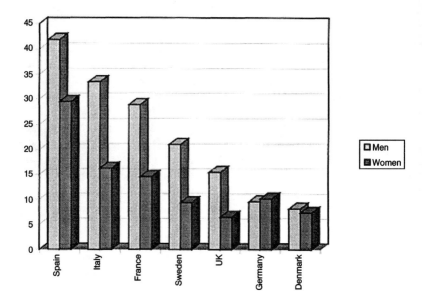

Figure 3.2   Percentage of under-25s unemployed in Western European
            countries (males and females compared, 1996)

Source: Eurostat Basic Statistics of the Community, 1997

countries of Europe. Young people were particularly badly affected
in all regions. Figure 3.2 indicates the percentage of the under 25s
which were out of work in different Western European countries. It
is evident that there are wide variations, but that in countries such
as Spain, Italy and France there is a substantial problem of youth
unemployment and it has also increased dramatically in Sweden.
In Germany and Austria, where there was traditionally very little
youth unemployment, it is starting to climb too. In most countries
young men are more likely to be unemployed than young women.
This may be because young women do not register, or once they
are married are counted as 'housewives'. However, it could also
reflect the fact that the new service industries favour the employment of women and the jobs which have disappeared are often the
'traditional' industrial male jobs.

    In post-communist countries unemployment has become a re-
cent and very dramatic problem, since these are economies with
little previous experience of unemployment and little ability to cope

with the phenomenon. The rapid fall in output and loss of export markets following the collapse of communism and the former communist trading arrangements led to a rapid rise in unemployment with young people being particularly vulnerable. In Poland 30 per cent of those under 25 were out of work in 1992, along with 20 per cent of those in Hungary. In Romania half of those registering as unemployed were under 30 and this figure was 45 per cent in Bulgaria. In the former Czechoslovakia, with the lowest unemployment, it was still the case that there were more than twice as many young unemployed as other groups (Eurostat 1993b). Long term unemployment is increasing in these countries and it is the unskilled who are the most likely to be unemployed. There are, therefore, features common to Western European countries.

By the early 1980s it was clear in Western European countries that the problem was not going to disappear and that beginning workers were structurally disadvantaged in the labour market. In Britain this meant that traditional apprenticeship and employment opportunities disappeared and everywhere new skills and styles of work were required. The institutional response was to create measures especially aimed at young people: they were therefore 'targeted' for intervention. Those countries such as Germany, Austria and Switzerland, where extensive training schemes already existed, expanded them still more to absorb a new wave of young workers. In those countries where training had previously been limited (such as Britain, France and Italy) more schemes were introduced. The schemes took a number of different forms which addressed either labour demand (adjusting the labour market) or labour supply (adjusting young people) and which are summarized below:

Demand-side schemes

1. Schemes to encourage employers to retain workers by paying them, for example, not to make redundancies. Examples of this are the various kinds of temporary work subsidy schemes that prevailed in the UK during the 1970s when unemployment was first a problem and were intended to balance the cyclical irregularities of labour demand. Another example is the 'Warteschliefe' schemes used in Eastern Germany after unification as a way of avoiding mass redundancies.

2. Schemes to encourage employers to employ more young workers – for example through a special payment for each employee, or as in Germany, by levying a payroll tax for *not* employing sufficient young workers (Koditz 1985).

3. The expansion of existing training places by employers. In Germany employers themselves expanded training places in response to the recession (Rose and Winangek 1990).

4. Extending the age of compulsory education. This was carried out in Britain in 1972 when the school leaving age was raised from 15 to 16. Although ostensibly for educational reasons, this reform was delayed until the onset of youth unemployment and conveniently reduces the size of the potential labour force – particularly amongst those likely to become unemployed, such as early school leavers. In some parts of Germany an additional school year was added.

Supply-side schemes

5. Training schemes inside the workplace funded fully or partially by state agencies. An example of this would be British Youth Training which paid an allowance to young people and placed them with employers. Employers got a free trainee worker, although under later versions of this scheme they had to contribute something towards the cost. This was used after 1992 in the Czech Republic where it was called the 'assistants and practicants' scheme.

6. Training schemes outside the workplace in special centres or workshops. Such schemes are often designed for those who are 'hard to employ' and provide specialist work training in a setting designed usually to simulate a work setting in some way. These exist in most Western European countries.

7. Job creation schemes involving various kinds of socially useful work. There are examples from many countries. These are usually jobs such as clearing cemeteries (schemes such as this exist both in the Czech Republic and Britain) or decorating churches. They are usually jobs which would not have been undertaken by normal municipal or other services. They are often organized by charitable organizations.

8. College courses for the young unemployed. Examples of this would be various German schemes for adding an additional vocational preparation year to the existing school-work transition. In Britain these were implemented too.

9. Grants to encourage small businesses and self-employment. Examples of this would be the schemes developed in the eastern regions of Germany or the Enterprise Allowance scheme in the UK. Similar schemes have been introduced into the Czech Republic and Poland but lack of resources and expertise means their impact has been limited.

10. Job Clubs for the unemployed to meet and overcome the demoralization associated with isolation and the many failed applications which unemployment brings. Job Clubs may offer facilities like a telephone or typewriters and may encourage skills such as how to write a letter of application or a personal résumé. In the UK, participation in Job Clubs can be a compulsory requirement for those claiming benefits.

11. Reduction of young people's wages in order to make them cheap to employ. This has taken place in Britain through a variety of schemes as well as by dismantling wage protection and is currently being implemented in France.

12. Giving credits or vouchers to young people for education and training, as was done in the UK.

Examples of all these can be found in many different countries. They resemble one another insofar as they involve some targeted intervention by the state. However, the problem with linking training to measures to deal with unemployment is that the training becomes devalued: training schemes start to acquire a bad reputation as 'warehouses' for the unemployed and commitment to such schemes falls. They also come under criticism for being open to exploitation by employers who are able to get a cheap (or free) young worker and do not always provide good training for them. There has been much discussion of these schemes in Britain and of the discourse of 'new vocationalism' generally (Finn 1987, Hollands 1981, Cockburn 1987). Individualization here meant that young people were responsible for managing their own training and employment with increasingly uncertain outcomes. Creations of 'portfolios' of skills and curriculum vitaes for all levels reinforced the idea of skills being something which the individual had to find and to carry around with them. Inventing CVs became a skill in itself.

In some post-communist countries the response has been to introduce 'intervention' schemes of various kinds based upon western experience and often using western aid from such sources as the ILO or the Know-How fund (Cranston 1992, Fabian 1991, Demcak 1991). In East Germany, the most developed and widely implemented intervention schemes exist because they could be funded from West Germany. In addition, new special measures were introduced which were designed to make vocational training less dependent upon large industries and to encourage the growth of the small business sector. In the former Czechoslovakia an active labour market policy was pursued which resulted in a decrease in the number of young people out of work and meant they were no longer seen as the most problematical group. However, in most post-communist countries, the dramatic rise in youth unemployment is not met by any initiatives or training schemes, and in spite of an enthusiasm for such solutions in principle, the hard pressed Labour Offices have been too concerned with trying to administer newly created unemployment benefits systems with very limited resources to be able to deal with any new intervention schemes. Although the rate of unemployment is not as high in the former Soviet Union, there is much hidden unemployment as people are registered at a place of work in order to be eligible for pensions and official benefits but in fact there is no work and they are sent home with no or partial pay and may even be working somewhere else, such as in the informal economy.

Another problem in the post-communist youth labour market is that young people are trained for the wrong jobs, since training and education was linked to the old heavy industries instead of the providing much needed new skills in service industries and information technology. The disappearance of traditional jobs and training places for young people that began as industries started to rationalize particularly affected the apprenticeship schools, home of approximately half the young people in Poland, Hungary and Czech and Slovak Republics. These training places had previously been tied to local enterprises and provided trainees for them, but now they have to find placements with private enterprises instead. In Poland those schools which failed to attract placements, and therefore pupils, were allowed to go bankrupt, whereas others in areas such as catering and distribution found themselves increasingly popular. This application of market criteria was a way of introducing some reform in the educational system. New market pressures forced schools to respond creatively in order to survive, since funds were scarce and reform was needed. Schools were accustomed to negotiating with employers for placements and fulfilling the needs of the local economy so many of them were able to find alternative placements for their students and some forced the students to find placements for themselves (Roberts et al. 1995). This flexibility is partly a response to a situation where there is an awareness that everything must change.

The expansion of training has therefore helped to prolong and extend the youth phase in most countries and the introduction of intervention schemes have contributed towards this. These changes have broken down the old patterns of secure, staged transition, created by modernization, especially in the post-communist countries, and replaced this with a more risky and uncertain situation where training and education is more indefinite. This also reflects changes in the labour market to which we now turn.

NEW TRENDS IN THE LABOUR MARKET

Modernization helped to concentrate workers into mass industries and to divide the labour market according to different segments and levels of skill. The mass production model found in both industry and in services has been termed 'fordist' after the alleged inventor of the production line (Amin 1994). In East Europe fordism was even more evident. In Western Europe, young people have different ports of entry depending upon factors such as their age, their qualifications, their gender, their ethnicity and where they live (Ashton and Maguire 1986). Some sectors of the labour market are reserved exclusively for young workers whereas in others they may be competing with married women or migrant workers. In this competition they are likely to be disadvantaged. Whilst some jobs may offer internal promotion and access to extended careers, in others there are only lower level jobs in the 'secondary labour market' which are likely to be low paid and casualized with frequent lay offs and redundancies. Thus the labour market is not an open competition with buyers and sellers of labour but is socially structured. However, the situation of where there is a clear layer of young workers going into menial jobs, as described by Ashton and Maguire (1977) or Paul Willis (1977), is likewise a thing of the past as labour market destinations are more uncertain and subject to frequent change.

The nature of work has itself been changing in recent years according to some sociologists (Lash and Urry 1987). The restructuring of the 1970s killed off some of the traditional manufacturing industries and with them have gone traditional male jobs and crafts. The globalization of economies, particularly the opening of frontiers for capital and industry in Europe, has had profound effects. Thus it is no longer necessary for all functions of the firm to be located in one place – manufacturing of cars can take place in Spain whereas the headquarters of the industry could be in Munich. The high social protection which characterizes many European labour markets raises the cost of labour. The post-communist countries have the advantage of lower wages in the competition for industry, but social protection is also high. Industries can move around in search of cheaper premises, often following regional subsidies, and some have moved out of Europe altogether into the third world countries which now produce the steel and ships which used to be made in core industrial regions such as Britain. The possibility of importing cheap fuel from Eastern Europe keeps low-paid Polish miners in work but means that mines can be closed in Britain and hence there is an international re-division of labour, even within Europe. This can mean rapid changes in skills and labour demand. This has been linked to changing styles of work sometimes termed 'post fordism' with a retreat from large-scale manufacturing and services and a movement towards 'flexibility' – that is, short term, temporary and part-time work, often on a contract basis. Although the extent of this is variable across Europe, this has replaced the expectation of a job for life and a person can expect to have to re-enter training or education and change career at several points in a life-time, which also blurs the character of age-status transitions.

The disappearance of full-time jobs for young people has been accompanied by the growth of part-time and casual jobs. A typical example is the growth of young people's employment in burger bars ('MacJobs') where pay is low, turnover is high and the workers are as disposable as the products. Furthermore, the expansion in education along with the simultaneous erosion of grants and stipends has meant that many young people work their way through college or training schemes by doing extra casual jobs. The formal labour market has shrunk, but the casual and informal one has grown. Students and trainees work in retail and catering jobs, in seasonal agricultural jobs and in temporary holiday relief both whilst at school and afterwards (Wallace 1987, Finn 1987, Griffin 1985). Unemployment has added to this, with large numbers of young unemployed in Southern Europe existing on casual seasonal employment. According to Coles (1995) a whole parallel labour market in some inner city areas absorbs many of those who are not in training, not in education and not in work, offering alternative, semi-criminal careers. The rewards from this can be much higher than those from low paid 'shit jobs and govvy schemes' (Coffield et al. 1986).

The development of a market for labour in post-communist countries increasingly resembles the situation in Western Europe. The most disadvantaged are the unqualified, the children of ethnic minorities, migrants and women. These groups find themselves at the bottom of the market. Young people are also more vulnerable than other groups. This has helped to fuel an increasing demand for education and has increased the relative disadvantage of minority groups. The nature of jobs has changed too in post-communist countries. For example, Koklyagina reports from Russia that young people are more likely to enter the services and catering sectors than heavy industries as in the past (Koklyagina 1992). Those with language and computing skills are likely to be in great demand, as salaries and fringe benefits become increasingly differentiated within labour markets. However, it is not necessarily the most highly skilled jobs which attract the highest salaries any more. In a recent survey in Poland a petrol pump attendant was earning more than a university professor (Roberts et al. 1995).

In post-communist countries too the 'shadow labour market' for working students is important since there are fewer grants than there are students and their value has fallen. As in Western Europe, the informal economy provides some compensation with opportunities for trading goods, for acting as salespeople, for selling small wares and services having increased. In areas of high unemployment, informal economic activity is the only way of earning a living; in agricultural areas there is the possibility of work on family farms. For example, informal activities were extensively practised in parts of Poland where goods could be bought from the eastern borders and either sold within Poland or further west at a profit. Young people would finance their holidays in Western Europe by bringing tradeable items with them, sometimes bought from Russian and Ukrainian traders who are not able to travel further west. Young people are able to pass easily backwards and forwards to the EU countries without visas from Poland, Hungary, the Czech and Slovak Republics and some use this to work temporarily abroad, earn money and bring it back or to learn a language.

These developments have changed the life conditions of young people in post-communist countries. Their transition period has become more protracted and the outcomes more uncertain: whereas in the past training led to a work placement, now it no longer does so. A study by Bertram (1992) in East Germany which has replicated the same questions to young people since 1972, found that young people have become more career oriented and more concerned with the prestige of the career they pursued. On the other hand they had lost some of their concern with doing socially useful work and had become more materialist and individualized in their goals. Titma (n.d.) found that in the former Soviet Union there had been changes in work values some years before *perestroika* and that material rewards and job security had already started to become important values. However, he also found continuity in the desire to do socially useful work and to see work as a source of prestige and creativity. In fact, young people are adapting more flexibly and readily to changing labour markets than are other groups. They are more open to learning new skills and they are more mobile.

In Western Europe, according to some surveys, a 'post material' attitude is developing among young people in the affluent countries. In Germany successive surveys have found the development of attitudes associated with self-fulfilment outside of work rather than career success (Zinnecker and Fuchs 1981). In Spain too, the response to the lack of employment opportunities was to eschew a conventional work ethic and see casual work as an advantage (Chisholm and Bergeret 1991). However, such trends should not be exaggerated. Other surveys in Britain found that young people on the whole wanted to work even when few jobs were available (Banks et al. 1992).

STRATIFICATION

In all countries the transition from school through education, training and into work is stratified, but these patterns of stratification are changing too with developments in industry and in education it-self. Furthermore, by casting a look across the European continent we can see more clearly structural forms of stratification than when we are looking at any one country. Next we consider some of the issues which stratify young people in the transition from school to work: educational and social background, gender and ethnicity. Although these are not the only forms of stratification, they are the best documented.

Educational Level and Social Background

In Western Europe social background has been a predictor of post school careers, with those from higher social backgrounds being more likely to have children who enter the higher levels of the labour market offering more extended careers (Ashton and Field 1976). Education played a mediating role and whilst it offered some opportunities for social mobility, educational success often reflected the social background of the person (Bourdieu and Passeron 1977). However, the extent to which this happen varied between different countries. In Germany the existence of an educational-administrative elite was associated with a strong tendency to encourage their children educationally and therefore to reproduce itself (Müller and Karle 1993). Indeed, some have argued that the school system actually prepares young people for specific sections of the labour market either through codes of behaviour transmitted by the system itself (Bowles and Gintis 1976) or through the sub-cultures created within the school or training scheme which encourage self selection (Willis 1977, Bates and Riseborough 1993). However, Jones (1987) has indicated that processes of social reproduction can be quite complicated because it is some time before young people reach their final class destination. Their first job on leaving school may not be the final one. The increasing competition and selection function exercised by the school mean that a high achieving 'track' with those destined for higher education, and probably higher careers, can be identified. These are an increasingly privileged group who not only have better jobs in the long term, but better life styles and access to material resources in the short term too.

Working-class school-leavers used to be identified by the fact that they mostly left school at the minimum age and went into work. They selected themselves by dropping out of the educational race at an early stage, but had the advantage of higher incomes and access to consumer culture in the short term. This is no longer the case. The collapse of the youth labour market since the 1970s means that those from working-class background go not into work but into unemployment or into schemes or college courses. They are now the most disadvantaged in access to employment. Their incomes are low or non-existent with more limited access to leisure and cultural resources. Their situation has deteriorated relative to other groups of young people and are described in one study as having 'no career' (Bynner and Roberts 1991). About 10–20 per cent of these constitute the 'educational subclass' who are alienated from school, disadvantaged in work and in training and likely to be unemployed. They are also increasingly likely to be the homeless, the runaways and among those falling into lives of crime (Coles 1995).

There is, however, a large group of young people between these two extremes who go into employment through various training and educational courses. These are a less easily definable group. The numbers in these different categories is variable between different countries – there are more, for example, in the 'no career' group in Britain than in Germany. What is clear is that the different strata of young people are defined by not just social background but also interaction with training and education systems. Amongst young people in extended transition, social strata are defined by these training and educational schemes rather than by the labour market which they do not enter until later.

In communist countries too, stratification according to social background was important although those from working-class backgrounds were more likely to be socially mobile on account of the policies of positive discrimination. Nevertheless, there was more similarity with western countries in terms of social reproduction than we might expect and variations could be better explained by the way in which a country industrialized than by the fact that it was capitalist or communist, according to Mateju (1990) and Andorka (1990). Although those with the best education did not necessarily receive the best rewards under communism, there was a strong tendency for the education elite to reproduce itself and where parents could not pass on property to their children, securing a good education for them was a prime value. The early educational expansion under socialism in countries like Bulgaria led to dramatic patterns of mobility. By the 1970s roughly one third of those in higher education came from educated families, 37 per cent from fathers educated only to secondary level, 23 per cent with fathers educated only to primary level and 3.7 per cent with even less education (Stefanov 1981, Dimitrov K 1986). In the post-communist situation, new forms of stratification have been emerging in these societies with the creation of a new economic elite – some of whom were also members of the previous elite (Mateju 1993). What is emerging is that the twin pressures of increasing demand for education at all levels and declining state funding means that there is an increasing number of people in higher education on the one hand (the shortfall in state funded places being met by the private and part-time degree sector) and growing illiteracy and a decline in educational standards on the other.

Young people become increasingly dependent upon the state or upon parents during this long transition, a subject which is further addressed in the next chapter (Jones and Wallace 1992). Thus social background has a new dimension, because it is increasingly the financial resources of the *parents* and the extent to which they are able or willing to support young people which will determine the resources of the young person. With education in post-communist countries being increasingly privatized, it is often the parents' ability to support young people which is important. Certainly in more home-centred societies such as exist in Central and Eastern Europe (see Chapter 4) those households with more highly educated parents were also more likely to have access to a range of consumer goods and were able to offer their children additional advantages such as travel abroad. In Western Europe too, the competitive advantages of young people who have to stay in an ever-extending education and training system could depend increasingly upon the degree of support and financial subsidy they receive from parents.

However, other forms of stratification are also emerging as important and regional differences within Europe are important. The difference between the Southern and Northern European countries is striking in terms of opportunities for young people and linked to this is an urban/rural divide which does not exist in urbanized counties such as Britain or the Netherlands. Where the urban/rural divide does exist, however, there can be great contrasts between the limited life opportunities of those in rural areas and those in urban areas with better access to educational and cultural facilities and more diversified labour markets. Rural deprivation continues to be a factor in the post-communist countries where rapid urbanization stripped the countryside of young people (Bridger 1989).

The concentration of educational facilities in major cities means that young people have to move in order to be educationally mobile. The migration of young people to urban centres such as Moscow also takes place because of the increased cultural resources there. However, in parts of Northern Europe rural areas can be quite prosperous and with good communications facilities need not be disadvantaged.

Other kinds of regional difference include the variation between labour markets. In a local labour market dominated by mining, for example, a different set of values would be transmitted to young people than one dominated by the electronics industries or financial services. The horizons of most young people are set by the prospects of the local labour market which also tends to create its own set of cultural values. An Anglo-German study, for example, found that there were wide disparities in young people's prospects between expanding and contracting labour markets within each country. In Germany such disparities were smoothed out to some extent by the existence of an elaborated training system, whereas in Britain young people relied more directly on the labour market (Bynner and Roberts 1991, Evans and Heinz 1994). Prospects in local labour markets affected the likelihood of staying at school and the likelihood of entering a scheme rather than a job directly. Similar disparities between local opportunities were found in Poland (Roberts et al. 1995). The lack of comprehensive 'intervention' schemes and the geographical reorientation of the labour markets (those near the western borders start to become advantaged rather than disadvantaged as in the past) mean that there is increasing diversification between labour markets for young people.

In this section we have tried to indicate that whilst the traditional factors such as social background continue to affect young people's prospects, the significance of social background may be changing with the effects of extended transition. The most disadvantaged are no longer those who enter the labour market at the minimum age, but rather those with no jobs or on poor quality training schemes. Other factors are also important in the reproduction of social advantage or disadvantage and to these we now turn.

Gender Differences

The educational reforms which we have been describing affected young women particularly. In the European Union the number of

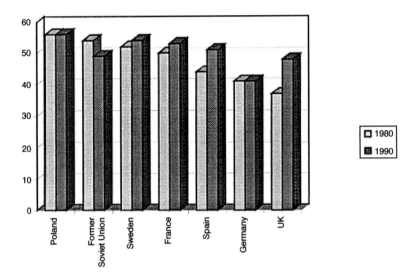

Figure 3.3   Percentage of women in higher education 1980 and 1989/90

Source: UNESCO Statistical Yearbook, 1992

young women in higher education rose from 45 per cent in 1983 to
49 per cent in 1993 and this reflects a much longer-term trend
whereby young women are catching up with and even overtaking
young men in the higher levels of the education system. In Central
and Eastern Europe too, young women were some of the main
beneficiaries of the reforms. In Bulgaria, for example, a very traditional patriarchal ideology had prevailed before the war which meant
that girls were not likely to continue in education beyond the minimum age and formed the majority of the illiterate population or
those with only elementary education in 1946. By 1956 they had
caught up with men in secondary education and by 1965 they formed
the majority in higher education and more than half of those with
a degree are now women (Semov 1972). Figure 3.3 indicates the
relative position of women within different educational systems
and it can be seen that in some countries they have overtaken
men. In general the percentage of women in higher education in
West European countries is between 40 and 50 per cent whereas
in communist countries it is frequently over 50 per cent. In all
countries, except for the former Soviet Union, the trend is for

the number of women in higher education to increase compared with men.

Some people argue that this illustrates that gender differences are dissolving in the late twentieth century (Zinnecker 1990). However, closer inspection reveals that women are concentrated in particular educational sectors in all countries, which tends to lead to lower paid jobs and 'feminized' professions. According to Krüger (1989, 1990) they spend a longer time in education only to get worse jobs. In Germany the multi-route educational and training system tended to encourage young men to raise their aspirations as they moved through it at each stage, whereas it had the opposite effect on young women who were 'cooled out' by the long period of training (Wallace 1994).

Once they leave education women still go into gender segregated sections of the labour market and this is evident in the training they receive. In those countries where training is highly structured, women are more often found within those sections of the training system which lead them to feminized careers routes. In Germany, for example, there are institutionalized lines of gender segregation in the professions that are pursued by women and those pursued by men, with some two thirds of girls concentrated in retail, clerical and hairdressing training; whilst males were far more dispersed through a variety of trades, these were nevertheless more recognizable as 'craft' and technical training (Bundesministier für Jugend, Familie, Frauen und Gesundheit 1986). Furthermore, whereas 73 per cent went on to do additional second stage training, only 27 per cent of females did. The schemes associated with girls are the ones most likely to last two rather than three years, leading to lower status, lower paid jobs (Mayer, Krüger, Rabe-Kleberg and Schütte 1983). Even in terms of apprenticeship pay, girls fared comparatively worse, getting only one half to one third of the pay in male-dominated occupations.

In Britain, the more *laissez-faire* approach to training nevertheless resulted in gender segregation. Training schemes were shaped by the character of the local labour market and by those who administer the schemes to a much greater extent than in Germany. Consequently, young women were found concentrated in schemes linked to traditional areas of female employment – mainly in 3 occupational training areas – whereas young men were spread across 7 occupational training areas. Thus, whilst the training group 'Installation, Maintenance and Repair' was 96 per cent male, that of

'Community, Health and Social Services' was 86 per cent female (Cockburn 1987). Sexist ideologies infused the training system, even where girls resisted it, so that even when they were introduced into non-traditional training they ended up doing female tasks – such as sewing the seat covers in car maintenance classes (Cockburn 1987, Stafford 1991). The off-the-job training often emphasized female comportment and presentation for young women. Youth training thus tended to reinforce gender ideologies rather than to undermine them.

Why was there this persistent pattern? Previously, women were not expected to have full-time careers in the labour market and a job was just something temporary, but this generation of young women do expect to spend most of their lives in the labour market. Young women suffer bias when they receive advice in looking for jobs and in their treatment from employers and trainers: a 'good job for a girl' is seen as service work and money is not thought to be so important for them because they are mainly concerned with getting married (Sharpe 1976). Furthermore, girls are socialized into family roles which tend to lower their aspirations for careers even where women no longer expect to give up work for a family. It is difficult for women who reject such gender stereotypes to maintain their stance (Stafford 1991). Female jobs tend to reflect the characteristics of family roles and the stereotypes of femininity and tend to be lower status and lower paid. More recent feminist work tends to emphasize the way which different kinds of work and training continually creates femininity rather than reflecting it (Adkins 1995).

In communist countries another pattern prevailed because women worked full time and gender equality was one of the proclaimed goals of socialist society. Women had to do the same jobs as men – often involving heavy manual work – and their production quotas were the same. It is evident from Figure 3.3 that women benefited particularly from educational reforms, being the majority in higher education in some countries. Young women in Poland were more likely to attend the general secondary schools (the equivalent of 'grammar' schools) than the secondary professional, vocational or apprenticeship schools, with the result that they were more likely to have a general education that equipped them for university (Roberts et al. 1995). But although boys and girls covered the same curriculum at school, young women nevertheless entered 'feminized' sections of the labour force – paradoxically some of these feminized professions, such as medicine, were the masculine ones in Western Europe. Even in East Germany, where gender equality was the highest, in 1987 women entered just 16 of the possible 259 professions (Nickel 1990). Childcare provision paradoxically helped to keep women in lower status jobs in the professional hierarchy because taking time off to look after children (up to three years) could discourage employers from employing women. In most communist countries women earned only 70 per cent of men's wages (Corrin 1992) and some evidence suggests, that it was very difficult for women to break into men's jobs. In rural areas of Russia, for example, women found it almost impossible to get into those agricultural trades with technical training with the result that very few of them ever became the tractor drivers who symbolized gender equality under socialism (Bridger 1989). Thus, although women had to do heavy manual jobs, this did not improve their general situation *vis-à-vis* men in the workplace.

Since marketization, women have suffered the highest unemployment in most post-communist societies (Einhorn 1992). Enterprises have cut childcare facilities and the right to long maternity leave means that employers are less willing to employ women (in Poland they have even sometimes made women sign an agreement that they would not have children whilst in their employment). In Eastern Germany, for example, they are in the feminized sectors and as income differentials widen, women are left further behind with the lowest wages and the worst employment prospects (Bertram 1993, Meier, Schmid and Winzen 1992). The possibilities for independence for young women have been weakened, especially in the former East Germany where there was the most support for women and the highest numbers of single parents. However, there are some brighter prospects too. Women, especially young women, are the best educated and since a general education is a more useful qualification on the labour market than training in a vocational trade or an apprenticeship, it could be that the long term prospects for some women are not so bleak. It is likely that new divisions will emerge for women in different labour markets and family situations.

It is thus evident that whilst women were some of the main beneficiaries of educational reforms, particularly in former communist countries, they do not necessarily benefit from this in the labour market. This tendency has been reinforced with the move towards market economies in post-communist countries.

Ethnic Minorities

The status of ethnic minorities takes different forms in the different parts of Europe and the extent of their disadvantage in both the short and the long term is variable. In Britain, those from ethnic minorities are disadvantaged in the labour market because they suffer disadvantage in the education system and because they are likely to live in parts of Britain hit by industrial decline and rising unemployment. Some ethnic minorities have a higher risk of becoming unemployed than others with Afro-Caribbean and Guyanese suffering 11 per cent unemployment in Britain as against 7 per cent of white people, 9 per cent of Indians and 17 per cent of Pakistani/Bangladeshi minority groups in 1990 (Social Trends 1992). Some research has indicated that even when they have higher qualifications, those from ethnic minorities find it harder to get jobs than their white counterparts (Roberts, Duggan and Noble 1982, Wrench and Lee 1983). The experience of job search amongst ethnic minority youth is affected by the direct discrimination they receive from employers and from indirect discrimination – the fact that their face does not fit the employer's stereotype of a conventional worker and the fact that the firm may rely on word-of-mouth recruitment through its existing staff (Jenkins and Troyna 1983). They are also more likely to use the statutory services in their search for jobs. Jenkins and Troyna (1983) point out that this means there is no necessary connection between qualifications and jobs and between qualifications and insulation from downward mobility in the case of Afro-Caribbean and Asian youth. Although training schemes were designed to compensate to some extent for this disadvantage they have the effect of labelling ethnic minority youth as a problem category and therefore further stigmatizing them (Solomos 1988).

In other countries it is the children of migrant workers who find themselves in the bottom layer of the educational system. In Germany, for example, they were amongst those who were found only in lowest level secondary schools (Hauptschule), who leave without educational certificates, who are less likely to find apprenticeship places and who drop out of the educational system. They are more likely to be over-represented in special schools for the handicapped and disadvantaged children. It is estimated that 65 per cent in this group had no training and this was a particular disadvantage in the German labour market where access to professions was through training schemes (Bendit 1985, Bendit et al. 1993). Although the official policy has been 'integration and normalization' (see Bundesministier für Jugend, Familie, Frauen und Gesundheit 1990) and various intervention and educational schemes have been introduced to address the problem, Bendit (1985) argues that there is a reproduction of disadvantage from one generation to another through the official training and education system. A comparison of the educational qualifications of minority youth with all Germans shows that whilst in general 24 per cent of German pupils gained the university entrance exam in 1988, only 9 per cent of those from ethnic minority youth did so and, whereas only 8.4 per cent of Germans left school unqualified, this was the case for 21 per cent of children from ethnic minority groups (Bendit et al. 1993). Various special measures and intervention schemes have been introduced since the 1970s to target ethnic minority youth but they still remain disadvantaged in the labour market overall. In France the young people of Arab origin are most likely to be unemployed and unqualified.

Roma children are the most educationally disadvantaged group in most Central and Eastern European countries. Many of their children do not attend school at all. In Bulgaria it is estimated that 60 per cent are illiterate. Roma children are also the most disadvantaged during the current transition from communism with high rates of crime, drug use, prostitution and infant mortality and with unemployment now between 50 per cent and 90 per cent in some Roma suburbs of Sofia. The post-communist contraction of state and labour market has affected them most severely.

Ethnic groups are also disadvantaged in other countries since they are often the first to be fired when jobs disappear. In all countries, fear of migration and increasing labour market protectionism mean that policies are introduced to advantage native workers over foreigners (Wallace and Palyanitsya 1996). However, illegal and unregulated labour markets are widespread throughout the region and it is in these sectors that foreign and ethnic minorities find jobs.

Therefore, some groups of ethnic and minority young people are likely to be disadvantaged in the new divisions of labour in Europe. In countries where ethnic minorities have existed for a long time, they are among those most likely to be educationally disadvantaged and unemployed. The children of new migrants are at least temporarily in the same position. Furthermore, they are likely to find themselves victims of a rising tide of xenophobia which has swept across Europe in recent years and which we explore in Chapter 6.

CONCLUSIONS

The review of education and training in Eastern and Western Europe has revealed some common features. In both sides of Europe the development of education and training systems has helped to generate age-status categories which corresponded to other life transitions and this was part of the process of modernization. The growth of bureaucratic national education systems, be it under communism or capitalism, created defined phases of full-time education, training for work, extended education and, finally, work. Under communist authorities developments took place later than in Western Europe and with far more government intervention, but the results were more dramatic. However, in recent years, a combination of educational and labour market changes has extended the transitional period and started to break down the distinction between defined life phases of work, education and training. This had already started to occur in Western Europe from the 1970s as youth unemployment, the introduction of various vocational training courses, along with the increased demand for higher and longer educational courses, made the youth transition phase much longer and more open ended. It started to become a process which one could step in and out of, changing professions and training over an extended 'post adolescence' disconnected from other life transitions such as marriage or childbirth or leaving home. In communist countries where age-status was more controlled and more uniform such changes are taking place with greater rapidity. Now unemployment, intervention schemes and a variety of new educational and professional opportunities have created a less structured and more insecure youth phase. The timing of life transitions still depends upon these levels in the educational-labour market hierarchy with those nearer the bottom having more accelerated life-transitions and those towards the top more prolonged ones.

Despite the enshrinement of competitive, meritocratic values, social origins still play an important part in educational selection, although these are overlaid by other divisions of ethnicity, gender and region. New groups of young people are emerging which are either advantaged or disadvantaged by the expanding education system – at the top are the 'students' with better lives and prospects (although this depends upon the extent of parental support) and at the bottom are the educational subclass who are most likely to be unemployed or perform unqualified jobs. Ethnic minorities are over-represented in the latter group. Young women have a paradoxical position as being increasingly better qualified, but nevertheless disadvantaged in the labour market. There are a number of other kinds of disadvantage and difference which we have not dealt with here: sexuality, disability, those leaving care and so on. These 'absent voices' have not been included in the dominant discourse on youth in Europe and hence we lack adequate statistics and information about them.

Hence, whilst modernization brought fordism, selective educational systems and a segmented labour market, which through co-ordinated welfare policies helped to structure the age-status transitions in a fairly uniform way (although there were differences according to class, sex and country), post-modernizing tendencies have undermined this. Youth age-status transitions have become confused and uncertain following changes in the labour market which have removed secure employment and changes in educational and training systems which have increasingly individualized their paths into work. Increasing differentiation of young workers along a number of axes (e.g. sex, (dis)ability, region, religion, ethnicity, etc.) means that standardized solutions are increasingly inappropriate.

4 Family Transitions

The age-status transitions of young people are defined crucially by their position within the family. Families were constructed by modernization and within state systems in different ways in Western and Eastern Europe and, within each of these regions, family organization differs between ethnic and cultural groups. In centrally planned economies state intervention was very deliberate and very extensive, which means that the traditional cultural distinctions between Northern and Southern communist Europe that we described in Chapter 2 were eroded. Nevertheless, families in each area of Europe develop their own sets of relationships within and outside of the state and their own styles of intergenerational relations. Whereas in some contexts – such as in some stages of capitalism and all post-war communist states – age-status transitions are tightly structured and predictable as factors of social life, they are now becoming more unstructured, unpredictable and diverse.

There is a tendency for young people to pursue increasingly independent life-styles both within the parental home and outside of it and this is associated with 'growing up' earlier as we discussed in Chapter 1 (Chisholm et al. 1995). The tension between the search for social and cultural autonomy on the part of young people and the requirements made of them by other family members, especially parents, for whom they are subordinate family members, are an integral part of our contemporary notions of youth. It is also a source of conflict in the family. In post-communist countries where support for children by parents was always strong, this tension likewise exists. However, such trends must be set against the increasing economic dependence of young people upon the family as their 'transitional' paths are extended. The tendency towards social and cultural differentiation amongst young people is thus counterbalanced against material constraints. The lengthening transition from education to employment and rising unemployment mean that young people have fewer resources of their own upon which to draw. Furthermore, their increasing desire for independent accommodation which results from this search for individual autonomy is not met by the existing housing markets. Those who are the casualties of this process include the rising numbers of homeless and marginalized youth throughout the European region (Hutson and Liddiard 1994).

Young women often feel these shifts in patterns of family transition most acutely and their needs and experiences are more likely to be at odds with existing structures of family and youth support. They are often more protected and controlled by parents and other family members on account of perceived sexual and other dangers. This tension may be particularly acute in Southern European countries such as Spain, Portugal and Greece where traditional family expectations may conflict with increasing demands for independence (Leccardi 1995, Deliyannis-Kouimtzi and Ziogou 1995). Gender is therefore a crucial issue in these inter-generational negotiations and changes. Important ethnic differences in family relationships occur *within* societies and regions too as work by Brannen et al. (1994) illustrates.

Changes in family transitions have been subject to the following trends which will be further described in this chapter:

- the fall in family size
- the postponement of marriage and childbearing
- the increase in single person and non-family households
- the rise in non-marital partnerships such as cohabitation
- the rise in divorce
- the increasing tendency towards non-marital childbearing
- the increasing tendency of young people to leave home for reasons other than marriage
- the tendency for women to see employment as a destiny for themselves throughout life
- the increasing autonomy of young people within the parental household.

These are all factors which affect young people's biographies and inter-generational relations. However, we should see family transitions as a series of separate processes, which may or may not be connected and in the following pages of this chapter we shall address each in turn:

1. Families: the transition from family of origin to family of destination.
2. Households: the transition from household of origin (usually but not always the parental one) to establishment of an independent household.
3. Housing: the transition from home of origin to independent housing.

These transitions are *connected together* in popular ideology of the family and 30 years ago were connected together in practice as well. However, they are increasingly becoming *disconnected* both from each other and from other life transitions discussed in other chapters as the economic situation of young people deteriorates, their transitions are extended and uncertainty becomes a feature of this and other aspects of their lives. These have implications for the relationships of young people with parents both inside and outside the parental home which are addressed in the final section of the chapter. Firstly, however, we need to consider some of the variations in family life in different parts of Europe.

FAMILY TRANSITIONS: IDEOLOGY AND PRACTICE

The idea of 'the family' is heavily overlaid with idealized normative models in each society. Each European society has an ideal of how people should meet, fall in love, get married, find a home and have children, gradually moving away from parental dependency. However, this is not so often realisable in practice and is variable between different groups and different points in time.

In North-Western Europe the dominant model of the 1950s and 1960s, for example, was for a man to be a breadwinner and to support a dependent wife and children at home. Such an idealized household would not include additional generations and it was assumed that on getting married (by their early 20s preferably) young people would 'leave the nest' and start families of their own. The proper way to found such a family was to enter a stable heterosexual relationship then have an engagement, a wedding and a 'housewarming' celebration. There were standardized ritual markers for each of these transitions and gifts from relatives and friends could help to offset the cost of setting up home. The regulation of sexuality was likewise part of this normative transition process: how, when and with whom it is appropriate to have sex was determined by the right and proper way to organize family life. These sets of transitions were therefore connected together and also connected with related transitions in the labour market – from education to work for example.

In the agricultural areas of Southern Europe more 'traditional' patterns of family life and inter-generational relations survived into the post-war period. In these regions, parents hold greater authority and the lives of children – especially girls – was heavily regulated. The modernization of the last few decades, especially following integration into the European Union, has led to new styles of family relations and a search for autonomy by young people. Pais (1995) argues that we can see this in terms of James Coleman's (1990) model of evolution between different kinds of inter-generational relations. In the first phase, that of rural peasant society, he argues, young people were integrated into the rural economy and children were seen in terms of their potential as workers for the household. The financial investment in children or in their education was minimal. Such was the pattern in rural Portugal in the past, and it still exists to some extent in the present. The second phase was characterized by the family exchanging wages for consumer goods in an industrialized economy. The child ceases to be a worker and the family starts to see the child in terms of an investment for the future and long-term source of social mobility. There is strong incentive to invest in the education of children. This is the situation with newly upwardly mobile, urban, middle-class families in Portugal. The third phase, the post-industrial society, is one where families are unsure whether education will lead to a better career or not. The economic and social functions of the family are transferred to other institutions. This is the case with the more established urban classes in Portugal.

Although James Coleman's model is an evolutionary one, we can see that the different styles of inter-generational relations can co-exist within a modern European society such as Portugal, but also within older industrial countries. Within northern industrial countries there are elements of traditional family expectations as well. Amongst ethnic minority groups in Northern Europe, especially those who migrated from the Middle East or from Muslim countries, there was a tendency to hold more 'traditional' ideals of parental authority and youthful subordination and respect, particularly with regard to the control of adolescent girls' behaviour. This was the case even in urbanized middle-class families, which held views of parental authority similar to those in more traditional parts of Europe (Brannen et al. 1994). Amongst British Asians, for example, family solidarity is still especially valued and can also be seen as a source of support for young people (Brah 1986). However, the inter-penetration of 'traditional' familial values with that of the individualistic late-modern society can best be illustrated in the case of communist and post-communist East-Central Europe. There the collapse of modern institutions and their replacement by post-modern chaos is most dramatic.

In socialist societies the ideology of the harmonious family existed too. The official ideology proclaimed that the state cared for the family better than in profit-driven capitalist economies, but the reality was that families were forced together in order to find self-help strategies for economic survival. This produced in practice very close-knit, multi-generational families. The modern socialist economy was based upon rationalist, universalistic criteria and yet, at the same time, family relations pervaded the whole state structure: family ties were used for social mobility and also as a form of punishment by the state. For instance, the children of dissidents and political defectors were often denied access to university or housing. The widely propagated rights to free medical services, education, employment and social security were in reality obtained through a family stratified system of allocation which was very unequal (Mitev 1988, Watson 1993). Parents strove to secure the best possible education, housing or other resources for their children and many things were obtained through family connections (Mozny 1994). Families would put their names down for flats which they would not themselves live in but which may become available to their children in 20 years' time. The family also provided an important source of privacy, comfort and creativity in a situation where public life was totally regulated and controlled. Hence, the ideology of the family was an important subject of propaganda, but also as a source of affective solidarity. In particular, inter-generational ties of mutual support and co-operation were emphasized: parents should care for and financially support children and grandchildren; children should depend upon parents and in turn support their own children in a long-term form of inter-generational deferred reciprocity.

The communist states did not necessarily have a consistent policy on the family. In societies which self-consciously aimed to transform and rebuild social relationships, the family was included as an object of deliberate intervention. After early revolutionary attempts to abolish the family in the Soviet Union, policies moved instead towards supporting it (Juviler 1992). In the post-Second World War period, there was a tendency towards more pro-family policies included the provision of maternity and paternity leave, later with pay, child benefits, maternity grants and so on, reflecting an awareness of the limitations of poor quality and over-crowded public childcare provision. By the 1980s an elaborate set of family allowances had developed in many countries, leading to something of a 'baby boom'. However, easy access to divorce and abortion along with the full-time employment of women remained an important feature of Soviet-style socialist states, proclaimed as a way of liberating women. With the limited availability of other contraceptive methods in many countries, marriage would often take place when the young woman became pregnant and subsequent to that abortion would be used to limit family size (Harchev and Mazkovskij 1978, Davin 1992).

The East-Central European countries, which became communist only after the Second World War, likewise emphasized the liberation of women through their participation in the full-time workforce and this was in stark contrast to the peasant and semi-feudal societies which they replaced. Whilst the material position of women within the family may have been improved, in fact this never led to the liberation of women because relations inside the family – and particularly gender relations – remained very conservative (Watson 1993). Women did most of the housework and childcare, often under very difficult circumstances (Corrin 1992, Kurzynowski 1990). There were also considerable variations within the former Soviet bloc, with the Central Asian republics retaining a more 'clan' style of organization with early marriage and large families, whereas in the Baltic States marriage was delayed and families were small (Malysheva 1992). Roma all over East-Central Europe traditionally had large numbers of children and were organized around more extended families and clan-type groups. There were also differences between urban and rural populations and between different ethnic minority groups. For example, in Bulgaria the Islamic communities of the Rhodopa mountains live in extended rather than nuclear families and preserve strong patriarchal relations with sanctions against divorce (Churenev 1984). Hence, although there was a certain conformity introduced by communism, gender relations were far from being homogenous.

In centrally planned economies it was possible to attempt to regulate fertility and demographic trends through active policy interventions. Romania represents the most extreme example of pro-natalism, having abolished abortion and contraception and introduced compulsory fertility testing of women. There was a tax on women without children and on childless couples over 30. The result was large numbers of illegal abortions, many abandoned and handicapped children and many undernourished and poverty-stricken households with too many mouths to feed (Davin 1992). However, other states also introduced pro-natalist policies in milder forms through family support policies. For example, in the 1980s in Bulgaria, a falling birth rate prompted such a pro-natalist campaign (Spasovska 1980). A decree by the Central Committee of the Communist Party, backed up by an impressive list of official organizations, announced loans for young people setting up households, increased child benefits to parents and the extension of paid leave for women with children to two years on the minimum wage. In addition, they could take unpaid leave for another year with no fear of losing their jobs.

Under communist modernization, age-status transitions were strongly standardized in the post-war period. Related to the age of finishing education, of beginning work and gaining access to housing, marriage and childbirth took place in more predictable ways than in Western Europe. However, this was not necessarily related to the age of leaving home nor that of ceasing to be dependent upon relatives as we shall see later. The important point to make here, however, is that on account of the imposition of a model of the family based upon state policy and the affective importance of the family for survival in 'unofficial' society, a particular model of inter-generational relations was widespread. Familial solidarity and help between generations was very strong.

With the end of communism, the ideology of the family continued to be important because it was still necessary for mutual self-help, particularly in childcare and financial support for young people (Wallace 1995). However, the reaction against readily available abortion in some countries (such as Poland and East Germany) and the abolition of workplace crèches along with heavy criticism of the protected labour market position of mothers are indicative of new trends. Now there is a tendency to see the more role-differentiated family of the man as a breadwinner with a dependent wife and children as being more attractive. This is reinforced in advertising where women are portrayed as housewives and glamorous consumers whilst men's role is now to go out and 'hunt' for money in a free market. In some countries the Church further reinforces a conservative model of the family and in Poland this has been very influential in parliamentary debates as well as social policies (Watson 1993). Furthermore, some of the new post-communist political parties have stressed the return to family values as part of their election campaign. Already from the 1980s Gorbachov in the former Soviet Union was stressing the need for women to return to their 'natural role' in the family as a way of curbing rising juvenile delinquency. However, the need for two incomes and the reluctance of many women to give up their jobs means that the majority of working age women are still employed full-time.

Modernization theory has often focused upon recent trends in family change (Giddens 1991, Beck and Beck-Gernsheim 1995). Whilst some have emphasized the changing relationships *within* the family – between partners and between parents and children – others have emphasized the fragmentation and reconstitution of the family itself. Examples of the first tendency have described the movement away from what is termed 'traditional' family roles where the authority of the parents is strong, where rules are strict and where children are expected to be obedient and subordinate, towards what is termed the more 'modern' family which is characterized by more negotiated rules between parents and children and within partnerships, and more flexibility in relations between generations. Relationships are no longer so fixed by tradition and seen as 'essential'. This has been documented by a variety of researchers in Europe (du Bois-Reymond et al 1995, Hartmann 1987). The second tendency, stronger in the Anglo-American literature, emphasizes the way in which the traditional two-parent, nuclear 'modern' family of the 1950s and 1960s is being replaced by the fragmented 'post modern' family, one which can have several sets of parents (the product of divorce, remarriage, cohabitation and lone-parenthood) from which one chooses close or distant relationships, or with whom one can choose to have no relationship at all (Stacey 1990). The increasing self-awareness of women as key actors both in the labour market and in the family contributes to such trends as they no longer uncritically accept family roles which are handed down by tradition and difficult to reconcile with their improved educational prospects and situation as workers in the labour market.

The 'modern' family was based upon the possibility of wage labour providing sufficient income for young people in order for them to establish an independent household and upon the existence of affordable housing. Both of these conditions have become more remote. Whilst the model of the ideal family may persist, in practice young people are seeking more diverse ways of entering it and many also reject the standard heterosexual couple union as the best and only way to live. Lack of jobs and extended education all undermine the way in which such a family was traditionally formed. Furthermore, strong traditions of family loyalty in both Eastern Europe and parts of Western Europe ensure that close links are maintained between parents and children even where there is the possibility to move away.

Family roles are also constructed through social policies such as social security, wages policy, pensions, education and housing (Finch 1989) and in many European countries there is even a Ministry for the Family. In countries such as Denmark the need to support young people's independence has been recognized as a goal of social policy, whereas in Britain there has been a contradictory approach to this with policies shifting backwards and forwards (Jones and Wallace 1992). The 'family' of social policies, however, often implicitly embodies the norms of the policy makers which are also those of the dominant group in any society in terms of ethnicity and social origin. The result is that non-standard family forms – for example those of ethnic groups such as Afro-Caribbeans in Britain, where the dominant group is white, or Roma in East-Central Europe, where the dominant groups are not Roma, or Russians in Estonia where the dominant group is currently Estonian – are pathologized as 'deviant'. States tend to idealize a particular set of family relations as being 'natural' or 'normal' and these also tend to reflect the values of the dominant group (Abbott and Wallace 1992).

Having described the background to these trends towards change in family life, we will now describe the different strands of transition in more detail.

THE TRANSITION FROM FAMILY OF ORIGIN TO FAMILY OF DESTINATION

Just as the transition from full-time education into full-time work has become extended, so the transition to family of destination has too. The age of getting married generally is rising in European countries. Table 4.1 compares the age of marriage in selected Eastern and Western countries. The countries of Northern Europe have the highest age of marriage, represented in this table by Denmark and the Netherlands. However, the UK, also one of the Northern Protestant countries, has a relatively low age of marriage reflecting perhaps the relatively accelerated transitions in the UK. There is a consistent 2–3 or more year gap between men and women, which may partly reflect traditions such as military service, but could also

Table 4.1　Age at first marriage: Eastern and Western Europe by sex

	Males	Females	Difference Males–Females in years
Czech Republic	23.27	20.69	2.58
Hungary	23.8	21.1	2.7
Bulgaria	25.0	22.0	3
UK	26.4	24.2	2.2
Spain	26.7	24.5	2.2
France	27.0	24.9	2.1
Netherlands	27.2	25.0	2.2
Germany	27.7	25.2	2.5
Greece	27.7	23.4	4.5
Italy	27.9	24.9	3.0
Denmark	29.4	26.8	2.6

Source: Chisholm and Bergeret 1991. Figures are for 1987. *Additional sources*: Mozny 1994 and *Statistical Year Books*, Poland and Hungary 1995.

reflect a very standardized model of age-gender relations in Europe. In some Southern European counties, represented here by Greece and Italy, there is a tendency for young men to marry later and young women to marry earlier than in other countries. In the Eastern European group of countries – Hungary, Bulgaria and the Czech Republic – the age of marriage is generally lower than in Western Europe for both men and women, reflecting the accelerated transitions which had existed in communist countries. In this group of countries, there was generally earlier age of entry into the productive economy and marriage was a factor in gaining housing and marriage grants. However, there has been a recent tendency for age of marriage to rise. In Bulgaria, whereas in the 1958–68 period most brides were below 19, this is now rare and most marriages take place between 20 and 24. Those in higher education have a more protracted transition into family life, as is the case in Western Europe (Wallace 1995b).

Social stratification also has an important influence upon family formation. These patterns of transition varied between different social groups according to their pattern of entry into the labour market. Those with more middle-class occupations marry at a later age than those in manual jobs. Hence, in the 1970s in Britain semi- and unskilled workers married some four years earlier than the professional and intermediate workers (Social Trends 1986). This can be explained by the fact that professional and managerial occupations required a period in higher education before training, in other words, a more extended transition. There are more opportunities for life-style experimentation amongst the university-going middle-class than other groups. Those at other levels, on the other hand, may need to stay at home until they married and for them marriage was an occurrence which could happen sooner rather than later (Sarsby 1983).

In fact the idea that getting married was the normal way to leave home dates only from the 1960s in Britain when the age of marriage dropped so that one in three brides were teenagers and marriage became a universal institution, available to all (in the nineteenth century, by contrast, many women did not marry). In this period, getting married and establishing a home were crucially inter-connected as a way of establishing adult independence. The tremendous importance attached to this at the time coloured the whole period between leaving school and finally getting married. In Leonard's (1980) study, the majority of young people remained at home until then.

Since that time the age of marriage has risen so that only one bride in eight is a teenager. However, despite these changing patterns, familial ideology still exerts a powerful hold over people's imaginations and their behaviour. In 1984 Wallace found that even though young people had children outside marriage, had cohabited, lived in squats and bedsits or were unemployed, they still believed that ultimately they were going to make a conventional transition into a family of destination including getting married, buying a house and having children – even when there seemed no material means of achieving this (Wallace 1987). In East-Central European societies there was very strong pressure to marry and marriage was nearly universal, as was childbearing (Mozny 1994).

More recently, there has been a growing tendency to cohabit rather than marry. There is also evidence that young people are more tolerant about cohabitation than other age groups. The British Household Panel Survey asked about attitudes to cohabitation and found that the older the respondent, the less tolerant they were of this style of living (*Social Trends* 1996). Increasing numbers of young people are also now living alone or sharing with others in non-family households. This has risen from 5 per cent to 7 per cent between 1982 and 1987 in the European Community as a whole and this also reflects a shift away from marriage and towards these alternative household forms (Chisholm and Bergeret

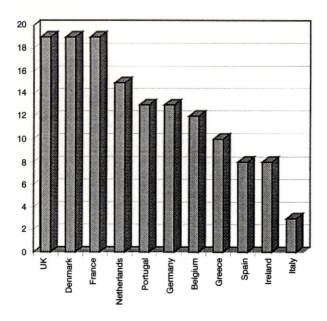

Figure 4.1   Percentage cohabiting in different European countries 1990

Source: Chisholm and Bergeret, 1991: 26. Drawn from Stastisches Bundes-amt, Bevolkerung und Ewerbstätigkeit Fachserie 1, Reihe 1, Wiesbaden 1987; Eurostat 1990, Eurostat Basic Statistics of the European Community 27th edn. 1990 Table 1.3

1991). However, there are considerable variations between coun-tries. Figure 4.1 indicates the rate of cohabitation in different Eu-ropean countries (data are not available for Eastern Europe) and it shows again the northern Protestant countries more likely to have this form of household arrangement than the southern Catholic ones. It seems that there is a tendency towards the individualiza-tion of living arrangements, with more young people living inde-pendently and more cohabiting in preference to getting married.

The age of having a first child has likewise been postponed with people across Europe starting their families on average one year later than a decade ago. The usual age of having first children is now in the late 20s for women (Eurostat 1996). In some countries, such as Germany and Italy, there has been an increasing tendency not to have children at all.

Despite the changes described above, those who fail to conform to this pattern are still considered to have 'premature' transitions, especially if they get pregnant before they marry, have illegitimate children, marry young, have families before they have a home and so on. Such behaviour is often attributed to ignorance, or deviance, especially in the case of lower-class or ethnic minority women. One US social scientist has characterized this as the 'problem' of the proliferation of the 'underclass' (Murray 1986) He argues that these patterns are part of a self-perpetuating 'culture of poverty' in lower-class communities and blames this at least partly on the sexual incontinence of the young people themselves. For lower-class young people, pregnancy was often seen (by researchers) as a misfortune, the product of insufficient use of contraceptives or ignorance (Schofield 1973). Social class is, therefore, an important factor in the way sexuality is perceived. Amongst middle-class young people, however, the possibility of sexual experimentation based upon periods away from home at college and looser, more unstructured relations between the sexes was seen as part of growing up (Aggleton 1987).

As Phoenix (1991) has argued, what is now considered 'too young' to have children (the teen years) was at one time considered the ideal age to have children and many of today's mothers would be considered 'too old'. However, such ideas of what is 'too young' or 'too old', 'too many' or 'too few' children are used in racist ideologies to condemn the family practices of ethnic or religious minorities such as Roma and Muslims. In general, however, teenage pregnancies have been falling rather than rising in most European countries.

Why has there been this tendency to postpone marriage and childbearing? First, it seems that the extended transition into employment means that other life transitions are correspondingly extended. This can be illustrated with the differences between countries and social classes which tend to reflect different speeds of transition in other respects. Secondly, rising unemployment can in some cases lead to postponed transitions or styles of transition being diverted in other ways such as by living together rather than marrying (Wallace 1987, Fagin and Little 1984), although other research suggests that unemployment can encourage young people to have children as an alternative form of status (Campbell, B. 1984, Willis 1984b).

A further factor is that marriage is no longer the main way of sanctioning sexual relations. The disconnection of sex from marriage can be found in attitudes to pre-marital sexuality which have generally become more liberal in every country – indeed, young people have led these trends with more tolerant attitudes towards all issues to do with sexuality – homosexuality, sex and abortion (Inglehart 1997). Successive surveys in Bulgaria have indicated a tendency towards greater tolerance of sexual relations outside of marriage, particularly among the urbanized populations (Mitev 1982). The highly educated are likely to hold the most liberal views and to favour more experimental, less 'traditional' sexual relations (Kjuranov 1987).

The early and universal marriage and childbearing behaviour in socialist states reinforced heterosexual conformity. In the Soviet Union gay and lesbian relations were often illegal or subject to harassment: homosexuality was regarded as a deviant illness. In many places it is still impossible for gay and lesbian people to openly declare themselves although there were some underground lesbian and gay movements and these have become more visible (Schenk 1993). Many of these have started to 'come out' more recently among youth sub-cultures, at least in Moscow (Pilkington 1996).

Young people are not sheltered from the sexualization of popular culture generally, which is no longer tied to other social institutions such as marriage but still very strongly tied to romantic heterosexual relations. Some studies have indicated that young women are often under considerable pressure to have sex and that sexual coercion or threatened rape may be a familiar experience for them (Halson 1990). However, in the late modern family, sexuality is something increasingly tolerated by parents and a subject of negotiation rather than taboo between parents and children (Brannen et al. 1994). Ironically, the increased awareness of sexuality leads to an increasing desire to protect young women, especially for parents to control them. The threat of AIDS has made many 'taboo' subjects common conversation and may have reinforced a certain sexual conservatism, although surveys carried out in Bulgaria found that young people felt that AIDS was little threat to them (Tonchev and Tomov 1989).

The transition to parenthood and the transition to marriage or cohabitation, like other transitions, have become increasingly disconnected. Unmarried parenthood had risen in many European countries. There is some evidence then that traditional moral norms about acceptable and unacceptable behaviour have shifted, particularly for the younger generation. For example, there was greater

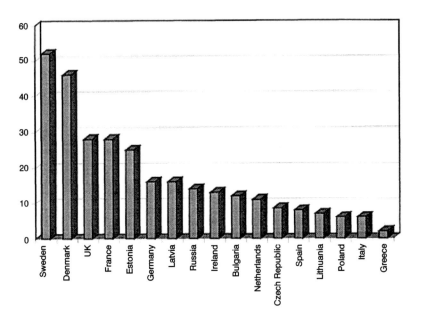

Figure 4.2   Extra-marital childbearing in Eastern and Western European countries, 1991 (percentage of all live births in each country)

Source: Socilogicky Aktualny, 1 1993: 22, Czech Academy of Sciences

tolerance of lone-parenthood across a range of different countries (Inglehart 1997). It is no longer a tragedy to become pregnant outside of marriage and young women to whom this happens no longer have to go into special homes or mental institutions, to give up their babies for adoption or to feel obliged to get married, as they would have done just a few decades ago.

Figure 4.2 indicates the rates of childbirth outside of marriage in the different parts of Europe. It can be seen that there are higher rates of this kind of family transition in Northern Europe, particularly in the Scandinavian countries, since in Sweden more than half of births take place in this way. However, extra-marital childbearing is also related to religion since Catholic Lithuania and Poland have lower rates than do the surrounding Protestant countries such as Latvia and Estonia. In general there is less extra-marital childbearing in most communist countries than in western countries, but even in the former communist countries it is rising: the percentage of

children born out of wedlock in Bulgaria increased from 3 per cent
in 1945 to 12 per cent in 1990 (Kjulanov et al. 1991).

The 'normal biography' in East-Central Europe meant that children followed upon marriage. Although the numbers born out of
wedlock have risen, this is considered undesirable in most Eastern European countries. There are, however, exceptions in sub-
communities with one quarter of non-marital births in Bulgaria
occurring in the Roma community where cohabitation was also more
common (Dinkova et al. 1991). Many mothers in former communist countries who had unwanted children, or who were not able
to support their children, put them in a state children's home. In
Bulgaria, this was the case with three quarters of the unmarried
mothers. Although there are special policies for lone-mothers, living conditions were hard and nine out of ten single mothers there
had difficulties making ends meet (Dinkova et al. 1991).

There is a general tendency for family size to fall with modernization. In Bulgaria it fell from an average of 6.3 children at the
turn of the century to 3.4 before the Second World War and 1.73
now (Statistical Year Book, Bulgaria 1991:36). A similar fall in family
size can be found in Western Europe where the average household
size fell from 2.8 to 2.6 people per household between 1981 and
1991, and this represents a much longer term trend (Eurostat 1996).
This is more marked in countries such as Germany and Italy. In
post-communist Europe the birth rate has fallen very dramatically
over the last few years, perhaps on account of the economic inse-
curity there.

There are therefore some common trends towards postponed family
building, decreasing family size and alternative living arrangements
throughout Europe, although these are stronger in some countries
than in others. There seems to be also some shift in the way in
which family relations and sexuality are seen – towards greater
tolerance and flexibility. This has affected the transition from family of origin to family of destination and de-coupled sex from marriage, marriage from cohabitation and marriage from childbearing.

THE TRANSITION FROM HOUSEHOLD OF ORIGIN TO
AN INDEPENDENT HOUSEHOLD

The transition to a separate household is also increasingly de-coupled
from traditional transitions into marriage. This is now seen more

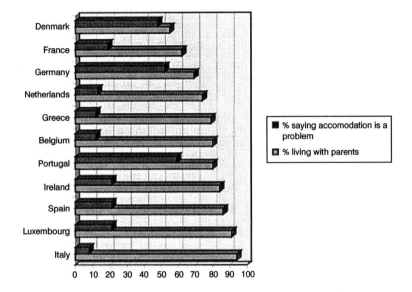

Figure 4.3   Percentage of young people living at home in different Western European countries and perceptions of accommodation as a problem, 1990

Source: Chisholm and Bergeret 1991: 23, drawn from *Young Europeans* survey, 1990

as a separate transition and a marker of independent adulthood irrespective of marital status. There is thus a growing diversity of household arrangements and more apparent 'choice' for young people in how they wish to conduct their lives (Hartmann 1987) and this may be at least partly because the extended 'post adolescent' transition discourages conventional family formation and encourages experimental forms of living.

Most young people in Europe continue to live at home whilst they are in their teenage years. Figure 4.3 indicates the numbers of 15–24 year olds still living at home in different Western European countries.

Figure 4.3 illustrates the fact that there was great variation in this pattern. Although overall there is a tendency for young people to live longer with their parents on account of their more protracted period of economic dependency, we can see that in Italy, Spain and

Ireland – the Catholic countries of the EU – this was more common than in more northern Protestant countries such as Germany, Denmark and the Netherlands or the UK. However, whilst in Germany, Britain and Denmark it was seen as desirable for young people to leave home, in countries such as Italy this was not necessarily seen as a problem at all (Chisholm and Bergeret 1991). This was also often the case in Central and Eastern European countries where young people did not usually think of leaving home unless they were married or studying or in military service. In the southern Catholic countries we can see more 'traditional' styles of living with more people living with their parents, fewer living independently and cohabitation being less significant than marriage – and this was even more the case in Greece. In Denmark by contrast, 25 per cent of the 15–24 age group lived autonomously in addition to large numbers cohabiting rather than being married (Chisholm and Bergeret 1991).

However, young people do not necessarily leave home for good. Rather, they come and go (Jones 1995, Young 1987). The common pattern was to move backwards and forwards from the parental home for a few years during this age-phase. Jones (1995), who has conducted the most extensive study of this topic, found that the most common reason for young people to leave home in Britain was in order to start an educational course, and this was followed by starting a new job. Other reasons for leaving home include to move in with a partner or simply to find more independence (Ainly 1991). It was more often young women who sought this kind of independence, perhaps because they may find family control more constraining. Others left home for more negative reasons including physical or sexual abuse, arguments with parents or step parents and even being thrown out by parents. According to Jones' study, these accounted for 23 per cent of all those who left home aged between 16 and 19 in Scotland. Most of those who left home lived in what she describes as 'transitional' accommodation – that is hostels, lodgings, shared accommodation with other young people in the privately rented sector and so on. This did not represent the final outcome of their household trajectory, but was usually temporary. In Germany, Gaiser and Müller (1985) likewise found that flats, hostels and shared accommodation was a common pattern for first setting up a new household.

But in what sense could it be said that these young people had 'left home'? In such accommodation they may return to parents to eat, to do laundry, for the holidays or when their course of education finishes. In Germany and Austria one way of accommodating the needs for autonomy among young people is to build them a separate apartment *within* the family dwelling. There are thus an array of transitional arrangements with respect to the household status of young people.

Communist modernization changed the patterns of leaving home in East-Central Europe. The early dislocations caused by rapid and forced industrialization in the Soviet Union created very rapid migration to industrial centres with large numbers of young workers living in hostels. By the 1970s this was no longer the norm, but it was still the case that those who wished to go to specialized trade schools (especially from the countryside) had to leave home in order to do so and these constituted 7 per cent of young people of the 14–17 year old age group (Ilynsky 1992). Low wages and the necessity of two incomes meant that young people could not in practice afford to set up home themselves. They thus relied upon family support for getting married and parents were crucial in obtaining favours for their children in the state system through co-operation and exchange (Raichev 1985). Thus, paradoxically, young people had to get married in order to be eligible for independent state support but in doing so they relied more upon their parents than ever. There was very strong parental obligation to support children and most parents wanted to help their children as long as they could irrespective of their own financial situation (Langazova 1985).

THE TRANSITION FROM HOUSE OF ORIGIN TO INDEPENDENT HOUSING

The ability to leave home depends upon whether there is housing to go to and young people have at all times been considered a low priority in governmental housing strategy: the assumption is that they should live at home. Forming a new household requires entry into the housing market of which young people form a very particular part. In much of Europe young people's position within the housing market has deteriorated in the 1980s. The increasing emphasis on owner occupation, the de-regulation of rented housing and rising rents have put much housing out of reach of young people. In addition, the redevelopment of city centres has reduced the number of potential homes where low rent accommodation was available

(Burton et al. 1989). The decline of state or council housing has also affected young people adversely. In all countries young people are disadvantaged as first time entrants onto the housing market. For example, in the UK where there has been an increased trend towards owner occupation it is difficult for them to raise money for a mortgage without a sufficient income or any collateral. In Germany and other countries where rents are linked to length of residence, this disadvantages new entrants into the housing market where they have to pay the highest rents. Thus, the number of young people who want to find their own home vastly exceeds the numbers who are able to do so (Gaiser and Müller 1985).

One effect of these pressures on the youth housing market has been a rise in the number of homeless young people over the 1980s. This is particularly evident in the UK, where young people, attracted particularly to London, are found sleeping in doorways in the city centre or in 'cardboard cities'. But it seems that the numbers have risen all over Europe (Hutson and Liddiard 1995). Evidence from Britain indicates that many of young people's housing needs are concealed by the fact that they may be living on friends' floors or in temporary accommodation and squats and therefore not count as homeless. The factors leading to youth homelessness have been listed by Hutson and Liddiard (1994) as follows:

- Leaving care. Those young people who were the responsibility of children's homes or state welfare services are much more likely to become homeless. Whilst in the UK these constitute only 1 per cent of young people, they are one third of the single homeless (Stein and Carey 1986).
- Victims of physical or sexual abuse. A large number of homeless young people are those who suffered such abuse. They were estimated to be 17 per cent of young single homeless in one Scottish study (Killeen 1988).
- Mental illness. Large numbers of the single homeless suffer from some mental illness. Policies of care in the community has meant that more of them are discharged from psychiatric hospitals.
- Crime. Those leaving custody are at high risk of becoming homeless and the young homeless are more likely to become involved in crime.
- Family breakdown and family problems. In Gill Jones' study carried out in 1991, 60 per cent of homeless young people said that the reason they left home was because of family arguments.

Carlen (1996), however, explains youth homelessness in terms of the gap between young people's incomes (generally declining) and the price of housing (generally rising). She illustrates how inappropriate many of the hostel solutions are to the problem of youth homelessness and shows that young people often preferred to fend for themselves. The young homeless were not just victims – theirs was also a life-style which met certain needs and a desire for independence and autonomy.

Homelessness is often linked to a pattern of moving around transient accommodation with periods of sleeping rough and to the fact that most of the young homeless could not return home. There is a range of emergency accommodation which will usually only take people for a limited duration and not if they are seen to cause too many problems, but the demand for places greatly outstrips the supply. In Germany some hostel accommodation is provided for homeless young people, although their numbers do not appear to be as high as in Britain, and in France there are also efforts to provide reception centres for them (Coles 1995, Gaiser and Müller 1985).

Thus, it is evident that not all young people are happy living with families or have families to live with. It is possible that were accommodation and incomes more available for them, far greater numbers would leave home. What is happening is that as youth are being re-defined as a dependent population, so there are large numbers of casualties who have no-one to depend upon or any desire to be dependent.

In former socialist countries it was very difficult for young people to leave home and form a new household because of the absence of sufficient housing. Three generational families were common and young people had to live with parents normally for a few years even after they were married. Consequently, in Bulgaria in 1977, 61 per cent of young married couples were living with parents and this was typical of other communist countries too. When young people left home to study elsewhere they lived in dormitories (about 13 per cent) and would return home to parents frequently. Others (about 29 per cent) rented accommodation (Radulov 1973). Consequently, many young people lived with parents until the age of 30 or more. Getting married was one way to secure independent housing – a survey in Hungary found that 12 per cent of women who married whilst at university did so only in order to stand a better chance of getting housing (Kosha 1985).

Although the official policy was to prioritize young families in access to housing, in practice this was seldom successful. The difficulties which this involved can be illustrated by the experience of lecturers at Sofia University. They would live in a dormitory for at least ten years, sharing a room with babies at first and then with growing children. When they at last received a flat somewhere in the suburbs and managed to furnish it, their own children would marry and live there with them. The flats themselves were often very small with 70 per cent of flats built after 1980 in Bulgaria having only one or two rooms (in order to maximize the number of dwellings being provided). In the former Soviet Union the situation was still worse with 'komunalka' still common – flats where several households shared kitchen and bathroom facilities. However, there were other variations between countries. In East Germany, for example, one of the wealthiest former communist countries, only 20 per cent of young families shared accommodation with parents.

The introduction of market reforms have not yet produced a full market in housing with flats and housing still being obtained through various family strategies for circumventing the regulations. In large cities the opportunities for commercial letting have driven up residential prices without necessarily substantially improving quality. Many state and co-operative flats have been privatized. On the other hand, an illegal market in renting has developed with co-operative and state or even private flats being sub-let several times over, often for exorbitant prices, making some of the ex-socialist countries as expensive to live in as the leading western cities. In some cases there are reports of intimidation to encourage tenants in desirable residential locations to move so that their dwellings can be re-let more profitably. East-Central Europeans, most of whom are still on incomes considerably below their western counterparts, are priced out of such a market. Most people continue to live in the suburban panel-built blocks of flats which stretch for many kilometres around socialist cities. The chronic housing shortages which existed before the reforms have since been exacerbated. The restitution of some property to its former owners and the impossibility for ordinary people to get credit (banks charged 40 per cent interest in Poland in 1992) means that flats stand empty at the same time as there is a housing shortage because no-one can afford to buy them. One traditional solution has been to build one's own house and there has been a spurt in new housebuilding on rural plots, but

this would advantage young people only as members of larger extended families.

Thus, in many countries, the search for independence amongst
young people leads to a desire for independent accommodation
(Jones 1995). At the same time the amount of suitable accommodation available has declined, as has young people's independent
income which reduces their scope for finding such independent
accommodation. Various alternatives emerge, from the use of transitional accommodation to homelessness. However, it is likely that
whether or not they manage to form a new household, the relationship with parents continues during and after the period of transition to a new home and it is to these inter-generational relations
that we now turn.

INTER-GENERATIONAL RELATIONS WITHIN THE HOUSEHOLD

Youth is a period of transition between families. Young people
can be dependants or independent depending upon their economic
activity, whether they remain in education and whether they have
formed households of their own. The erosion in the income of young
people due to their extended education and training, rising unemployment and the deliberate cuts in their incomes and grants which
have accompanied this, means that young people are living with
their parents for longer periods of time and are more likely to be
financially dependent upon them (Jones and Wallace 1992). However, relationships with parents have changed. According to the
British Social Attitudes survey of 1987 most parents felt that they
were more liberal with their own children than their parents had
been with them (quoted in Roll 1990). In a comparative study of
the 1950s and 1970s by Allerbeck (1976), in Germany there were
similar trends reported with parents valuing independence and self-
determination more, whilst they valued subordination and obedience less than in the past. This change was also noted in other
studies around Western Europe (see Chisholm et al. 1995).

In East-Central Europe there is a strong moral obligation for
parents to support children throughout their lives. Surveys carried
out in communist countries indicated that parents felt obliged to
provide housing – including an independent home – for children
as well as an education. Although education was free in communist

countries and students could receive a stipend after their first year, having a student at home was, nevertheless, a financial burden for parents who had to pay for books and clothing, and many parents also paid private tuition to help their children pass entrance exams. For their part, young people did not pay board money to parents, nor participate very much in housework and this was consistent in surveys carried out both in the former Soviet Union and elsewhere (Mazkovskij 1982). The responsibility of children and young people in the household was only to 'study well'. Young people expected help from parents through all their major transitions in life (Mitev 1988).

One such transition was the birth of children. With women working full-time, grandparents provided crucial resources in the support of young families in this respect. Although the state provided public childcare, it is estimated that only 30 per cent of the costs were met by the state (Radulov 1973). Women could take up to three years off to care for children, but only a small number took advantage of this and most turned to their parents for help instead so that in 1980s in Bulgaria, for example, 68 per cent of young people used parents on both sides of the family for help in babysitting. For young people studying who had children (there were many in this category) grandparents were similarly an important source of help.

Grandparents started helping with children from the beginning and would take over responsibility for childcare as soon as the mother returned to work. One common practice, if the grandparents lived in a different dwelling to the young family, was for the children to spend considerable time and holidays at the grandparents'. As well as helping with children, grandparents provided other services, such as queuing for goods and doing housework – tasks which were essential in the struggle for existence under conditions of chronic shortage. Nowadays, family help is still preferable to publicly funded childcare centres and many of these have been closed in any case, as factories have rationalized or been privatized.

In post-communist countries parental assistance continues to be very important. The costs of education have risen with grants being eroded or cut out completely and students very often having to pay fees to go to college or university and also for school. The rising costs of education mean that young people are even more dependent upon parental support in order to continue their studies. Low incomes for young people mean that they are still not able to set up independent households (Roberts et al. 1995). However, a major contrast is that in some households the parents are no longer better off than the younger generation and in some cases the substantial dependence of children upon parents was starting to be reversed. As market relations disrupt old patterns of earning, so young people sometimes find themselves to be the main earners in families and under these circumstances their contribution to household resources could form an important part of household resources, particularly in poorer families (Wallace 1995). As the communist social safety net collapses and has not yet been replaced by sufficient safeguards for social security, the family remains an important resource.

Thus, with the extenuation and de-coupling of transitions for young people, relationships with parents can be very important, not only because young people are likely to live with them for long periods of time, but also because parents continue to be important even after young people have left home altogether. There is a paradoxical tendency for young people to have higher demands for autonomy at the same time as they are dependent upon parents for longer periods of time. This puts a certain amount of strain upon family relationships which can be resolved by allowing more independence within the natal family or may even result in the young person leaving. This may be particularly acute in working-class homes where previously young people left the nest and became financially independent earlier. Ironically, social policies which insist that parents should be increasingly responsible for their children's behaviour fly in the face of this increasing differentiation within the home and may put further strains upon family relationships, with parents complaining that they are unable to control their children and are increasingly unwilling to do so (Jones and Wallace 1992).

CONCLUSIONS

The chapter has explored some of the issues of age-status transitions in different social contexts. Whilst factors such as entry into work, marriage, sexual relations, childbearing and leaving home were all linked together in the 'modern' style of family such as existed in the 1960s and 1970s, these factors are increasingly becoming de-coupled as transitions take place in any order and are reversible. This trend is particularly discernible in the Northern European

Protestant countries, perhaps because of the tradition of individualism in these countries and here we can see all kinds of alternative household forms becoming more common. In the countries of Southern Europe and in rural areas more traditional styles of family life, with connected transitions, are more common. In the ex-communist countries age-status transitions into marriage, independent household and family life were previously strongly regulated on account of the formal planning of the economy, although now there is more postponement of transitions and some evidence of experimentation in family forms. There is also some variation according to ethnic group – as there is in Western Europe, although we lack sufficient material to document this adequately.

There is a general tendency for age-status transitions to reflect patterns of transition from school to work. As this is delayed, so are transitions into the family and this is most marked among those entering higher education in each country. Those in higher education in all countries are more likely to experiment with new styles of residence and family forms. It is possible, therefore, that the expansion of higher education will lead to increased flexibility in family and living arrangements.

In many ways the idealized patterns of starting a family and leaving home were rather similar in different parts of Europe with love, marriage and economic independence being aligned. However, they were not realizable in many contexts. The relationships between generations in the family likewise depend upon such social and economic contexts and in Eastern and Central Europe young people were even more dependent upon parents than in Western Europe. Nevertheless, the lengthening transition in Western Europe creates new roles within families as dependency is increased. This results in somewhat contradictory situations where a young person can be recognized as an independent citizen and yet still be financially dependent upon parents. The tendency has been increasingly to recognize the role of individual family members.

These family roles are further complicated by what some have called 'post modern' trends. The fragmentation of family relationships, the increasing diversity of life-styles and forms of living, the movement backwards and forwards between one status and another instead of a progressional movement, are all well developed in Western Europe and we are beginning to see similar trends in East-Central Europe too. With the breakdown of old structures of support and control we would expect to see such tendencies accelerating.

However, the breakdown of traditional structures of support and increasing individualization leaves increasing numbers of young people not only unemployed, but without family support (or escaping from family confinement) and in some cases homeless. The 'post modern' welfare state is unable to provide adequate solutions for them and such 'modern' solutions as confinement to institutions are also increasingly inoperable.

The nature of the transition from one to another household helps to construct gender roles and here we have been seeing women's roles becoming more fluid with women being seen as both participants in the labour market as well as being domestic workers in both parts of Europe. However, this may also make life more difficult for them as they are required to do two lots of work – in the home and in the labour market. This is certainly the case in Eastern and Central Europe where most women continue to work inside and outside the home despite a recent 'backlash' against their participation in the labour market and cuts in state expenditure which mean that they increasingly have to find their own 'private' solutions for childcare.

5 Youth Culture, Sub-Cultures and Consumerism[1]

Youth are defined by distinctive cultures and consumer markets and, following post-modern tendencies, such cultural factors become increasingly important for understanding social groups (Lash 1990). Often sub-cultures are espoused in opposition to mainstream or official culture and each generation of young people is able to creatively construct new styles and identities, building upon and breaking away from previous styles and fashions. Young people have taken advantage of new communications technologies as they have become available – record players, cassettes, videos, satellite TV, magazines, computers – in order to create and communicate their sub-cultures. Even the iron curtain proved unable to seal off young people from youth cultures which spread rapidly across East and West Europe creating a common cultural identity as 'young'. Youth cultures and consumer identities have therefore been very important in the social construction of youth in different global contexts, but this has often taken the form of a 'post-modern' antithesis to official attempts by dominant cultures to construct youth as an age category.

Capitalist consumer markets have spread youth cultural styles throughout the world so that they form part of a 'global culture' and this was further assisted by the crumbling of the iron curtain. This helps to create an idea of 'youthfulness' originating in western capitalist countries and particularly the USA with its domination of media culture. For young people in other countries the American model of youth can represent a 'dream of modernity' to which they aspire (Leichty 1995). However, it is not necessarily mainstream culture which is communicated. For German youth immediately after the Second World War, motorbikes, along with rock and roll brought in by the American troops, represented a model of youth which formed the basis of city gangs and an alternative

---

[1] An earlier version of this chapter appeared in *Youth and Society* 28 (2): 189–214

to the previous constructions of youth described in Chapter 2 (Lindner 1985). More recently, hip hop music and break-dancing, a culture associated with Hispanic and black youth in run down inner cities, became a world-wide phenomenon appealing to many different young people (Rose and Ross 1994). Thus, although youth culture may originate in one context, it may be re-read and re-interpreted in different ways in other contexts.

In this chapter we examine the role of youth culture, sub-cultures and styles in different social contexts and the official reactions of dominant regimes towards them. We look at the way mass media serve to create and define particular visions of 'youth' – ones which are often disembedded from one context and re-embedded elsewhere, sometimes becoming a form of political subversion.

YOUTH AND POPULAR CULTURE

We make an analytical distinction between *youth culture* generally, that is, youth as an element of the media-conveyed culture of consumption, on the one hand and *youth sub-cultures* which are more stylistically specific on the other. Although, ultimately, these two categories merge into one another, we begin by analyzing them separately. Young people have had a distinctive role to play within consumer culture within which they have been a specific market and a source of creative change. From the early development of mass consumer culture in the post-war period, youth were identified as a particular target group and this was associated with them having a new position as consumers. As early as 1959 Mark Abrams identified the 'teenage consumer' as a numerically significant section of the population with some surplus income as their wages, he claimed, had increased at twice the rate of that of adults compared with the pre-war period: 'their "discretionary" spending has risen by probably 100 per cent' (Abrams 1961:9) he concludes. This was linked to the changing position of young people within the family as it was no longer necessary to hand over all their money to parents and they could spend it on clothes, popular music, magazines and commercial entertainment through which they set consumer trends. Young people, particularly working-class young people who had wages to spend, were thrust into a new and conspicuous prominence.

In the USA, where consumer society developed more quickly,

sociologists such as Talcott Parsons and Eisenstadt (1956) developed general theories of youth. The peer group, encouraged by consumer culture and the differentiation of roles within the nuclear family, was seen as a form of socialization to adulthood: a way of helping young people make the transition from the particularistic values of the family towards the universalistic values of wider society. Youth cultures therefore had a 'function' in integrating young people into society. However, this functionalist approach tends to assume that this operated in a universal way, when, as we shall see, it tended to work in different ways for different social groups. Furthermore, this approach tended to see youth culture as a way of inculcating conformity to society rather than resisting it.

Many saw the development of mass commercial culture as a negative one. The Frankfurt School of Sociology, for example, through the works of Marcuse (1968) and others, saw people being cynically manipulated and duped by mass culture, as having their 'real' needs replaced by artificial ones in a vacant and homogenizing addiction to advertising, imported American culture and popular music. Young people were supposed to be particularly susceptible to this kind of media indoctrination. Richard Hoggart (1958), for example, deplored the vacuous commercial culture which was replacing the indigenous community traditions (as he saw it). More recently this sentiment has been echoed by Seabrook (1982) who describes the young unemployed as alienated from any 'real' community and excluded from, but nevertheless fascinated by, the tantalizing pleasures of the consumer culture which surrounds them.

Indeed, the Albermarle Report (1960) in Britain argued that efforts should be made to tempt young people back into youth clubs in order to pursue more elevated and supervised pursuits and there were efforts to round up the 'unattached' (that is, unattached to youth clubs) who were thought to represent the greatest problem in this respect. In this 'modern' phase, youth cultures were associated with a particular stage of life, that between starting work and 'settling down'. Adolescence was seen as a time of freedom and 'fun', an escape from adult responsibilities. For Hoggart, for example, youth was for working-class young people a 'brief flowering' before being dragged down by the weight of adult responsibilities and family commitments. The emphasis on fun, pleasure and hedonism embodied in youth popular culture was encouraged by the development of consumer culture so that this was a disruptive hedonism and at the same time commercially exploitable. Later, as consumer culture later became more generalized in the post-war period, so youth was no longer confined to a 'brief flowering' but rather the pursuit of pleasure and style came to characterize all stages of life.

The post-war period was characterized by the spread of an infrastructure which made new forms of participation in mass culture possible. The increase in leisure time and the individual ownership of the technology for transmitting cultures offered the opportunity for larger markets, but also more individualized participation and choice. To begin with, the technology associated with music and listening to music was important, with radio stations taking advantage of the increased ownership of radio sets, record players and tape recorders, followed by the more portable and convenient cassette recorder which allowed the easy recording of music. Listening to music has also become the most popular pastime – a dramatic change since the early post-war period (Lindner 1985, Damm 1985). This was followed by increased possession of other consumer goods – motorbikes, bicycles and cars – which enabled greater movement and autonomy outside of the home. From the 1960s, TV watching became standard entertainment with the near-universal ownership of TV sets, and with the introduction of cable and satellite TV, videos and the increasing privatization of telecommunications, more and more specialist broadcasts could be received. Furthermore, young people are increasingly likely to have such technology to themselves in their own bedrooms. Since the mid-1980s the increasing use of compact discs and computers allow more access to visual as well as aural communication and these technologies allow privatized consumption of mass culture by individuals or small groups. The video market too has expanded with 60 per cent of homes in Britain owning videos and 19 per cent having home computers by the 1990s (Social Trends 1992). In future, combinations of these technologies will make the international transmission of styles and cultures even more accessible. This allows the differentiation of young people within the family – they can increasingly retreat to their own rooms and own life-styles (Hartmann 1987).

This has led some to identify a form of 'individualization' in these activities: young people's activities and goods are increasingly controlled by them rather than subject to external control. There have also been changes in the forms of social activity young people en-

gage in. The evidence seems to suggest that more loose, unstructured leisure time, particularly parties outside of adult control, have
become more common (Zinnecker and Fuchs 1981, Damm 1985)
resulting in greater leisure time independence. There have also been
changes in the extent of parental control over this period. One
indicator of this is that, whereas in 1968 2 per cent of males in
Germany and 1 per cent of females had no restrictions on when
they should arrive home, in 1978 it was 48 per cent and 42 per
cent respectively (Damm 1985). Thus the increasing independence
of young people is possible through youth and consumer culture.

Participation in youth cultures and this form of unsupervised
unstructured leisure, however, is not equally enjoyed by everyone.
This is a phenomenon associated with urban areas where there are
places to meet, cultural 'scenes' to colonize and where there are
centres of communication for fashions to spread. In the rural parts
of Europe, such trends are not so well developed. Young people
have less opportunity to find out about such things and their activities are absorbed more into local community events: the fairs
and carnivals, the fire brigade and Red Cross, which involve all
age groups. The use of young people's labour in agriculture also
allows young people less recreational time (Wallace et al. 1994).
Young women also have less access to leisure, being more likely to
have to do housework in all countries and being more restricted
by parents (Zinnecker and Fuchs 1981, Griffin 1985).

From the 1970s there was a change in the way in which youth
popular culture was interpreted. Youth culture became less something which was outside and more an integral part of popular culture generally. The more recent generation of sociologists, brought
up on rock music themselves, saw popular music in a more positive light. Frith (1978), for example, rejects what he describes as
the 'Leavisite' tradition of snobbery towards popular music and argues
instead for its creative and progressive qualities. It is not, he argues, just a product of commercial exploitation, but also a question of the creative output of young people themselves, who have
access to more cultural forms and modes of expression. Whilst on
the one hand, it was true that capital was concentrated increasingly in the hands of large transnational companies and in order to
be successful, music had to be internationally appealing – bland,
non regional, non political – on the other hand, music became increasingly differentiated. Popular music had an important meaning
for different sub-cultural groups, as we shall describe in more detail

Youth in Society

later, Willis (1990) has argued that popular music makes an 'unarticulated' appeal and can appear to be rebelling against what is perceived as 'normal' life. Music also makes a space for the creation of small group or individual following of particular styles and fashions so that, instead of constituting an undifferentiated 'mass culture' or a culture clearly defined by class layers, it became differentiated according to styles and taste. This led sociologists to analyse popular music as a cultural phenomenon and a succession of studies of punk (Laing 1985), Acid House (Redhead 1990 and 1993), hip hop (Ross and Rose 1994) and other styles followed. The study of popular music became a genre in its own right.

A shift also occurred in the analysis of young people's magazines. The early feminist analyses of these magazines tended to be very critical of their style and content and the 'teeny bopper' culture which they promoted, describing it as 'one of the most highly manufactured forms of available youth culture – it is almost totally packaged' (McRobbie and Garber 1976: 220, Sarsby 1983, McRobbie 1978). They described young women as graduating from one type of magazine to another in age-specific bands. The magazines gave them detailed instructions on clothes and behaviour and included advertisements for cosmetics and clothes to help them attain these ideals. They were devoted to a more or less non-stop narcissistic concern with femininity. By the 1990s, however, such magazines were devoted less to patronizing instructions on how to be feminine than on how to develop an authentic personal style – from a 'modern' emphasis upon age specific conformity to a 'post-modern' emphasis on differentiation. The new magazines are keen to respond quickly to the development of new styles and taste amongst young people rather than trying to guide those tastes (McRobbie 1991, Lury 1996).

Whereas the earlier studies were concerned with what was produced in the popular media for young people – assuming that they were the passive consumers of such output – more recent studies emphasize the creativity and selectivity in the way these messages were received. In the 1980s a new approach to youth cultures developed, one which instead celebrated the variety and opportunity offered by consumer culture. McRobbie's own auto-critique illustrates this as she moved from seeing young women's magazines as examples of commercial exploitation, towards looking at the different ways in which young women read or interpreted such literature and expressed themselves creatively through it (see McRobbie

1991). Young people did not simply passively absorb all the advertisements and media images directed at them; instead they selectively interpreted them and re-appropriated elements for their own purposes in a re-reading of cultural texts outside the full control of the purveyors of mass media (Nava 1992). Paul Willis (1990) exhorted us to look at this as 'grounded aesthetics' of young people's cultural activity. Far from young people being the passive and defenceless victims of commercial media as portrayed by Seabrook, Hoggart and others, they are in fact some of the most sophisticated audiences of such messages, being a generation brought up in a world of visual signs. The development of new media such as videos, recording and publishing technology made it possible to produce or copy materials relatively quickly and cheaply, thus making the styles also more accessible through less commercialized media such as 'fanzines'.

One could argue that the influence of mass media culture over popular styles was reversed. Hence, although hippie and punk styles may have begun as reactions against commercial culture, with the rejection of mainstream materialism by the former and the flaunting of the debris of commercial culture such as safety pins and plastic bags in the latter, they were both in turn absorbed into mainstream styles and even haute couture – Zandra Rhodes, for example, produced diamond studded safety pins and expensive, 'designer' ripped jeans (Hebdidge 1979, Martin 1983). Now 'trend spotters' from magazines and fashion houses are sent out to mingle in the discotheques and city streets. McRobbie (1991) claims that feminism and other counter-cultures also affected women's magazines as those aimed at young women addressed more serious issues and 'alternative' magazines, such as *Spare Rib*, gained a wide circulation. The power rather than the powerlessness of the consumer became more emphasized (Nava 1992).

Moreover, although young women had previously been portrayed as those most subordinated to consumer culture, they were now analysed in terms of the power which this brought to them in exercising consumer choice. There are also attempts to reinterpret retrospectively the more conservative mass culture of the past as a way in which different femininities were constructed – and resisted. Lesley Johnson (1993), for example, looking back to the 1950s, sees a number of different dimensions to the construction of femininity in popular culture and a number of ways in which women could actively express their identities through this. Men's magazines and advertising directed at men has also taken on aspects of narcissistic pleasurable consumption as the images of the 'new man' have helped to create alternative masculinities, influenced by gay sub-cultures.

This way of looking at youth culture is influenced by 'post modernist' ideas. The extensive production – or over production – of images, signs and styles encourages a re-assembling of common identities around different themes. People can develop individual tastes and styles based no longer upon social position in the class systems or in relation to the means of production, but according to these free-floating images, as 'consumer tribes' and symbols can be reinterpreted and their reinterpretations reinterpreted in an endless 'pastiche' of styles (Lash 1990). Hence, for example, rave culture of the 1980s used symbols such as tie-dyed garments and 'smiley' symbols from the 60s' youth cultures but re-cycled them in the context of new sub-cultures (Redhead 1990 and 1993). Rather than a dominant youth culture there are a variety of different 'scenes', some continuing from original sub-cultures (such as rockers, heavy metal), some re-cycled from the past and some using elements of other sub-cultures to forge new styles. Youth culture is characterized not by a definitive set of characteristics which can be described and catalogued, but by its evanescence and ephemerality. A person can dip into many different styles and music as the sub-cultures rapidly come and go.

This attention to consumer culture inherent in more post-modern perspectives has resulted in the celebration rather than the critique of commercial representation and a fascination with advertising and symbolic culture. Attention is diverted from the structural inequalities which this conceals. However, access to consumer culture is to a greater or lesser extent determined by incomes and incomes are unevenly distributed (Jones and Wallace 1992). With very high youth unemployment in many parts of Europe, this is an important factor. Another problem is that in analysing style, culture and representation, young people themselves disappear from view. Some cultural sociologists still emphasize the importance of understanding the material context from which the styles arose and the actual activities of young people rather than only their representations (Willis 1990).

The increasing dependency of young people upon the household and family results in their dwindling economic power at the same time as increasing participation in consumer culture is possible.

This paradoxical situation means that new consumer groups emerge as significant. For example, rather than working-class young people being identified as the significant consumers – as in the 1950s and 1960s – these are increasingly unemployed or languishing on low incomes or on training schemes. Rather, it is students, mostly middle-class, who emerge as the most leisure-rich consumer group. They have both greater access to more forms of consumption and a greater inclination to take advantage of them being subsidized both by state and by parents (Roberts, Campbell and Furlong 1990).

POPULAR CULTURE IN EASTERN EUROPE

In the communist half of Europe commercial cultures were not allowed to develop as the regimes prioritized production over consumption until the 1970s and the inefficient distribution system in an economy of perpetual shortages ensured that consumer choice was minimal or non-existent. Furthermore, the mass media were controlled by the state, which broadcast television and radio, controlling the output in cinemas and other places of entertainment. Despite these limitations, mass culture had an important impact. In communist Bulgaria and in Russia youth cultures also developed from the 1950s onwards, encouraged by the increase in leisure time, increasing urbanization with concentration of young people in geographical spaces and the spread of mass media and access to consumer technology such as tape recorders and radios. By the 1960s and 1970s, youth cultures were widespread amongst people between the ages of 14 and 28. Although they were met at first with animosity, by the 1980s youth culture began to be seen as a normal part of young people's behaviour.

Time budget studies carried out in the 1970s found a considerable rise in the amount of free time enjoyed by young people – they did less housework and less paid labour than their equivalents in the 1950s (Pateva 1982). This trend was consistent across all groups, although girls did more housework than boys and the amount of free time rose with educational level. Communist ideology encouraged 'active' – that is socially productive – leisure, such as participating in sports or folk-dancing, rather than 'passive' leisure such as watching television or listening to music, but young people were more active in the former as well as the latter pursuits (Pateva 1982, Mitev 1982).

From the 1960s and 1970s there was what sociologists identified as a 'revolution in the mode of living' (Mitev 1982). The number of objects for 'cultural use' such as tape recorders, TV sets and radios increased sharply between 1962 and 1974 but most of all amongst young people. Thus, although young people had the lowest incomes of all groups in communist society where access to goods and income was based upon seniority, they nevertheless owned a higher share of tape recorders and other media technology (Mitev 1982). It was common for young people on getting married to buy first a tape recorder and only thereafter a cooker! In Russia young people were ingenious in inventing ways of creating records for reproducing music, fashioning their own music instruments and sound systems, all of which was carried out in private flats (Riordan 1989a).

Music was particularly popular with young people in communist countries and here it was the international styles which were important, even though young people had limited access to them (Western music was broadcast for about 5 per cent of the time – otherwise they had to listen to it from foreign broadcasts, if they were able to reach them). Surveys carried out in Estonia by Mejnert (1987) found that in 1984 40 per cent of young people listened to Western music everyday and even in 1974 pop music was followed by 96 per cent of the young people up to age 19 and 77 per cent of those up to age 29. Age, rather than social status, was the differentiating factor in musical tastes. Younger age groups also visited discotheques – which were restricted in number – and developed localized sub-cultures within them.

Cinema was similarly very important for the spread of mass culture for young people, particularly in the 1950s and 1960s when it was the most popular form of entertainment. Occasionally it was possible to see Western movies, which developed a theme of youth within a mass culture. However, the dominant diet was of Soviet 'socialist realist' films which addressed social problems in a didactic way and invariably had a happy ending since the purpose of cinema was to educate rather than only entertain (Stefanov 1975). (This prompted the joke: Is it a good film? No, it's Soviet.)

However, participation in youth culture also involved 'symbolic production' through developing distinctive styles of hair dressing, dancing and clothing. For young people in eastern block countries where consumer choices were non-existent and even basic commodities in short supply, obtaining fashionable clothing, such as jeans, was a major achievement. Nevertheless, they went to great lengths to collect money and procure such items. Unlike in Western Europe, the planned socialist economies were completely unresponsive to youth styles and tastes which were developed outside rather than through the official distribution system. In the 1950s, the 'stiliagi' in Moscow developed their own 'stylish' models of dress which differentiated them from what they regarded as the shabby banality which surrounded them and was revived in their followers in the 1980s (Pilkington 1994). Participation in youth culture distinguished urbanized and non-urbanized youth, but also different ethnic sub-cultures: dancing and music were important components of the cultural activities of Roma youth who developed their own taste in colourful, flamboyant clothes and tattoos, outside mainstream society (Georgiev 1978).

The spread of mass youth culture which we have described in Bulgaria was a manifestation of the creation of a distinctive collective identity for youth, separating them from other sections of society. It created a new mentality in which hedonism was a basic principle. Hedonism was alien to the old values, both those of the pre-war non-industrial society and those of the post-war society of socialist transformation, when hard labour and personal sacrifice were sacralized as leading goals. The studies which documented the transformation in culture from the 1960s found distinct generational changes in the way in which people spent their time and the value they attached to different activities. This implies that the development of a youth culture helped to transform people's lifestyles towards a more consumer and entertainment dominated values – a distinct contrast to traditional Eastern European society. This helped to create a communication barrier between the older and younger generations in societies where this was not supposed to 'officially' exist. However, rather than a generational war, Pilkington (1994) recommends that we see these cultures as part of an interlocking set of generational relations, since they coexisted with strong familial solidarity.

The authorities were suspicious of every activity which differentiated people from the conformity to the officially sanctioned norm. They wished to impose 'ideologically pure' norms for young people's dress, behaviour, music and artistic pursuits. This control over cultural preferences was called 'aesthetic education' and consequently, youth cultures were proclaimed an 'ideological diversion'. Rock music in particular was subject to political hostility, being explained as ideological indoctrination by imperialistic forces (Sarkitov 1987) and even social research on youth was justified in terms of the part it could play in aesthetic governance and ideological struggle against Western influences (Stefanov 1978). In the most extreme instances it was blamed for the revival of fascism. The cultural struggle took the form of intolerance to youth styles such as beards, jeans, long hair and short skirts and this could be justified not by reference to Marxist theory so much as to gerontocratic conformity and intolerance of anything which deviated from it. Young people with long hair or beards had them cut off on the spot by police officers (although they protested that Marx and Engels themselves had sported flowing hair and beards!). The carefully purchased and treasured jeans were ripped, badges were torn off and girls wearing short skirts were stamped on the thighs with an official seal! Young people's gestures were seen as 'acts of sabotage against the state' and for this reason their importance was magnified both by the authorities and by young people themselves. In this way, youth cultures became a major vehicle for confrontation between the 'older' authorities and the younger, more creative and style-conscious generation.

A similar process happened in Russia where music became popular amongst young people from the late 1950s and Western sub-cultural artifacts, music and information spread rapidly amongst young people through informal channels (Riordan 1989b). From the late 1960s the Beatles became particularly popular and there is still a memorial to John Lennon in Prague, previously a symbol of protest and now a tourist attraction. Rock music had a huge unofficial following and very soon Russian groups emerged with their own distinctive approach to rock music. Paul Easton (1989) points out that in Russian rock music the lyrics were more important than in Western music and these expressed joking cynicism and alienation. He attributes the popularity of rock music to the fact that during the Brezhnev years there was growing alienation of young people from the system and disillusionment with socialist values and particularly from Komsomol, the organization which was supposed to represent them. Youth culture and music filled a cultural gap, giving the opportunity for creativity and self-expression. As in Bulgaria they were first of all resisted by the authorities and then in the 1980s there were attempts to incorporate the music and the personalities which were by that time very famous, by broadcasting the music on state radio and offering concert venues. Members of the youth sub-cultures that developed around rock music were against doing regular work and preferred instead part-time work or work which required little commitment from them in order to spend more time on rock music. They were also against military service. In Poland distinctive rock groups such as Manaam developed from the 1970s with their own following. It would be wrong to say, therefore, (as the authorities did) that these were simply Western imports.

The way in which Bulgarian authorities fought back can be seen as typical and took two main forms. First they tried diversion by attempting to win over young people by staging official collective events which would typically include music, entertainment and activities which could be officially controlled and gave the right ideological messages. However, these staged events were not popular with young people and they were unwilling to participate in them (Stefanov 1975). Secondly they acted repressively by tightening control over schools and university programmes and finally by passing a decree in 1987 which forced students up to the age of 18 to wear uniforms, short hair and allowed them out after 8pm only in the company of their parents and only to approved venues. Such clumsy efforts at control provoked even more outraged disapproval from young people who interpreted this as a violation of their rights as citizens. As one young man put it:

This order is unconstitutional. Since I am 18 years old, I have civil rights and the prohibition on me visiting theatres and restaurants and ordering me to put on my pyjamas is not right. Why is it possible for me to be allowed to vote alone but not to visit a restaurant except in the company of my mother? Perhaps the President thinks that participation in an election is of less importance (Mitev 1988: 94).

In Russia there were similar attempts to first of all condemn and later incorporate youth popular culture through the reform of the Komsomol. Pilkington (1994) argues that the issue of youth became increasingly politicized through the *glasnost* era. There it ended not in the overthrow of the regime by popular movements but rather in the weakening of state authority and the loss of direction in youth policy. The result of such oppressive measures was to politicize the conflict. However, it was not a struggle by youth for a share of power that was important, so much as a confrontation between those who had the power to impose their tastes and cultural standards and those who wished to escape such control and to pursue their own tastes. Although this did not begin as a struggle to question the legitimacy of the regime, when young people were cast in the role of agents of alien capitalist interests in this way, they began to re-consider their attitude towards the state.

However, other, more reform-minded, party officials saw this struggle as provoking unnecessary antagonism and recommended that crude state intervention be replaced by a tolerance of youth taste and individualized differentiation, using youth culture as a 'social safety valve' for youthful energy and enthusiasm (Michajlov 1986). Such reformist recommendations did not win much favour. Yet the 1980s saw the growing importance of youth sub-cultures which helped to further break down this old order so that the authorities were forced to tolerate them, being increasingly unable to control them.

In Russia, the issue of controlling the explosion of youth sub-cultures during the 1980s took the form of trying to distinguish those who could easily be incorporated into the official youth provision, those who could be wooed to acceptance and those who were simply anti-social, to be suppressed. The association of some sub-cultural groups with fascism was of particular concern to the authorities for whom the use of the swastika symbol, such as that used often as a joke by punks in London, was anything but playful given the bitter history of Russia's experience of the Second World War. This resulted in some quite imaginative efforts by Komsomol members to offer opportunities for bikers, for example, to practise their biking in controlled circumstances and to negotiate between them and the traffic police, with whom they were in constant collision (Pilkington 1994). However, as in Bulgaria, many sub-cultures rejected the idea of becoming incorporated into official structures and institutions and the reform activities of the 'grass roots' Komsomol organizers was often frustrated by conservative colleagues higher up the hierarchy.

YOUTH SUB-CULTURES

So far we have looked at youth cultures as an aspect of consumer society and mass media more generally. Now we shall consider more youth sub-cultures as more specific in time, place and style. The term is used rather loosely to denote specific local activities and also to describe more widespread styles such as 'punk', 'hippie' and so on.

There have been a number of ways in which sub-cultures have

been approached by sociologists and these have been extensively reviewed by Brake (1980, 1990), Pilkington (1994) and Wulff (1995) among others. This approach began with the study of delinquent groups in the USA in the 1920s and 1930s and was later reproduced in Britain and elsewhere. The most common approach until recently was to focus on working-class young men and their assertion of a 'space' as a source of control between home, work and school (Ashton and Field 1976, Corrigan 1979, Willis 1977, Robbins and Cohen 1978). Since they were granted little status in the outside world, young men created their own sense of status and this was linked to the fact that this was the group with the highest disposable incomes. Sub-cultures according to Brake (1980) were associated with a particular style of dress and behaviour, a particular argot and a particular kind of music and these were a response to the 'contradictions' in the parent culture and in the world around them. These early sub-cultures, mostly associated with small, localized groups, provoked angry reactions from adults and from mainstream society who associated them with violence, sexual promiscuity and lack of respect for adult values. However, as these 'anti-social' elements were given considerable publicity, the sub-cultures spread to other areas and became more generalized in Britain. One famous example of this were the Bank Holiday fights between Mods and Rockers which were analysed by Stan Cohen as 'moral panics' which paradoxically served to further enhance the sub-culture (Cohen 1972). The condemnation of such 'folk devils' by the mass media encouraged a 'backlash' that 'something should be done' which further encouraged others to imitate the sub-culture.

Cohen's work was further developed in by the Center for Contemporary Cultural Studies (CCCS) and others (Hall and Jefferson 1976, Mungham and Pearson 1976) who used variants of Marxism to show how different youth sub-cultures represented different social classes. Although only a small minority of young people joined such sub-cultures, they could be seen as a 'metaphor for social change' representing in dramaturgical form the issues facing more conformist youth. They rejected the notion of age as a theoretical concept and argued that youth cultures should be understood by reference to class (Murdock and McCron 1976). They also rejected the 'classless' conception of youth put forward by the media. Another influential perspective was that of Phil Cohen (1972, 1997) who indicated that the class contradictions which young people faced were related to material changes in their own neighbourhoods – the decline of the working-class communities following the destruction of the old houses in urban renewal programmes, the building of tower blocks and the drift to the suburbs, the decline of many traditional jobs in the East End of London. Skinheads, he argued, tried to recreate 'magically' the lost solidarity of their parents' class and hence provided 'solutions' at an symbolic level to these contradictions. At the same time it posed a symbolic resistance to the dominant hegemony dictating 'correct' behaviour by both drawing on working-class traditions and providing some innovations. In addition, more ethnographic approaches looked at car thieves (Parker 1976) or cultural groups in housing estates (Jenkins 1983) to understand the importance of sub-cultures for working-class young people. Some of the best publicized of these cultures was that of the football supporters who would violently defend the honour of their club against other fans and who followed British football teams around Europe.

The perspective developed by the CCCS was enormously influential in understanding youth sub-cultures and was used for analysing such groups all around the world from Sydney to St Petersburg. The CCCS approach of classifying and describing sub-cultures in terms of their class location and describing their behaviour and style was imitated in many different contexts. They described Teds, Skinheads, Rockers, Mods, Hippies and so on as an historical procession of class-based groups. Others, such as Hebdidge (1979, 1988), have tended to emphasize the spectacular aspects of sub-cultures and their emphasis on style itself as a signifier, cut loose from material conditions. Hebdidge analyses youth styles as a kaleidoscope of gestures, as reactions to one another as much as to social conditions. By the 1990s it became more difficult to identify the class components of sub-cultures such as 'punk' or 'Acid House' which tended to be eclectic in their social mix and to become incorporated very quickly into mainstream fashions (Redhead 1990). Furthermore, the 1980s saw the very rapid production and reproduction of sub-cultures as old ones were invented, new ones revived and some, such as Acid House in Britain or stiliagi in Moscow, adopted some of the styles of previous sub-cultures as self conscious 'quotations' (Pilkington 1994). The development of sophisticated and reflexive sub-cultural awareness and the media search for new trends and styles amongst youth resulted in a very rapid turnover of sub-cultures. This means that styles which were intended to shock mainstream culture were very rapidly absorbed back into mainstream culture and turned into commercial consumer artifacts. This reflexive relationship between sub-cultures and commercial culture is reflected in popular music as we previously described, but also in fashions, dances and vocabulary. The display of the body, the adoption of fashionable styles becomes something for everyone, not just for youth. Furthermore, such sub-cultures were no longer so strongly associated with youth as older sub-cultures, such as hippies or rockers, continued to exist along with many of their increasingly older adherents. Thus, even age as an aspect of youth sub-culture started to dissolve (Lury 1996).

Steve Redhead (1990) argues that not only is the analysis of youth sub-cultures in terms of a succession of symbolic resistances to class positions impossible to sustain in the 1980s, but that it was probably a mistaken approach even previously. Drawing upon Baudrillard, he argues that sub-cultures can better be analysed in terms of ecstatic spectacle, escape and attempts to have fun. He bases his ideas on the study of 'rave culture' associated with large parties of up to 5000 young people drawing upon a range of sub-cultures and meeting at venues in the countryside or in warehouses. Indeed, 'having fun' became almost a social movement as there were attempts to legally prevent such organized parties from taking place and to introduce a 3 am curfew on dancing.

The traditional studies of sub-cultures were predominantly about white, male working-class youth. This prompted criticism of the absence of other groups and studies which aimed to document those other groups. Hence, studies of black and Asian young people emerged (Cashmore 1987, Back 1996, Pryce 1979), as did studies of more middle-class sub-cultures (Aggleton 1987) and a strident feminist critique encouraged more studies of girls' sub-cultural activities which we address in the next section. The ethnographic tradition of studying small groups of young people as sub-cultures continued, however, as can be seen in the contributions to Redhead (1993), Pilkington (1994) and others.

One of the interesting features of the ubiquity of sub-cultures since the 1980s is their internationalization. Styles and music can be spread very rapidly across international frontiers, especially using new media technology, but is a punk in Moscow the same as a punk in Manchester? What meaning do such sub-cultures have in different international contexts? For example, whereas in Britain 'punk' was seen as both 'dole queue rock' and the result of alternative artistic movements originating in art colleges (Laing 1985), in Germany the 'punk' sub-culture was not so much a response to rising unemployment as in England where it originated (according to Lindner 1985) but to the increasing institutionalization of youth as an age-phase and to the 'hippie' orientation of the parental generation. The punks were nicknamed the 'Null Bock' generation (Lindner 1985, Preuss-Lausitz 1983) because they rejected everything – not just the consumer and moral values of the restoration but also the critical values of their parents. The critical middle-class had by this time become installed as the teachers, youth workers and social workers of the system and these were the people that the new generation came into contact with (Linder 1985, Preuss-Lausitz 1983). Being the generation most subject to competition for educational and training places, they were also the generation most likely to reject or reverse such aspirations in their sub-cultures. 'Null Bock' was also the reaction against the extension of adolescence and the increasing dependency of youth upon parents, education and training (Büchner 1990). Thus, similar sub-cultures in different parts of Europe were the result of different pressures and took on different meanings.

YOUTH SUB-CULTURES UNDER COMMUNISM

The concept of sub-culture is useful too when considering the expressive behaviour of young people in the ex-communist countries of Eastern Europe. Under the former regimes youth cultures were a form of 'resistance' because any non-conformist expression of style became an act of defiance, even if it was not intended that way. The idea of youth sub-cultures developed in a West European context can therefore help us to understand the development of stylistic resistance and small alternative groups under the former regimes, particularly during the latter decades of communism. We have already touched upon the threat which youth culture posed to communist authorities during the 1950s, 60s and 70s. By the 1980s these regimes were suffering economic crisis and it was evident to many that living standards were falling far behind the consumer oriented Western Europe, which some were able to watch on their TV screens. Attempts to respond somewhat to the consumer demands of their citizens resulted in a growing dependency upon foreign loans in many countries, during a decade squeezed by an international debt crisis and rising interest rates. The stagnation in the labour market and in young people's prospects was further compounded by the ideological exhaustion of the regimes. In the last decade of communism youth cultures ceased to be seen as threatening and became more widespread. The state monopoly on broadcasting and the arts was undermined by the spread of new media technologies such as satellite TV and the clandestine circulation of cassette tapes and later videos, which could be easily copied and pirated. Music replaced cinema as the most popular form of entertainment, accessible to small groups and helping to create a private space around which small sub-cultures could develop in a way not conceivable in more collective forms of entertainment (Mitev 1988).

Whilst in the 1950s small numbers of young people had modelled themselves on the 'beats' and in the 1960s on the 'hippies', in the 1980s sub-cultures became both more common and more diffused. Punks appeared even in Russia, where they were termed 'British horrors' and sub-cultures took on a self-conscious form of stylistic political opposition (Svitek 1990, Riordan 1989b). The enthusiasm for music allowed personal tastes to be developed outside of 'official' state control and could be interpreted as a reaction to the devaluation of words into official slogans: music, by contrast, offered a direct, hedonistic and sensual form of expression beyond, and incorruptible by, linguistic communication (Mitev 1985a). It was also diametrically opposed in form to the technological orientation of the official Komsomol organizations with its progress-dominated 'movement for scientific and technical development' (Okeanov-Dimitrov 1989). Thus the pleasure seeking aspect to music offered an escape from the rationalistic-technological official values and, in doing so, subverted them.

However, music was not the only basis for creating youth sub-cultures. Participation in certain sports as both actors and fans also constituted a basis for the formation of youth sub-cultures. Small knots of young people followed football teams, football players or started skate-boarding cliques, developing their own rituals of interaction and specific values. This too could be seen as a reaction to the over-bureaucratized, over-formalized state organization of 'mass physical culture and sports'. Playing sports in non-formal, non-official groups was a way of searching for self-identity and expression under a communist regime. Thus these groups became known as the 'non formals' and could encompass a variety of activities from local neighbourhood gangs to alternative social movements.

Young participants in these small, spontaneous groups, which developed in many places throughout Eastern Europe, saw sub-cultures as a style of living and a way of searching for authentic self-realization, created and reinforced by group identity. These offered an escape from the discipline and formal regulation of daily life. Whilst official policy and media treated all these groups as the same, for young people the specific characteristics of each group made all the difference in the world and this explains the clashes and sometimes even outbursts of violence between sub-cultural groups, as happened in Kazan in Russia (Pilkington 1994). In Russia such groups became based increasingly on territorial control: gangs of youths from one suburb would fight those from other suburbs and those from one sub-culture would hunt and fight those from another (Riordan 1989b).

The sub-cultures of the 1980s were fundamentally different to the mass youth culture of the 1960s and 1970s. Whereas in the former times a common love of rock music and unconventional dress had fused young people into a general force as 'we the restricted' against the gerontocracy of 'they the restricters' (Stojchev 1989), the later youth sub-cultures represented a different phenomenon. They were dispersed into different kinds of groups and cliques with different identities and purposes. However, there were still important differences between these and western sub-cultures. Sub-cultures in eastern bloc countries could not be so easily identified with particular social strata, but rather with age and with region, with whether they lived in an urban or a rural context. The spread of such cultures was a manifestation of the conflict between formal institutions and the non-formal forms of youth spontaneity and initiative; between an official, state-supported culture and an unofficial more direct and meaningful form of cultural expression. This espousal of alternative forms of expression led to conflicts within the home too (Mitev 1988).

Research on youth sub-cultures was carried out in the early 1980s in Bulgaria in spite of official pressure, but the final report was censured: officials stated that no such groups existed. Nevertheless, the report (which carried the stamp 'top secret' and is now a bibliographical rarity) found that there was a definite change in the formation of sub-cultures in the 1980s with more groups being formed and more members in them (Mitev 1984). The most numerous group were the 'poppers' who were teenagers from the elite grammar and specialized schools. From wealthy homes, they were able to visit restaurants frequently and use imported tobacco and alcohol. Heavy metal followers also existed and these were mostly workers of between 20 and 22, along with students in technical schools. Hippies were mostly students in higher education, especially in arts and humanities faculties of universities, whereas the punks were mainly from evening schools, professional and secondary schools. They aimed to be the most provocative: 'Not everything can be explained in words. . . . We are generally against every theory' (ibid.: 9). Rocker groups were associated with the cult of the motorbike (even though not all of them owned motorbikes). Music was very important for all these groups – 'Through their songs the punks express that they have their freedom, that they do what they like' (Mitev 1984:19). However, non-formal groups were also concerned with styles of clothes, poetry, songs and theatre performances – all manner of forms of 'self expression'.

In the Soviet Union there was a veritable 'youth revolution' in the 1980s as *perestroika* allowed the emergence of groups that had previously been underground and encouraged the formation of new ones. Some of the best known include groups who wore western clothes and followed western fashions (the *muzhery*). As a reaction, other, anti-western groups formed, one of these being the 'Lyubery' named after an industrial suburb of Moscow. They practised physical fitness and set themselves up as vigilante groups who attacked westernized youth and aimed to rid their areas of corruption. One initiation ceremony was to beat up punks. Riordan (1989b) attributes their existence to the bleak lives of young people in the industrial cities who were envious of the more cosmopolitan existence of young people in the big cities where there was greater access to cultural resources. Another group which he identifies are the 'Afgantsy', veterans from the Afghan war who were unable to settle back into civilian life and were embittered by the changes they found on returning to their homes. Like the Lyubery, these were 'muscular socialists'. These became the objects of recruitment by nationalist parties, and there were even some fascists sporting neo-nazi insignia. Rockers were an already well established group who emerged into greater prominence with *perestroika*, and these were joined later by punks. To some extent these were only anti-establishment posturing: 'If Pravda's for it, I'm against it' in the words of one group member (ibid.: 135) but there was also a tendency for neighbourhood gangs to form who became involved in drug taking, black market trading and other forms of illegal activity.

There was a large number of people studying the youth sub-cultures at this time in Russia according to Pilkington (1994) and numerous explanations were offered by psychologists and sociologists for the presence of such groups. During the *perestroika* period, explanations began to emerge which did not simply follow the line that these were examples of western subversion. Rather, they were explained in terms of the mental 'sickness' of the adherents (many punks, for example, were treated for mental illness) or in terms of the contradictions of late Soviet society, or because of their alienation from official structures of power. Pilkington (1994) offers a fascinating and comprehensive analysis of these explanations.

Studies carried out in the Czech Republic also found youth sub-cultures had formed by the 1980s. One group had a western orientation and was mainly consumer oriented. For them the communist system prevented them from pursuing the consumer life-styles which they believed they would be able to do in 'the West'. They frequented discotheques, wore western clothes and were concerned with having and spending money. The second group was more idealistic, associated with movements for ecology or social reform. In religious areas they were also associated with religion. The final group was the 'negatives' who were mostly working-class and apprentice youth who joined punk and other opposition sub-cultures and were sometimes involved with drug-taking. Theirs was not so much a political protest as a desire to shock (Stastna 1988 unpublished report).

Although in Britain sub-cultures were associated mainly with working-class youth – at least in the early decades after the Second World War – in communist countries they were often quite privileged groups of people. The rockers who could gain access to motorbikes and those who were able to dress in western clothes were children of privileged elite parents who could afford to subsidize this kind of life-style: it was out of reach for normal youth. Therefore, ironically, it was the sons and daughters of the elite who espoused this kind of cultural protest.

In Bulgaria, the reaction of the authorities to youth sub-cultures in the 1980s was in some ways similar to that of 20 years earlier. The hostility was more open this time and became a topic of concern at the highest levels of the party hierarchy where the 'non-formals' were declared as one of the three main enemies of society according to a circular letter by one of the party secretaries (Raychev 1989). The Communist Party engaged the official youth organization, the Komsomol, in the struggle against non-formal youth activities. In a report to the Central Committee of the Youth League at its XV congress in 1987 the main strategy was proclaimed to be 'to foresee and prevent the possibilities of negative, anti-social directions in their (the youth groups') activities . . . and to start categorical action with no hesitation' (Stojkov 1987). The sub-cultures were declared as 'alternative' or 'negative deviations' and were accused of being agents of capitalist countries, or simply indoctrinated by them. Many such activities became criminalized and Ovchinskij (1987:86), after a survey of 386 such groups in the Soviet Union carried out between 1981 and 1986, found that nearly half the leaders had been sentenced in court and spent time in penal institutions. Noting that the legal offences of the non-formal youth groups were very wide, ranging from stealing to 'group hooliganism', the author warned of the danger of 'such seemingly sub-cultural deviations' leading young people further into a life of crime. However, attempts to suppress youth sub-cultures served to further alienate young people. As one said:

I want to dress as I like, to listen and watch punk groups over the radio and TV. They do not issue punk music and even if it is introduced it would be forbidden because they are afraid that people would say immediately that this is a western tendency and it is not compatible with socialist ethics, that youth should not be corrupted. In this way I became embittered (Mitev 1984).

Other, more moderate, attempts to stop the formation of such groups used instead what we might term a tactic of 'diversion'. This took the form of attempts to direct young people's tastes and activities into more 'normal' or conventional directions through administrative measures. State institutions such as the radio and the schools competed to counteract every new wave of music or style with old models, propagating a return to the sentimental music of the 'town shlagers' of their parents 20 years before or encouraging amateur art activities (Mitev 1988).

This strategy was grounded in the explanation of youth sub-cultures as mere imitations, copies of western styles with no cultural roots in Eastern European countries. The explanation preferred to ignore the fact that new styles and music had also developed *within* communist countries and some of the information were spread from there. As one respondent put it:

It should be taken into consideration that gramophone records of heavy metal are issued in the USSR and that the badges and stripes that we wear are made in Hungary, another socialist country. They are not a western influence (Mitev 1984:19).

The 'imitation thesis' claimed that youth sub-cultures were rooted in the specific conditions of capitalist countries where 'youth is poor, hungry and unemployed' and hence there were no reasons for such deviant behaviour under communism where such conditions did not apply (Lisovkij 1985). Therefore, youth who participated in such activities were accused of 'political apathy and lack of elementary political culture'.

However, this explanation of duplication and mimicry of western sub-cultures does not explain all the variations which were found in Eastern Europe. Lisovskij (see Mitev 1985a) described sub-cultural groups in Russia which had no counterpart in West Europe. The 'Teljegas' defined themselves as a patriotic group and wore a *teljega* – a type of jacket which had been common after the Second World War. All over Eastern Europe music fans followed musical groups which adapted popular music in a national context and often achieved a considerable national following. In Poland, for example, there were a number of waves of passing fashions of this kind. In Russia in 1983 alone, 42 music bands were disbanded by an order of the Ministry of Culture because they 'did not meet elementary moral-aesthetic criteria' (Lisovskij 1985, Kozakevitch 1985).

A more popular explanation for youth sub-cultures and the following of music in Bulgaria was that this was an aberration, a means by which young people escaped from the 'true' problems of society. Sub-cultures were 'a substitute for the true self-realization of youth' (Mitev 1985a:63). It was also claimed that, in escaping institutional regulation, young people were merely trying to avoid their citizen's duties (Okeanov-Dimitrov 1989). This explanation led to a third 'solution' to youth sub-cultures: one of incorporation. This was pursued by the Komsomol who tried to incorporate such groups within its organizational structure by accommodating 'groups according to interests'. This legalization and recognition of diversified groups was aimed to 'prevent their development into forms of protest or de-socialization' (Mitev 1988). This approach accepted sub-cultures as a normal part of youth behaviour which may be 'alternative' to existing institutions but not necessarily hostile to them. This strategy, recommended by the Youth Institute, tried to steer a course between repressive measures and complete tolerance. This approach tried to channel the aberrant forms of 'self-realization' into more recognized official organizations; to formalize the 'non-formal' groups. The groups 'according to interests' were granted access to premises and up-to-date technological equipment in return for incorporation and surveillance by Komsomol. These new tactics of incorporation, whilst recognizing youth sub-cultures, were an improvement on the clumsy efforts of the Komsomol in previous decades. However, they were still unable to fully institutionalize youth cultures.

Even these limited attempts at incorporation were met with fear and suspicion by senior party and Komsomol officials. They feared the disruption and fragmentation of the Youth League, seeing this as a rupture in its organizational unity. They accused the new strategies of 'tearing apart the organization and leading to a drift towards breakaway groups', thus causing a 'reduction of organizational-political influence of the Youth League' (Balkanski 1981). In the Soviet Union too, there were attempts to incorporate 'non formal' groups into Komsomol during the 1980s rather than suppress them, or deny their existence, in a belated attempt to reform the Communist Youth League. However, it was too late: the growth of the 'non formals' was by this time uncontrollable.

The analysis of the 'problem' of youth sub-cultures under communism and the different solutions which flowed from that analysis all reflect a view of such spontaneous and non-formal activity as a threat to the mainstream institutional activity. Strategies of repression, diversion and incorporation all admit a fear of such forms of collective or individual expression. Although youth groups made no attempt to challenge political power, they challenged the regime by undermining the very basis of its functioning – authoritarian power and conformity. In fact, sub-cultures sprang more from a desire to escape than to confront and allowed a cultural 'space' where alternative identities could be formed (Svitek 1990). This was therefore a kind of spontaneous, unorganized protest which confronted the old, orthodox and conservative generation with new, fresh and spontaneous values.

YOUNG WOMEN AND SUB-CULTURES

The early feminist critiques of sub-cultural theories, such as that of McRobbie and Garber (1976), pose the question: can the absence of young women in sociological accounts be explained by the fact that they were really not active in sub-cultures, or were they rendered 'invisible' by male researchers? It is likely that the radical male researchers who did the field work into youth sub-cultures identified with the excitement, the machismo and the icono-clasm of masculine sub-cultures which made them in turn critical of the role of the home and family which young women appear to represent: 'The writers, having defined themselves as against the family and the trap of romance as well as against the boredom of meaningless labour, seem to be drawn to look at other, largely working class groups, who appear to be doing the same thing' (McRobbie 1978:39).

McRobbie and Garber answered their own question by arguing that young women were not present in male sub-cultures – apart from as girlfriends and hangers-on – because they have their own cultural forms of expression based upon the retreat from male defined situations into an alternative culture of 'femininity' based around the girls' bedroom and being a 'fan', which is seen here as a very restricted role. Working-class girls' sub-culture was portrayed as peripheral to that of working-class boys and to the working-class as a whole and as being the victims of packaged and commercial-ized culture which led them to be absorbed into an ideology of romance (Sarsby 1983, Sharpe 1976).

An alternative view of working-class girlhood emerges from the study of young delinquent women, girls in gangs and young black women. In these studies young women are seen as more actively participating in sub-cultural groups or as forming their own sub-cultural groups or gangs and being critical of male superiority (Fuller 1980, Shacklady Smith 1978, Wilson 1978, A. Campbell 1984). De-spite this defiance, however, they still felt compelled to conform to the 'oppressive triangle' of love, sex and marriage in order to legit-imize their participation in street culture. Sue Lees (1986) illus-trated the way in which control was exercized over young women through the use of negative sexual labelling, particularly the label of 'slag'. Barbara Hudson (1984), using a more Foucauldian ap-proach, considers instead the contradictions between the discourses of youth, encouraging experimentation, storm and stress and those of femininity which encourage instead more passivity and conformity. Nevertheless, young women managed to create their own cultural spaces with friendship groups (Griffin 1985).

The feminist emphasis upon gender as an aspect of sub-cultures led some people to reconsider the role which masculinity plays within them. The necessity to assert masculinity through talk or through behaviour leads young men towards aggressive posturing, extremely sexist language and homophobic discourse and at times even real violence (Wood 1984, Mac an Ghaill 1994, Halson 1991). Masculine codes of conduct, it seems, oppress not only women but also men themselves.

In studying young women in Soviet society, Hilary Pilkington (1992a, 1992b) found that during the *perestroika* period young women were largely absent from descriptions of the many youth sub-cultures which were starting to develop there. Young women were portrayed in terms of their sexual relations with gang members, such as with rocker bike gangs for example, or disapprovingly in terms of their promiscuous sexual activities or involvement in prostitution. However, in her own study of one sub-culture she found that girls predominated, dressing in more masculine 'chic' styles in the manner of favourite female popular singers whose style and self-assertion were admired. They manipulated commercial culture in order to develop their own styles. On the other hand, she finds considerable reference to the sexual regulation and subjugation of young women by youth gangs. Gang rape was an accepted way of controlling young female members in many parts of the former Soviet Union and from the *perestroika* period onwards, prostitution offered an apparently easy route to money in order to participate in new consumer styles. In her follow-up of the Moscow youth cultural scene in the post-communist era, Pilkington (1996) found greater use of drugs, the increasing importance of the club scene, the increasing influence of nationalist and chauvinist politics upon youth cultures (including the appearance of 'skinheads') and an emerging gay and lesbian scene which was formerly heavily suppressed. There was greater diversification of youth cultures and some influence of national politics, a subject we take up in the next chapter.

YOUTH SUB-CULTURES AND ETHNICITY

In the USA, sub-cultures were frequently studied in terms of ethnicity (see for example Whyte 1943) and this developed from the classical 'urban ecology' approach to their understanding. In Europe, however, the study of sub-cultures looked mainly at white youth. Nevertheless, the presence of ethnic groups, especially black ones, was seen as having a significant effect on white sub-cultures which adopted black vocabulary, music and styles even whilst defining their identity through racism. Hebdidge (1979) and Chambers (1985) even argued that youth culture has been a process of continual dialogue with black music and sub-culture, even when it was suppressed to an 'underground' strand of popular culture.

Jazz from the USA took root in many parts of Europe and became influential in shaping musical tastes and black American soul music later came to dominate discotheques from the 1970s onwards. From the late 50s reggae music was imported into Britain by immigrants from the Caribbean and marketed through specialist ethnic record shops and labels for that community only. However, its influence soon spread as 'reggae' music and its various variations became part of mainstream popular culture. Some of this drew on elements of 'Rastafarianism', a Jamaican cult which drew upon pan-African ideas (Cashmore 1987, Chambers 1985). The 'dreadlocks' of the Rastas became a popular emblem although there were only a small number of real adherents, the vocabulary and symbolism – for example the red, green and gold hats – were more widely adopted as elements of style throughout the world, especially by young black people. This and other black consciousness ideas were promulgated through reggae music. Through the use of sound systems, DJs developed their own distinctive commentary through 'rapping' – talking over the music – a form of rhythmic poetry expressing the condition of black youth, which in some variations was antagonistic towards white society. Nevertheless, rapping was soon taken up in many countries and many languages, used to express a range of feelings and issues which had little to do with the experiences of urban black people in the USA or Caribbean islands where it originated. This could be seen as an example of the 'post-colonial' character of musical styles and sub-cultures. The 'hip hop' music, clothing and dancing which accompanied it began as a 'street theatre' among ethnic groups in blighted city districts of New York and was also seen all over the world (Rose and Ross 1994).

The importance of black Americans for American popular music and the dissemination of their styles through the domination of US mass media has been a new source of meaning for young black people all over the world in very different communities. However, it also influenced youth in quite other contexts. In Hamburg during the Third Reich, for example, young people who were unwilling to conform to homogenizing demands of the youth organization and nationalist politics, identified with black American jazz and swing music as that of an oppressed group – but oppressed in quite a different way (Polster 1989). In travelling to Southern Africa, black American music has interacted with African music to create 'township' jazz which could in turn be reimported into mainstream Western European musical styles. There is thus a 'post-colonial' dialogue between different cultures through popular music. Nor is it only black young people who have used musical sub-cultures to forge new ethnic styles. In Britain young Asians have combined disco music with traditional Asian sounds to create 'Bhangra', sometimes in combination with other ethnic sub-cultures, whilst young Muslims in Arab countries have also developed their own musical styles and identification through music (Schade-Poulsen 1995). The energy, vitality and originality which ethnic groups are able to bring to popular music has helped contribute to the diversification of popular culture and more post-modern styles of cross-cultural identification.

However, the other side to this 'post-colonial' diversity is the increasing racism, nationalism and intolerance which is also expressed through youth cultures – something we address in the next chapter.

CONCLUSION: THE END OF YOUTH SUB-CULTURES?

Youth sub-cultures have taken on different forms under different conditions. In the communist world they were a form of expressive escapism against formal disciplinary control and the over-regulation of youth as an age group, whilst in Western Europe they were interpreted as a form of escapism from the regulation of work life, made possible through possession of an income. Now that repressive control in Eastern Europe has vanished and in Western Europe working youth in a conventional labour market become increasingly rare, would we expect youth cultures to disappear?

We argue that this is not the case. The removal of some of the formal structures of an oppressive state and the increasing disappearance of affluent working-class youth mean that youth cultures are not formed so often as reactions against this experience. But it is evident that in the 1990s some new dynamics are operating. The interaction of leisure with new consumer markets and technologies has meant an expanding range of styles and choices for young people whereby all the previous youth cultures are simultaneously present. The generally greater acceptance of popular music and sub-cultural styles is indicated in the fact that the BBC World Service publicizes a range of music and analyses their styles: from 'Seattle grunge to Birmingham Bhangra' as they proudly announce. English teaching programmes translate and explain the text of popular songs as popular music moves from the margins to the mainstream. Communications technologies have made possible the broadcasting of stations devoted to specialist musical tastes.

However, at the same time independent youth incomes have fallen. The evidence would seem to suggest that it is now students who are the most active participants in youth cultural activities whereas working-class youth on training schemes, unemployed or on reduced wages are not so easily able to participate (Roberts, Campbell and Furlong 1990). These latter groups are most likely to be excluded from cultural participation. The escape from institutionalized regulation and control is that of the college, the university or the training scheme rather than the job or the state organization. It is no longer a case so much of Saturday-night escapism being the only form of excitement because young people can escape all week in the more relaxed organizational environment of college or university. Further and higher educational institutions offer the additional advantage of subsidized cultural activities, 'student unions' and a variety of clubs for organizing leisure events. Such institutional settings are perhaps more tolerant of individualized styles and tastes which may allow more fluid and evanescent sub-cultures. Moreover, it is evident that young people can move around between sub-cultures and utilize different aspects of mass culture to suit their own needs.

The early penetration of western mass culture following the opening of the Eastern European societies after 1989 took the form of a wave of pornographic and violent literature and media which was cheap and easily sellable. At the same time, the institutional arts have collapsed following the withdrawal of public subsidies and steep price rises which put other forms of culture out of the reach of young people. The national folk culture and music which had been fostered under communism was replaced by an internationalized pop culture. A retreat from ideologies and official, institutionalized politics means that more privatized forms of consumption and leisure have been further encouraged. The circulation of cassette and video tapes is still important, made accessible by the extensive 'shadow' market of illegal copies. One recent survey found that two-thirds of the households in which young people lived in Poland had a video player, one-third had satellite dishes and over 90 per cent had record or cassette players, which was not far behind many Western European countries. But the videos are at present mainly copies of western movies, often junk ones (prompting the joke: Is the movie good? No, it's American).

Research in a number of post-communist countries seems to indicate an increasingly peer-group and youth-centred pattern of cultural interaction (Molnár 1992, Kjulanov et al. 1991). This has been interpreted as a reaction to the dissolving world of adults where older authorities have been displaced and discredited – a response to anomie rather than repression, of under-determination rather than over-determination. Peer groups offer a mode of communication and socialization in values and attitudes, sexual and social preferences. The old values and certainties with which popular opinion clashed were replaced by a period of rapid change and increasing uncertainty. Stable pay structures and inter-generational relations are replaced by ones of fluidity as young people are left to find their own age-status transitions in an increasingly diversified world. One product has been the rapid circulation of evanescent styles and sub-cultures and the co-existence of a variety of sub-cultures – but no longer as oppositional 'resistance'. There is also, in turn, a reaction against the 60s-style 'alternative' dissident generation in the sharp cut suits and severely short hair of the young 'businessmen'.

However, there are still important regional differences, with access to cultural consumption concentrating in big cosmopolitan centres. In rural areas the levels of individual consumption are extremely low or non-existent and most leisure time is spent with family and friends rather than consuming commercial leisure (Roberts et al. 1995). Consumer items owned by households are a shared resource and this is why the 'privatization' of consumption described by Jung (1994) is important because new technologies give access to international mass culture which can be enjoyed without leaving the living room. The generational changes and self-assertiveness of youth need to be seen in the context of very family-centred societies where solidarity to one's own family still usually takes precedence (Pilkington 1994, Wallace 1995).

To return to our earlier question: is this the end of youth sub-cultures? It seems that the proliferation of sub-cultures and their absorption into commercial mass media, rock and fashion industries has on the one hand resulted in the increasing importance and acceptance of them but, at the same time, youth as a cultural force is dissolved. Youth cultures are endlessly recycled through retrospective nostalgia (60s parties etc.) and also through 'quotations' such as 'sampling' – the replaying of excerpts of previous songs re-mixed together using computerized technology. Youth becomes style and style is for everyone. Youthfulness is still important but it is no longer only young people who should be youthful: everyone should keep abreast of styles and fashions and maintain vigilance over their bodies to keep them youthful. Youth is no longer a 'brief flowering' between education and work but rather an extended period, which can carry on to middle age and afterwards.

However, young people are still a creative and innovative force in this process. They have helped to 'juventicize' society, the words of the Romanian sociologist Fred Mahler. Even those increasingly marginalized youth such as the so-called urban underclass in the USA are able to create new styles in dance and music which can inspire people at the other end of the world. The globalizing of youth as an idea, as a style and as a commercial product is both an example of cultural colonization of countries where 'teenagers' did not previously exist, but also encourages new configurations of ethnicity, meaning and belonging in an increasingly disembedded world.

Whilst youth culture and youth sub-cultures can be seen as ways in which youth are defined, or indeed, define themselves, the absorption of youth cultures into mainstream commercial culture also leads to the undermining of a distinctively youthful styles. The commercialized and idealized view of 'youth', previously associated with a stage in the life cycle, becomes detached from the reality of life for most young people. As it becomes something to which everyone should aspire, the problems and misfortunes of young people are forgotten or ignored. Some young people are themselves excluded from 'youth'.

6 Young People's Political Values and Participation[1]

Throughout this book so far we have argued that youth was the result of the construction of age-specific categories through the process of modernization and we have illustrated how these were more 'strongly' constructed under some political state regimes than others. But is 'age' a sufficient basis for political mobilization or representation? In this chapter we explore some circumstances under which genera-tion does indeed serve as the basis for a political movement and we also consider the political orientations of young people more gen-erally. Since 'youth' is necessarily a transitory phenomenon, because people grow up and therefore leave youth movements, age serves as a rather different basis of 'interest' or political organization than do other forms of social structure such as ethnicity or social class.

In considering youth and politics in East and West Europe, we must take a broader definition, to include the political participa-tion and representation of youth at different levels of the political structure, their integration or disaffiliation and their activities which support or subvert the social order of the societies in which they live. This is not because we see youth as an 'essential' or norma-tive social group; rather we use the framework of 'youth' as a so-cially constructed group within the context of particular nation states and particular political systems. Young people's position within political structures is a factor for constructing youth in the same way as is their place on the labour market. Since this group can be both subordinated and privileged, their activities have greater or lesser significance at different points in time and one of the fea-tures in which we are interested is the way the activities of youth can have important political consequences at certain critical his-torical junctures. Some questions we address are: why do youth coalesce into a political interest group at certain points in time? How does their political involvement relate to their position in the social structure? What impact does this have on politics generally? What sorts of issues do youth become involved in?

---

[1] An earlier version of this chapter appeared as 'Why do youth revolt?' Kovatcheva and Wallace (1994) *Youth and Policy* 44: 7–20

The attitudes and activities of young people cannot but be shaped by the events taking place around them. When there are dramatic historical changes young people play a very important part and this can serve to politicize them and to create 'youth' as political force. Such changes would include the civil rights movements of the 1960s, the protests against nuclear weapons and environmental destruction of the 1970s and 1980s and the popular movements against repressive governments in state socialist countries in the late 1980s and 1990s followed by the rise of nationalist populist movements.

Such changes affect everyone. So why should youth be a particular focus? Some have argued that psychologically youth are in an unstable life-stage and this would account for their more radical and romantic tendencies and for the inevitable conflict of generations (see Schneider 1990 for a review). However, we would not support such arguments. Rather, it seems to us that young people encounter political and social institutions or events less encumbered by the weight of previous socialization than do their older contemporaries and that their transitional position between family of origin and family of destination and between education and work makes it more easy for them to adopt critical or oppositional postures: they have invested less in the status quo than have older people. However, age alone does not lead to a likelihood of political activity. This requires crystallization through external political and social events. In this way we can identify the influence of 'generations' in politics (Mannheim 1952) and this has led Braungart and Braungart (1990) to argue that distinct political generations can be identified dependent upon the interaction of historical periods and generational cohorts. In Europe we can see the influence of the Second World War on creating a certain generational consciousness – an awareness of hardship and a more conservative, more puritanical orientation towards the post-war status quo. The fact that it was young people who were largely active in wartime resistance or fighting helped to forge the consciousness of that generation. The post-war generation of the 1960s, growing up in an affluent society, was more concerned with consumption and leisure than the older generation, producing a certain generational conflict in both East and West Europe. The rising youth unemployment and media saturation since the 1970s, along with the numerical decline in the numbers of young people, help to bring into focus a new set of issues and new political constellations. Now the rise of nationalism and ethnic politics does the same.

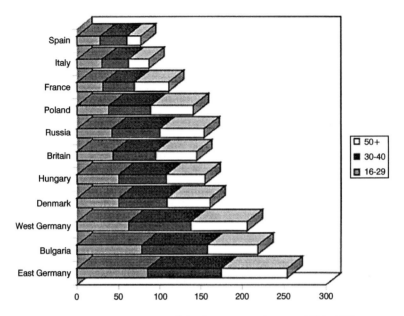

Figure 6.1. Interest in politics by country by age 1990–1993
(percentage who said they were 'very interested' or 'somewhat
interested' in politics in each age group)

Source: Basanez et al. 1997 World Values Survey of 43 countries 1990–1993

PATTERNS IN YOUTH POLITICS

The romantic idea of youth as 'idealistic' assumes that they are
believed to be more inclined towards involvement in extremist politics.
In particular, it was believed that rising unemployment and the
direct experience of economic collapse may push young people
towards extremist politics as happened in Germany in the 1920s
and 30s. However, successive post-war surveys have indicated that
young people are generally not politically radical, even in conditions of high unemployment. Recent studies of young people's
political orientations found that patterns of political support tend
to follow those of parents and the regions in which they grew up
(Evans and Heinz 1994, Banks et al. 1992, Bynner and Roberts
1991).

Most young people are not interested in mainstream politics at
all – and neither are most adults. Figure 6.1. shows the numbers of

people who said they were 'very interested' or 'somewhat interested' in politics. There does not seem to be a radical East-West
split in this respect. In those countries where the adults were interested in politics, so were the young people and vice versa. In
some countries many people, both young and old, were interested
in politics – for example in the two Germanys (perhaps because of
the unification issues in the early 1990s when the survey was carried out). We could hypothesize that the interest in politics may
have been because some particular political event was taking place
at the time of the survey.

In one comparative survey of Britain and Germany covering 16–19
year olds, only about half of respondents said they would not vote
or did not know how they would vote (Bynner and Roberts 1991).
In more economically depressed regions in Britain even fewer young
people expressed an interest in conventional politics or political
parties and this was more evident the lower down the socio-economic
hierarchy they came from (Banks et al. 1992). Furthermore, most
of the young people never talked about politics at home with their
parents as it was thought to be a rather dull subject (Corr, Jamieson
and Tomes 1990). However, interest in politics varies with the level
of education: the higher up the educational system, the more interest
in politics (Banks et. al. 1992). Thus it would appear that the more
a young person is integrated into society through their education,
the more interest they have in the way that society is governed. At
the other pole, the unemployed are politically marginalized and
perhaps increasingly 'disaffiliated' from dominant political and social
system and also the least likely to vote – although this in itself
could be seen as a radical political gesture.

Although young people do not show great interest in joining
mainstream political parties in most countries, they are much more
likely to engage in direct political action, including occupying buildings, participating in unoffical strikes, signing petitions, joining
boycotts, joining demonstrations and so on (Basenez et al. 1997).
This seems to imply at least some level of youth idealism.

When they are interested in politics, young people show different political sympathies to adults. We can see from Figure 6.2.
that there are generally more left wing people in Western than in
Eastern Europe and many of these are young people. This may
reflect the disillusion with socialist or communist politics following
the revolutions of 1989 and afterwards. However, we should bear
in mind that by the mid 1990s socialist and reformed communist

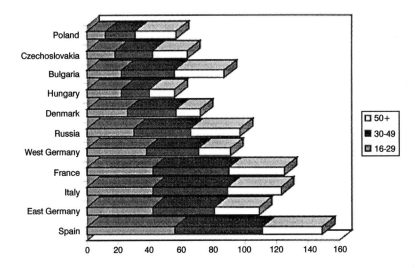

Figure 6.2 Left-right self-placement by age 1990–1993
(percentage placing themselves on the 'left' in each age group)

Source: Basanez et al. 1997 World Values Survey for 43 countries 1990–1993

parties were doing very well in elections in the region and in many countries had taken power. This disillusionment may therefore have been a temporary phenomenon to be followed by disillusionment with the *alternative* to socialism. Furthermore, whereas in Western Europe young people are more likely to be left wing than were adults, in Eastern Europe, the reverse was the case. This corroborates other data which show young people more in favour of the new regimes in Eastern Europe and of market capitalism than the older generation (Wallace 1997). In Eastern Europe being left wing is associated with the conservatism of the former communist regimes rather than being for radical change of the social order, whereas in Western Europe it is more likely to be the other way round.

Nevertheless, there are circumstances in which young people can make a political impact. Among the highly educated group, student politics and protest at the end of the 1960s reflected a radical disaffection with the political system. Riots in many university cities such as Berkeley, Paris and Berlin, and a flowering of an alternative political consciousness left a legacy in the development of counter-cultural movements such as radical left, feminist and alternative religious movements (Rootes 1990, Brake 1990). Although these may not have had a direct impact upon mainstream party politics, they did have an effect upon popular culture and perhaps a delayed effect upon political culture as many of the radical ideas for ecology, feminism and so on did enter mainstream politics many years later. More recently, there have been protests throughout Europe in the 1970s and 1980s against US military bases, against nuclear power plants and nuclear arms and against environmentally damaging projects such as dam, airport and motorway building. Young people have been very active in these movements, although again outside of mainstream politics, and it is these issues which have helped to shape the consciousness of the present generation. Sexual as well as gender politics have occupied the generational consciousness with a more visible gay and lesbian community also willing to take to the streets on occasion. Therefore, it is not so much the conditions of young people or mainstream political issues which have mobilized youth: it is alternative issues.

In general, young people do not seem to mobilize so readily in favour of their own interests. The introduction of educational fees and the erosion of student grants in Western European countries such as Britain, the removal of social security and housing benefits did not provoke much protest. The major exception perhaps is the recent wave of protests by young people in France over the lowering of their wages in favour of a training allowance, provoking mass student demonstrations in March 1994. Neither was much of a stir caused by the rapid introduction of educational fees and the deterioration in conditions of life for young people in Eastern Europe, despite their successful political activism only a few years previously.

Some would argue that the disaffiliation of young people from mainstream political life means that they turn to other kinds of expression such as 'passive alienation' which can express itself in rioting (Ridley 1980) or crime. Perhaps the riots of 1981 and 1985 and the 1990s amongst deprived inner city centres throughout Britain can be seen in this light. The social and economic changes experienced by working-class young people shape their attitudes and behaviour in many ways – in the post war period they were the first to encounter and to shape the 'consumer society' and later on they were the first to suffer from rising unemployment, deteriorating public services, homelessness and escalating ethnic tension. Although less likely to join political movements, they have been important in shaping the 'cultural politics' of youth sub-cultures which have taken on a different dimension in the context of the 'new Europe' (see Chapter 5). It is they who have confronted police and fought other groups in a struggle for control of the streets and shopping malls (Presdee 1990). Such unarticulated and spontaneous actions can also be seen as an indirect form of political protest.

YOUTH POLITICS IN EASTERN EUROPE UNDER SOCIALISM

The establishment of the communist system in Eastern Europe meant the ending of autonomous youth political activity and the organization of youth into 'official' youth organizations. Prior to this, the main political involvement of youth had been in the nationalist revival and liberation movements which led to the collapse of the Austro-Hungarian and Turkish empires and also to social revolutions like that in Russia in 1917. There had also been a variety of other youth political, cultural and sport groups. Student demonstrations were an established form of political protest, especially where the 'intelligentsia' were seen as the bearers of national consciousness. Examples include student demonstrations which resulted in the closure of Sofia University in Bulgaria in 1907 and Charles University in Czechoslovakia in 1938.

We have already described the way in which young people were created as bearers of the 'bright new future' under communism in Chapters 1 and 2 and the way in which this was associated with the lack of any real power or autonomy for young people. This powerlessness existed at the same time as a 'strong' construction of youth within the political and social structure: they were the builders of the socialist future and enjoyed representation as an age group at various levels of the political and state organizations. For example, within the Communist Party itself youth were represented as an age group, as they were in parliament. Their most important representation was through the Communist Youth Leagues. However, this was in many ways a way of controlling youth and keeping them at a distance from any real power (as we analyse in Chapter 2). In practice, they were rather alienated from these structures, but alienated in a silent, unobtrusive way. For young people, politics was a tool for managing society and was perceived as an activity over which common people have no influence – the realm of the authorities, of those above (Marody 1991). Indeed, retired people were, in practice, more politically active than youth in most activities such as attending political meetings, writing letters to public officials or making proposals at public meetings (Mitev 1982).

Under these conditions of forced political and stylistic conformity, anything which deviated from officially-sanctioned activity and behaviour was seen as threatening to the authorities. Thus we could say that everyday life was over-politicized when even small gestures of personal self-expression were seen as threats to the political authority of the system and rendered deviant activity. This of course made such actions all the more tempting for some and resulted in a constant struggle over cultural expression as we saw in Chapter 5. Although it was very difficult for young people to openly adopt such sub-cultural styles, they became an important source of unofficial culture. For young intellectuals there were informal clubs which discussed various problems from arts to morality through samizdat publications. However, even dissident clubs tended to discourage young people from becoming too actively involved for fear of 'ruining their future'. Since any kind of political expression was forbidden except through official channels young people carved out space for autonomous activities in other ways. In Lithuania they joined choirs, in Latvia they cultivated gardens, in other countries they helped in family projects to build country homes and they also participated in informal economic activities such as trading (Gomulka and Polonski 1990, Csepeli and Orkeny 1992, Smollett 1986).

YOUNG PEOPLE AND THE POLITICAL TRANSFORMATIONS AT THE END OF THE 1980s

Given the general exclusion of young people from the political process and their political apathy and cynicism it seems surprising that they played such an important part in the 'gentle', and sometimes not so gentle, revolutions of 1989 and afterwards. In fact, there had been the growth of political movements through the 1980s with such young people playing an important part in such things as 'Eco glasnost', an ecological movement in Bulgaria, and in Solidarity in Poland from its formation in 1980–81. Many demonstrations were organized by students over ecological issues. One example in Plovdiv was a protest at the official decision by the central authorities to tackle the vole population by poisoning them – an agricultural exercise which was so clumsily executed that it killed most of the local wildlife in the food chain. Students arrived in the city carrying strings of dead birds and rodents which they had picked up from the surrounding fields as a protest. Young people demonstrated over the Gabcikovo-Nagymaros dam on the borders of Hungary and Slovakia.

Why was it that young people suddenly became an active political force? It has been suggested that it was precisely the labelling of youth sub-cultures as subversive activity which may have helped young people to form a more critical detachment from the system than other groups (Kabátek 1990). Another explanation lies in the fact that this generation had been born after the terrors of the Stalinist era and after the invasion of Czechoslovakia following its experiment with reform communism in 1968. This generation was therefore not as frightened of military intervention or the more extreme forms of political repression, such as deportation to concentration camps or execution, as were their predecessors. Having had no direct experience of the Second World War, this generation could see little reason for the continued occupation of their countries by Soviet troops. Finally, since much of the most militant activity came from students, we could argue that their position was the most unsatisfactory. Full employment along with economic stagnation and gerontocratic forms of elite recruitment meant that many were forced to take jobs for which they were over-qualified on graduation. The extraordinary success of the socialist educational reforms in creating a relatively large university educated population in what had sometimes been semi-literate societies over the space of one or two generations helped to raise meritocratic aspirations enormously and these aspirations could not be fulfilled except by participating in the Communist Party. This led to increasing discontent amongst educated groups.

This generational explanation is supported by the student activists interviewed by Kovatcheva in Bulgaria. For them, anyone associated with the former regime bears responsibility for the guilt of that regime: 'there was no open protest, not even the slightest attempt – nothing to wipe the shame from their [the older generation's] faces' in the words of one student. In other words, anyone who conformed to the previous regime bears the responsibility of guilt for that regime (in fact this is not a very accurate assertion because there were many individual protests, especially in 1968, but it is indicative of the feelings of the present youth activists).

Another expressed the opinion that the political culture of the country could only change once all of those 'born in slavery' were dead.

It was a demonstration by students in November 1989 in Wenceslas Square which led to the toppling of the communist leadership in Czechoslovakia and young people's participation in the 'singing' revolution in Lithuania helped to trigger the changes there. In some countries young people's demonstrations led to violent confrontations as in Tiananmen Square in China in 1989, in Romania in 1990 and in Tadzhikistan in 1991. In Bulgaria it was student occupations of university buildings in 1990 which prompted and accelerated changes in the governing elite. The first wave of occupations throughout the country began soon after the parliamentary election of June 1990 when it became clear that the former Communist Party had gained the majority of seats and ended at the beginning of July with the resignation of President Mladenov. The second wave of demonstrations in November through to December was better organized and prompted the resignation of Prime Minister Lukanov and his socialist government. In the Ukraine student demonstrations and hunger strikes forced the resignation of the Prime Minister and withdrawal from the Russian-dominated Commonwealth of Independent States which replaced the Soviet Union. Further demonstrations in 1992 forced the resignation of unpopular Prime Minister Vitold Fokin. Thus, it was student demonstrations that played an important part in triggering the major political changes in the region.

In Hungary the Alliance of Young Democrats was formed by a few dozen university students in 1988 as an alternative to the Communist Youth League and this was Hungary's first independent political organization (Pataki 1993). The age limit was 35. In the 1990 elections and subsequently it proved to be one of the most popular political parties for both younger and older voters because it represented a new, fresh generation untainted by involvement in the system. This was clear in their election poster which pictured two repellent and wrinkled old communist leaders kissing each other in greeting juxtaposed with an attractive young couple embracing. The slogan invited the population to choose between them. The election campaign included a popular music song and other youth cultural referents. The style of the Young Democrats was unconventional and they wore blue jeans and T-shirts in Parliament or grew their hair long in defiance of contemporary conservative norms.

In Poland young people joined the 'flying university' in the 1980s

– an unofficial alternative university held in the private homes of professors – organized the Catholic Academic Youth and participated in the crucifix revolt in 1984 when the authorities tried to remove crucifixes from classrooms. They also organized against military service. In Romania, students organized protests and demonstrations in Timosoara in 1989-90 and in Bucharest and set up the Free Student Union. In the then-existing Soviet Union students and young people were prominent in the various protests by national liberation struggles in Lithuania, Georgia and Armenia, in Latvia and elsewhere and in all countries occupied by Soviet troops there was increased resentment against them. In the DDR it was students at the Humboldt University who led some of the demonstrations and protests and in Leipzig they joined candlelight demonstrations.

The increasing importance of mass media in influencing public opinion and politics means that this kind of symbolic political gesture, designed to attract attention and capture the public imagination, can be more effective than mass rallies or mass party membership. The peace, ecology and anti-nuclear movements use such symbolic gestures very effectively, as when Greenham Common missile base was surrounded by singing women holding hands and attaching personal artifacts to the wire fence. In Eastern Europe, the politicization of youth cultures discussed in Chapter 5 meant that they were well practiced in symbolic protests which later took the shape of theatre plays and dramaturgical gestures such as the satirical burial of communist 'Good Fortune' by students in Bulgaria. However, mass rallies were used too, as in the gathering in November 1989 in Wenceslas Square which brought down the regime in Czechoslovakia. Generally speaking young people eschewed any membership of formal organizations, preferring the kind of organization developed through the 'non formal' sub-cultural groups. Despite the temporary power which such symbolic protests held, they did not coalesce into formal political organizations or movements, but rather tended to evaporate once the protest had been made. This illustrates the weakness of such form of protest as well as its strength: when the powers against which it was ranged collapsed, so did the opposition.

This prominent role of youth in pressuring change towards democracy in East-Central Europe suggests some comparisons with the student movement in the western countries in the late 1960s. However, whilst the student movement in Central and Eastern Europe

began with protest leading towards changes in the political system
and then later moved towards reform of universities, the student
movements in the West started as local incidents protesting against
university authorities and only later moved towards broader political issues (Rootes 1990, 1980). The research on student radicalism
in comparative perspective and of Kovatcheva on the student movement in Bulgaria reveals a deep, moral anxiety amongst student
activists (Habermas 1969, Kovatcheva 1995, Bertaux 1990). The
protest campaigns in the welfare capitalist and post-communist
societies, although varying in their demands and tactics, manifested
a common desire for self-expression and more meaningful political
participation. The student movements in communist countries were
more directly successful. Their direct impact can be traced in important personnel changes in the governing elite, in election results, in changes in the legislative systems and in new constitutions
which no longer privileged the leading role of the Communist Party.
This implies that at moments of an extreme crisis in political legitimation, youth, especially student protests, can represent a new
force of change and can have a profound political influence.

YOUNG PEOPLE IN POST-COMMUNIST POLITICS

Although young people played such a key role in toppling the communist state authorities in many countries, in most places this activism did not continue for long. In the more western post-communist
countries (Hungary, Czech Republic and Poland), the official Communist Youth Leagues disappeared and were not replaced by any
equivalent organization. Whilst young people are no doubt thank-
ful for this relief from official duties, it means that young people's
interests are no longer represented, even in token form, at any
level of society. There are no longer quotas for age or gender, as
in the past. When the election system was opened to competition
at a national level in 1989 in the then Soviet Union, there was a
significant decline in the number of young people elected to the
USSR Congress of People's Deputies. Among the 2249 deputies
only 187 were aged under 30 (8.3 per cent), although 40 per cent
of these seats were guaranteed to the Komsomol under the 1988
Election Law (Lentini personal communication). However, there
were also new opportunities for young politicians who were seen
to be untainted by the former political regime and could not be

held to political ransom on that account, as was the case with many of the older leaders. Many very young people became prominent in politics – it was possible to find Ministers in their early thirties. Although individually, there was a rejuvenation amongst the leadership, young people no longer existed as a political group. Indeed, youth have disappeared as a strongly constructed category as other interest groups have emerged.

Instead, there emerged a variety of shifting and fragmented parties, organizations and interest groups, along with a profusion of youth unions, societies and federations which rapidly come and go. Very often such organizations have already dissolved by the time their emergence is announced in the media. In Bulgaria, Komsomol was reconstituted in 1990 but as a 'non political' organization, while a small part of its members formed a Socialist Youth Union. The weakness of such organizations was partly due to suspicion towards any organized activity requiring discipline and structure – an attitude inherited from the over-organized past (Kovatcheva 1995). Young people prefer to pursue semi-spontaneous movements rather than organizations which would require a more routinized activity. Whereas in the past the enemy was obvious and could be confronted, in a situation of political and economic liberalization responsibility is de-centred and it is difficult to see whom to blame. There are also other outlets for the politically and economically ambitious, for example in business.

The Young Democrats in Hungary, who traded on their youthful, untarnished political image in the early 1990s, had to adopt more conventional styles of activity. The age limit of 35 for membership has been abolished and members now nominate older and more experienced candidates. They have also abandoned their blue jeans for suits (Pataki 1993). The Young Democrats also lost their innocence, now being accused of corruption and authoritarianism. In the more traditional Ukraine the student organizations reflect those of the dominant political alignments, so there is not so much a disappearance of old formal structures as their re-grouping. Thus along with the reconstituted Komsomol, there is a Students Union, a pro-socialist, pro-Russian organization, and the Union of Ukrainian Students, a western oriented, nationalist organization based mainly in Western Ukraine and supported by the Ukrainian Diaspora. These organizations reflect the main political power blocks in a divided region.

In the elections immediately following the transformations of 1989/

90 voter turnout was high and young people participated actively in this, with voter turnout something like 75–80 per cent in Bulgaria, for example. Young people were more likely to vote for the new anti-communist parties (Tonchev and Jordanova 1991) and this was also found in a recent survey in Poland in which it was evident that young people were most likely to vote for reform parties such as the Democratic Union rather than the communist and socialist alliances which in fact won the recent elections there (Roberts et al. 1995). However, this initial electoral enthusiasm has been replaced throughout the region by political disillusionment. Now voter turnout has dropped considerably as young people and others no longer see any point in participating in elections and the early very high aspirations for democracy have not been met. In Hungary, young people have turned once more away from politics (Molnar 1992) and in Poland 35 per cent of young people said that they would not vote at all in the next elections whilst 31 per cent were undecided (Roberts et al. 1995). Qualitative interviews revealed a general cynicism about politicians and the political process which was felt to have little connection with young people's daily concerns. There was a similar disillusionment with the role of the Church in politics, although it had enjoyed substantial support during the communist period. This perhaps means that young people in Eastern Europe are becoming more similar to their western peers. As in western countries, it is the better educated, particularly students, who are more likely to have an interest in politics and more likely to engage in radical activism rather than mainstream politics (Roberts et al. 1995).

Gender plays some part in youth participation in post-communist politics. Women's equal access to political citizenship was officially proclaimed by communist ideology and was reinforced through formal legislation. There were quotas for women in political institutions with representative functions like parliament but their number in central and regional party committees – where real decision-making took place – was very small. Data indicate that in the post-communist period things are taking a turn for the worse. For example, in Hungary 21 per cent of those in parliament were women in 1985: in 1990 there were only 7 per cent. The corresponding figures for the Soviet Union are 32.8 per cent in 1984 and 15.7 per cent in 1989. In other post-communist countries the figure is even lower (Dahlerup 1991).

Whilst women were active in dissident groups in the region, such as Charter 77 in Czechoslovakia, they have tended to disappear from the post-communist political scene. Some of the most well-known groups organized by and for women are done on the basis of women's traditional roles rather than against them. For example, in Prague and in Bulgaria there was a campaign by mothers to demand clean air for their children. This can be attributed to the economic crisis and the necessity for household survival strategies of which women form an essential part (Balbo 1987). However, a closer scrutiny reveals the continuing influence of traditional gender ideologies dominating Eastern European societies where women carried not a double but a triple burden: housewife, productive worker and political activist (Kjuranov 1987). After the start of the transformation traditional gender ideologies were even strengthened by the common disenchantment with communist ideology and its version of women's liberation.

When age is taken into consideration, women's access to politics is even more restricted. Kovatcheva's (1992) study on the student movement indicated 4 to 5 times less female than male presence on the governing committees of the two occupations and the different newly formed student organizations. Perceptions of women students who took part in the organization of the occupations were heavily sexualized both by non-participating students and by adult society in a fusion of gender and age stereotyping. The most common negative images used by opposing parties was of red old woman – comparing the socialist party to an unloved, ageing woman – and 'blue young hooligan' for the supporters of the Union of Democratic Forces.

Feminism is not popular in Eastern Europe. This attitude can be explained by the fact that the introduction of liberal economic ideologies has tended to reinforce a conservative model of the family in which the man is the main breadwinner and by the fact that in Eastern Europe women would frame the gender question differently than in the Western Europe (Wallace 1995). As Ferge (1990) has argued, the argument that 'personal is political' is directly contrary to the common desire in post-communist countries not to let the political into private life. In addition, there is a lack of feminist research into women's issues and instead a tendency to continue the Soviet practice of seeing 'isolated shortcomings' of gender equality as a 'side product' of studies about 'more substantial issues' (Voronina 1988). This reflects the common attitude of not accepting gender problems as important or as being in need of any policy

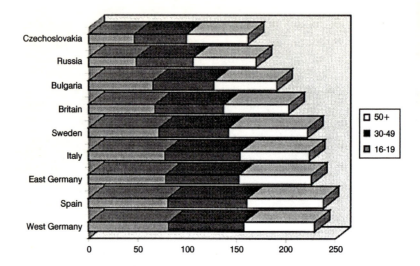

Figure 6.3 Attitudes towards women and work by age 1990–1993
(respondents were asked 'Having a job is the best way for a woman to
become an independent person' (per cent strongly agree or agree)
in each age group)

Source: World Values Survey 1990–1993, Basanez et al. 1997

solutions. However, a new feminist politics is also emerging (Mueller
and Funk 1993).

In Figure 6.3 it is evident that in Western European countries
young people value gender liberation through work more than older
cohorts. However, in Britain, Sweden and in Eastern European
countries where there was more likelihood that women were working outside the home, the situation is reversed: older generations
preferred the employed woman as an option. This perhaps reflects
the disillusionment with emancipation which we discussed previously.
In the countries of Southern Europe which experienced delayed
modernization, there is even more affirmation of work for women
as a means of independence. It seems, therefore, that those countries in which women's participation in public working life was strongly
institutionalized are the ones where young people are least likely to
see this as a form of independence. The exception is for East and
West Germany where women's independence through work was valued
in both countries, with very different experiences of this in practice.

Young people are in a state of confusion and uncertainty in post-communist societies, but this reflects the general confusion of the political situation. There is a battlefield of conflicting social and political theories, reflecting the rapid state of change in societies which have lurched from one system to another in the space of a few years. There are few stable political tendencies – for example, in Poland almost none of the parties in the first government exists any more. The confusion in public life is reflected in political attitudes expressed in many surveys where old stereotypes are mixed with new beliefs (Georgiev and Zhelev 1992). There is not always a clear right-left divide in politics around which parties and groups are aligned and political alliances rapidly come and go. Politicians often have more following than do their parties or other institutions which they represent (Marody 1991). The orientation towards persons is linked with an inclination to assess their qualifications in moral rather than meritocratic terms which means that politicians are open to accusations of past or present corruption or collaboration with the communist authorities. This trend can also be seen in an attraction towards colourful political personalities rather than concrete programmes (Schöpflin 1991). For example, the Canadian émigré Tyminski received a quarter of the vote in the 1990 presidential election in Poland – a situation which was replicated in the Bulgarian presidential election in 1992 in the case of George Ganchev, who brought from his stay in England the image of a self-made man instead of any clear political programme. Politicians are usually seen as being in politics for their own benefit rather than because of any ideas they represent. The disillusionment of young people with politics is not difficult to understand in these circumstances.

Nevertheless, there is evidence of a generational shift in post-communist attitudes. The results of a survey of 11 post-communist countries found that younger people rejected both the communist political system and the communist economic system more than older generations. Although they may be cynical about the present political situation, they were certainly not nostalgic about the past (Rose and Carnaghan 1994). Furthermore, 'pro-capitalist' economic values were more likely to be found among younger men than among older people and women, implying that the younger generation were looking forwards to a market-oriented future (Wallace 1997). Perhaps this reflects those who are 'winners' and 'losers' in the changes.

One of the results of the student protest campaigns throughout the region was that increased participation on different levels of university decision-making was conceded – from one third in Bulgaria to one half in the former Czechoslovakia of the representatives on the main university committees. In Donetsk there is 20 per cent representation on the equivalent of the academic Senate. The system of electing professors and those in key positions means that students can potentially have a very important means of political leverage through these committees. However, fewer than half of the student representatives in academic assemblies and councils at Plovdiv University have ever attended a session of these committees and this was true for other universities as well. In Prague the students are disillusioned with this representation and feel that it achieves very little (an attempt by Sociology students to reduce the amount of statistics they had to learn failed to have any effect). This behaviour confirms the observation of Bok (1991:3) on Hungarian and Czech systems of higher education, that despite their prominent role in the change from communist to democratic regimes, students seem 'apathetic and uninterested in participating actively in the university governance'. Although young people express concern about the archaic methods of teaching and assessment, low quality of some lecture courses, difficulties with getting the necessary information and acute shortages of equipment, these attitudes have not yet produced mass student activism. Having developed the consciousness about the need of changes, students lack the motivation to put them into practice. Their realistic fear of unemployment and conviction that there is no relationship between their academic performance and their access to finding a good job are all factors that discourage students from their efforts for restructuring the system of higher education. Over the last four years fees have been introduced into higher education and the costs of studying have risen considerably as students now have to pay more for accommodation, for books and for other materials. In many countries fees for university study have now been introduced or are being discussed. Students have failed to react to this privatization of their institutions and to the worsening conditions of study. There have been few political protests over these changes. In Bulgaria in the beginning of 1994 Sofia University was occupied with the demand for a larger share of the state budget for higher education. This was accompanied by the organized protest of those financing their studies themselves. However, in contrast to previous protests, the interest among student population was low. The occupation spread over few other universities, but it failed to win any change in state finance for universities.

Young people can quickly mobilize again when the political or economic situation changes. Although the Bulgarian students had de-mobilized after the occupations in 1990, they were protesting again in the winter of 1996/7 in the Serbian Republic and in Bulgaria. Rather than being apathetic towards politics, young people become involved in direct and indirect action when they are sure that they can make some impact, and in situations of acute political crisis.

YOUNG PEOPLE'S POLITICAL VALUES

It is claimed that young people are more likely to espouse 'post materialist values' – associated with self-fulfilment and self-expression in all countries – than were adults. According to Inglehart (1990) and colleagues, on the basis of a comparison of 43 different societies over time, there is a shift in political values which accompanies modernization. In 'traditional' or developing societies there is more concern with primary economic needs and a more rigid adherence to authority and traditional or religious values: these are termed 'materialist' values. However, with growing affluence these needs are fulfilled and there is a shift instead towards 'post materialist' values concerned with aesthetics, life style and other goals. Furthermore, these more advanced industrial societies are moving towards a 'postmodern' phase with the break up of affiliation to traditional parties based upon class or religion and a move towards concern with issue politics and political movements such as environmental concerns, movements to do with abortion rights, recognition of gay and lesbian equality, women's issues and so on (Inglehart 1997). The hypothesis of Inglehart and colleagues engaged in this study is that there is a generational shift in political attitudes because young people experience a different set of values as they grow up and tend to carry these with them through life. This results in what could be termed a 'juventicization' of society. Post-materialist values are evident in all parts of Europe as Figure 6.4 indicates. However, it also indicates that former communist countries (except for East Germany) had less 'post materialist' values in general. The people in the more affluent and 'western' oriented post-communist societies, such as Poland and the former Czechoslovakia, were more likely to hold 'post-materialist' values.

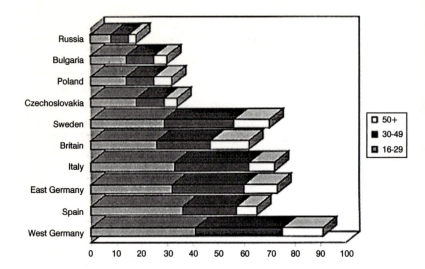

Figure 6.4   Post-materialist values by age 1990–1993 (percentage in
each age group who held post-materialist values)

Source: World Values Survey 1990–1993, Basanez et al. 1997

Young people are also conspicuous in movements for gay and
lesbian rights, New Age travellers and so on. They are more likely
to be tolerant of ethnic groups, foreigners, homosexuality and sexual
emancipation (Basenez et al. 1997). The general European trend
is for young people to be identified with new social movements
and 'post-modern' politics.

YOUNG PEOPLE AND POPULIST POLITICAL MOVEMENTS

Although young people are not very active in mainstream political
movements, in one particular area they have received a great deal
of press attention – their participation in movements of the 'new'
neo-fascist right. In particular, there is the association between a
skinhead sub-culture and the neo-fascists. Skinheads began as protest sub-cultures in the 1980s in the most western communist societies and have spread gradually further eastwards. However, under
the influence of their western neighbours they turned from small

cultural forms of protest into more organized political groups after the changes of 1989/90. Unlike other forms of youth protest, these are mainly youth from the lower social strata and are overwhelmingly men. In Britain it seems that it is mainly those from depressed areas who are likely to turn to extreme political solutions (Roberts and Parsell 1990), although in Central Europe it seems that these are mostly young people who are in work. Rather than the 'lumpen' image which skinheads have in Britain, in Central Europe they portray themselves rather as disciplined vigilantes who undertake physical training and try to keep the streets clean of foreigners and criminals. They seem to enjoy some support from police and population for this.

Originating in East London in the early 1970s, the skinheads were associated with a tough, fighting masculine image, support for particular football teams and racism (Cohen 1997). They are characterized by a distinctive uniform of rolled up jeans, shaved heads and 'Doc Marten' boots. This image spread to Europe as a result of roving football club supporters and their media coverage. It was only later that they began to be recruited into neo-fascist parties such as the British Party and the National Front and began to adopt nazi symbolism such as the 'Sieg Heil' salute.

Skinheads were active in Germany through the 1980s and were associated there with the revival of 'neo-fascist politics'. In the 1990s, however, racism is increasing all over Europe, including Britain, and far right movements have enjoyed something of a revival. Racist feelings and racist attacks are on the ascendant throughout Europe and some parties previously associated with the political fringe have had considerable electoral success in Austria, Belgium and France. These parties have capitalized upon the fears of immigration generated by the opening of the borders to the East. In Germany, skinheads have attacked mainly Turks, but also homeless people, mentally and physically handicapped, and homosexuals. In the Czech lands and Hungary they are thought to number about 6000, according to the popular press, and have targeted their attacks mainly against Roma. In Pardobice 300 skinheads marched through the city centre shouting 'Czech lands for the Czechs' and 'Gypsies to the gas' in February 1993 and later in the year a youth was beaten to death by skinheads. Attacks on Vietnamese are also a common occurrence but are seldom reported to the police. The Czech skinheads eschew the neo-nazi symbolism because of the unfavourable historical associations it holds in a country previously occupied by the Third Reich. In Germany the 40 000 or so right-radical sympathizers published their own magazines with names such as *Skinhead Zeitung, Frontal* and *White Power*. In each country skinheads follow particular kinds of bands and music, often with racist lyrics. In 1992 in Germany they accounted for some 1600 attacks and 17 deaths (*Spiegel* 49/92) whilst in Britain there were seven deaths attributed to such causes in 1992. One of the best known of these attacks in Germany was on 23rd November in Mölln when a whole Turkish family were killed in a fire attack. However, this was only one of many fire-bomb attacks and beatings (Hockenos 1993).

Some attribute the growth of these far right groups in Germany to the problems of unification and opening the eastern borders (Hockenos 1993). Factors include the collapse of the former East German economy, the very high rates of unemployment amongst people accustomed to full employment, the crisis of ideology amongst those for whom the promise of the West turned out to be a disappointment and the general disorientation of youth brought up in disciplinarian organizations now finding themselves in a post-communist confusion. The politicization of immigration has affected Germany as well, so that the skinhead attacks are directed against the refugees and asylum seekers and the seasonal and foreign workers who have entered since unification from or through Eastern Europe.

However, German researchers from the Youth Institute stress that there is no simple explanation for the rise of right wing violence and that it is not only associated with young people. Racist attitudes are more likely to be espoused by adults than by the young and the skinheads represent only a small minority of young people (Schneider 1990, Hoffmann-Lange and Eilders 1990). They also point out that many of the explanations which have been advanced for accounting for neo-fascist youth groups are not equally valid in both halves of Germany. Thus, for example, the dramatic rise in unemployment or disillusionment with capitalism does not explain skinhead activities in West Germany or elsewhere.

The skinheads are perhaps an extreme example of a much publicized minority group, but the revival of nationalism and the mobilization of young people in such nationalist movements is a new dimension to cultural politics which is far more significant in the context of fragile economies and democracies and the weak social integration in Eastern Europe than it was in Britain where it originated. They can be compared with nationalist and authoritarian socialist youth movements such as the Afgantsy – vigilante groups of Afghan veterans – and the Luybery in Russia. Both of these youth groups are pledged to fight what they see as corruption and western decadence in their society (Riordan 1989b). Youth sub-cultures in Moscow have also been influenced by the growth of chauvinist politics (Pilkington 1996). Far more sinister than the marginal skinhead youth groups are the nationalist demagogues which have arisen in the region and have the capacity to stir up a witches' brew of potential xenophobic and racist attitudes from positions of power within the state apparatus. The mobilization of young people through war, as in the former Yugoslavia, encouraged the development of sub-cultures based upon predatory masculinity which, with the breakdown of law and order which accompanies civil war, were tragically destructive.

Despite the association of young people with racism and political extremism described above, systematic comparative analysis shows that the majority are in fact more *tolerant* than other age groups. Young people are more tolerant of foreigners and less likely to see themselves as nationalist than are other age groups. Furthermore, they are also more tolerant of other kinds of 'difference', whether sexual, political or ethnic, than were other age groups and generations. It was older people who are more likely to hold stereotypes about minority groups (Basanez et al. 1997).

CONCLUSIONS

To summarize, the situation of youth politics in communist and post-communist societies can be characterized by one of an over-politicized age group (in reality one expressing cynicism and apathy) which can quickly mobilize to become a creative political force but which can later rapidly demobilize again into apathy. The current situation can be described as one of confusion and uncertainty with a range of unstable groups coming and going, but one underlining the growing importance of national or ethnic identities in politics.

In Eastern Europe the official category of 'youth' as a modern political construct has disappeared along with the official youth organizations and many forms of youth representation in the political structure. However, because youth occupied an over-politicized space, their activities acquired a political character. This political consciousness was only a temporary and transient articulation of interests which were later replaced by a rapidly changing plethora of groups and interests which have yet to cohere into a clear political map.

The alternative non-politicized articulation of interests through a strong civil society has yet to emerge in many places.

In Western Europe young people remain both politically and economically marginalized because they do not represent a strong political force, despite the existence of formally organized youth wings in Churches, political parties and so on. A large minority do not vote at all and are not even interested in mainstream politics. Their marginalization from mainstream political representation means that youth concerns seldom appear on the political agenda – youth and their growing economic marginalization remain unchallenged. Under normal democratic systems, 'youth' is not a category sufficiently strong or cohesive enough for permanent political mobilization – a 'weak' model of youth prevails – and this changes only under certain heavily ideological regimes such as communism, fascism or nationalism. In some post-communist countries, nationalism is being used at present to mobilize young people under a strong concept of youth.

Instead, most young people are active in more 'post-modern' forms of protest – symbolic and cultural challenges to the dominant system of rules and regulations and to dominant values and assumptions of good taste. These are often spontaneous and ephemeral. Young people use 'cultural politics' of youth styles which are also implicitly critical of the dominant order. These 'cultural politics' can move from symbolism to more or less explicit political identification in some circumstances and thus help to articulate the interests and experiences of sub-groups of young people. Under both capitalist and the former communist regimes they could be a subversive influence, but in the latter case they could also be a more direct political threat because of the politicization of everyday conduct.

Issues that young people in both East and West Europe are most concerned with are issues of the environment and social justice rather than 'mainstream' politics. In both East and West Europe, most young people are cynical about 'mainstream' politics and alienated from the political process. However, under some circumstances, when there is an overall crisis of legitimacy in the dominant order, youth politics can play a pivotal role, for example in the 'evenements' of 1968, or in the changes of regime in 1989 in Eastern Europe. This is not so much the product of youth organizing as a coherent interest group, as of young people, particularly students, being seen as a 'new force' against the 'old order'.

7 Conclusions: Postmodernization and the Deconstruction of Youth

In this book we have attempted to show some of the ways in which youth are constructed at different historical periods and within different state formations. By comparing capitalist with state socialist systems and 'post-industrial' with 'post-communist' systems we have tried to chart elements of change and continuity. Whilst our data derives mainly from contexts with which we are familiar, it is evident that in the former socialist countries the forced homogeneity of political and social orders is rapidly diversifying and such countries as the Czech Republic, Bulgaria, Russia and Ukraine are developing in very different directions. Rather than convergence, there is divergence. By contrast, the European Union is now imposing more uniformity on Western European states than had existed in the past and it is easier to draw comparisons between them. At any rate it is easier to find comparative statistics which make the kind of analysis presented here for Western Europe more accessible.

Our argument is that whilst modernization constructed youth as a social category, postmodernization is deconstructing youth. The evaporation of concepts of youth intervention mean less forced participation for young people, but also less state support, leading to individualization and privatization of young people's problems and the social exclusion of some groups of young people from mainstream life.

It is evident on both sides of Europe that similar economic and social forces have shaped – and are shaping – developments there but that these forces have different impacts depending upon the social, cultural and historical configurations of the society. For example, whilst all states have experienced modernization and industrialization, this has taken place in very different ways – in some cases through capitalist free market development (with more or less state direction) and in other cases through rapid communist modernization. Although the character of modernization and industrialization is disputed, they nevertheless created state bureaucracies and state-directed institutions such as education systems which have served to define age-status categories. Furthermore, state bureaucracies have used age as a principle for classifying and regulating citizens – for example, in access to voting, pensions, punishments and rewards and so on – important as an organizing principle in all modern state systems. However, the implications of this are very different. In some states, youth are identified as a target for intervention, whereas in others this is less the case and hence there are both 'stronger' and 'weaker' models of youth constructed under different state and social systems. Communist, fascist and nationalist states construct a very strong model of youth since youth was the group with the strongest potential to be mobilized and upon which rapid modernization could be built (Mitev 1996). Within welfare capitalist societies there are contrasts between stronger and weaker constructions of youth – as for example between Germany and Britain.

The homogenizing tendencies associated with modernization have given way in recent decades to countervailing postmodernizing tendencies. The growing importance of culture and particularly youth culture in defining social groups is evidence of this and has helped to undermine 'modern' communist regimes based upon rigid categories of 'youth' defined by biological, developmental or materialist concepts. Youth culture, by contrast, is more non-material in form, relying on the transmission of styles and music, and it is also expressive and evanescent. Other postmodernizing tendencies associated with young people include the increasing non-correspondence and fragmentation of life course transitions and their diffusion across different age groups. Whereas through industrialization, youth had been associated with a specific age between school and work, when courting, hedonism and experimentation took place before settling down to family, household and job, it is now an indefinite period. Family, household and job no longer coincide and are quite remote or even undesirable goals for many young people.

Also associated with the postmodern erosion of traditional social classes and occupations is the social exclusion of a substantial fraction of young people (some 40 per cent in some regions) who are more or less permanently sub-employed. As the economic independence of all young people has been undermined through the withdrawal of state support, the contracting and privatizing of the welfare state and the increasingly lengthy and indefinite extension of the youth phase, those unwilling or unable to resort to parental support are stranded. There is evidence that young people in this situation create their own lifestyles through crime or through the informal economy and informal mechanisms of support (Carlen 1996, Coles 1995). These are not so much the working-class disadvantaged (formerly the objects of state intervention and concern) as the non-working class disadvantaged and the state is concerned with them generally when they break the law or cause a public nuisance by sleeping in doorways. Otherwise solutions for them are privatized and individualized as responsibility is shifted back towards the individual or the family or the voluntary sector.

Rigid divisions associated with sex and 'race' also start to dissolve with postmodernization. Essentialist notions of sex and a woman's or man's role for which they must be educated have been challenged by postmodern theorists (Butler 1990). Young people have led the way in forging new roles for men and women which broke with the past. Under market capitalist regimes this has meant increasing androgyny and the movement of women into higher education and into men's jobs (although there are also limitations to this). In the former communist countries, it has meant increasing differentiation as a reaction to the forced homogenization of the sexes. Similarly, 'race' was previously associated with immigrant groups or with categories of 'black people', 'jews' and with scientific theories which were products of modernity (Bauman 1989) resulting in 'holocaust' or 'apartheid' resolutions. By contrast, second generation young people are developing a range of hybrid and creative styles using elements of diasporic, post-colonial and local cultures (Back 1996). Recognition of cultural difference rather than assimilation or apartheid have become the governing concepts. However, a counter reaction to this is the aggressive assertion of ethnic chauvinism among some sub-cultures and among some political leaders. Such 'postmodern' recognitions and tolerance of diversity may be an ideal among academic writers such as Bauman (1992) but it is not necessarily very widespread within populations of Europe generally. The erosion of nation, race, gender cleavages and taken-for-granted age categories is also a threat to their assumed ideas of what is natural and normal, inherited from the past.

Next we shall summarize the contents of each chapter in order to show how we have developed this argument. In the first chapter we considered theories of youth and the ways in which these were used to legitimize various kinds of intervention by states, political parties and voluntary organizations in the lives of young people. We considered developmental theories, social theories, critical theories and theories of youth developed in communist countries – not just as descriptions of intellectual history but as active models of intervention. In this chapter we also considered the main arguments for modernization and postmodernization, but rejecting the view that modernization is linear, uniform or leading towards convergence in European societies. Finally, we considered sources of differentiation in youth, in particular ethnicity, gender, class/educational level and differentiation according to different regions and parts of Europe. Postmodernization has led to an increasing awareness of different sorts of differentiation and their importance for young people's experience of growing up in Europe. However, it makes it more and more difficult to impose an homogenous age-stratified concept of youth.

In the second chapter we took an historical look at modernization and postmodernization of the life course. We considered the way in which industrialization, urbanization and the expansion of the state had helped to construct youth as a social category. Our argument was that although 'youth' may have existed previously, modernization created an idea of the life-stage associated with precisely calibrated time and used age as a way of classifying people and distributing services. Through legislation for working conditions, for education and in order to 'save' young people from crime a particular idea of youth was born. However, most important were voluntary youth movements of various sorts which helped to construct a model of youth as objects of intervention which was later absorbed by the welfare state. Although at first churches, sports organizations and trades unions were important everywhere in attempting to deal with the problems caused by industrialization, in East-Central Europe youth organizations became increasingly politicized. In countries taken over by either fascist or communist regimes, youth were more or less compelled to spend much of their spare time in youth organizations and were seen as the bearers of the 'bright new' future. However, the youth organizations were also a method of surveillance and control over young people. The creation of professions associated with young people followed these patterns as the non-democratic countries created a political cadre of youth leaders linked to the Communist Party, whilst in democratic countries the youth professions struggled with various models of intervention and professionalization. The collapse of communism also led to the disappearance of the youth organizations but also to increasing problems for youth of unemployment, lack of recreational facilities, along with the continued lack of housing – problems which were increasingly privatized and individualized. In Western Europe postmodern ideas of fragmented transition and de-centralized authority led to notions of 'empowerment' and 'leading from below'.

In the third chapter we considered transitions in training, education and work. Just as modernization helped to construct universal education systems and therefore an age-specific entry into employment, postmodernization led to indefinite and extended education and training, casualized jobs and perhaps no certainty of permanent work. In the early stages schooling was geared to the labour market at different levels and towards male and female skills; these more standardized routes have given way to more androgynous and less clearly stratified pathways into work. Rather, people move in and out of training, school, college and work at different levels. This means that rather than being 'young workers' on leaving compulsory schooling, young people are more likely to become trainees or students for longer and longer periods of time. This is true as much for those from upper social backgrounds as those from lower social backgrounds. These changes occurred partly because the nature of work itself started to change following postmodernizing tendencies towards temporary and insecure employment with frequent skill changes. As welfare states retreated and a market model of welfare and education started to predominate, so strong concepts of intervention also disappeared and pathways through an array of education, work and training schemes were individualized and privatized at all levels. These changes have been a feature of Eastern European as much as Western European societies – only in post-communist countries the changes happened more rapidly. When considering the different social groups within youth, however, we find that young women have in many ways benefited from changes in education and the work place: they are no longer held down by 'modernist' ideas of their roles and status. Furthermore, ethnic groups are better able to assert their 'difference' and to resist assimilationist policies. Postmodernization brings greater freedom as well as greater chaos.

In Chapter 4 we looked at family transitions, and the way in which the two-parent, gender structured nuclear family, institutionalized in various ways by modern state systems, served to structure the passage from home of origin to home of destination. In both communist and welfare capitalist countries, this was supposed to take place in a structured and orderly way, coincident with labour market transitions to a full-time job (even if, in practice, lack of housing may not have allowed it to happen). Now new trends in family formation led by young people including single households, cohabiting, single parenthood, the coming out of gay and lesbian relationships and the increasing fragility of family bonds such as marriage has led to these transitions no longer being strongly structured or predictable. German and continental social theories have emphasized the increasing negotiation and flexibilization of roles between parents and children and between partners, whereas Anglo-American social scientists have emphasized the postmodern tendencies in family relationships leading towards fragmentation and differentiation. Rather than being imposed upon young people, relations with relatives can be chosen. However, this is combined with lack of housing for young people in all parts of Europe and their decreasing economic independence, leading to problems of homelessness and social exclusion. The retreat from welfarist models of youth intervention means that here is a privatization and individualization of the problems of family transition – it is up to you to find solutions for housing, childrearing and partnership yourself (or to hope for support from parents). In post-communist countries the strong traditions of family solidarity, especially between generations, mean that they are more likely to seek family solutions, whilst in Western Europe, young people increasingly simply have to fend for themselves.

In Chapter 5 we looked at the most 'postmodern' tendencies of all and those were associated with youth culture. We distinguished between youth as an aspect of popular culture in general and stylistically specific youth sub-cultures. Popular culture became more and more important as an aspect of late twentieth century society, something which pervaded everyone's lives. Youth sub-cultures were at first more class and regionally specific but were soon taken up by the mass media and spread everywhere. Young people participated through following popular music, fashions and styles and age-specific literature. In the communist countries listening to popular western music and adopting sub-cultural styles was a form of subversion and we describe the various ways in which the authorities reacted with repression, with denial or with attempts at assimilation. None of these was successful, but they did serve to politicize youth sub-cultures into a form of resistance. This helped to undermine those regimes which were revealed as ridiculous in their reactions and quite out of touch with young people's needs. By the 1980s and 1990s youth sub-culture proliferated and, as in Western Europe, took many and diverse forms with the continuation of previous sub-cultures at the same time as new ones were being created. Furthermore, rather than being seen as subversive they were quickly adopted by popular culture and used by politicians and commercial interests for publicity. Communications technology and commercialization meant that youth cultures and sub-cultures (it became more difficult to distinguish them) could be spread very rapidly around the world, creating a general model of desirable, hedonistic youth as an aspiration. However, this generalization of youth as a social category also dissolved it as an age-specific phenomenon, because 'youth' is seen as something everyone should aspire to. The modernizing tendencies to construct youth as an chronologically defined category was undermined by these postmodernizing tendencies.

In Chapter 6 we considered young people and politics. We considered both their participation in politics and the political values and attitudes which they supported. Young people are leading the world in every country in the espousal of 'post-materialist' values associated not so much with physical survival but with self-fulfilment and self-expression. They are associated with the replacement of a work-achievement ethic with a leisure-expressive ethic. In general, however, they are not very interested in mainstream politics and large numbers do not vote at all. Instead they are more interested in the sorts of 'new social movements' associated with postmodern politics, including ecological issues, animal rights and issues associated with women's, sexual and racial emancipation. In general they are more tolerant in their attitudes than are adults. Young people are also involved in more 'symbolic' politics of style and we saw in Chapter 5 that these sub-cultural politics can become politicized under some circumstances. In the 1980s and 1990s right wing and nationalist political movements came to be associated with particular youth sub-cultures, especially 'skinheads', and these have been spreading through Europe from Britain where they originated. However, as with youth sub-cultures we should be aware that the same style can have different meanings in different places. The chapter also considered how under some circumstances youth could mobilize as a political force, for example in the revolutions in Eastern Europe at the end of the 1980s, but one which was temporary and confrontational rather than long term and organizational in character.

Table 6.1 Contrasts between modernization and postmodernization for youth

Modernization	Postmodernization
Youth defined by precisely calibrated age	Youth as an age group dissolves
Work-achievement ethic	Leisure-expressive ethic
Distinguishing youth by male and female (separate schooling, youth provision etc.)	Mixed provision
Ethnic groups defined as 'immigrants', assimilationist model through social policies	Range of ethnic hybridization and differentiation through youth cultures Multi-cultural models
Separations by class/education linked to levels of the labour market – more education for some and work or training for others	More and more education and training for everyone
Youth culture associated with specific 'courting period'	Youth culture associated with all periods of life
Youth as a period between family of origin and family of destination	No clear division between family of origin and family of destination – perhaps no family of destination
Working class most disadvantaged youth	Non-working class most disadvantaged youth
Politicization of youth movements and youth as bearers of the bright new future	De-politicization of youth
Conventional right–left politics	New social movements

Young people are associated with post-modernizing tendencies in European societies and we can summarize these in Table 6.1.

We can see that these postmodernizing tendencies intersect with all areas of young people's lives. But they also affect the construction of youth itself. In Western Europe postmodernizing tendencies could be seen developing over several decades alongside modernization, but accelerated by the collapse of traditional industries, the growing fiscal pressures on the welfare state and the rise of then 'new right'. In Eastern Europe there was a very sudden plunge into de-industrialization and postmodern *laissez-faire* privatization and individualization. These societies lurched from one system to another, although there are also important lines of continuity. In the countries of Eastern Europe experiments in privatization of state assets, the withdrawal of the state and rapid commercialization were introduced in a very radical way, ideas which were often still only being discussed in Western Europe. In some respects, therefore, especially in terms of these economic experiments, Eastern European societies were leading the West rather than vice versa (Mestrovic 1994). Young people, however, felt the brunt of these changes and were also the leaders of these changes under both systems.

We have described the processes whereby 'youth' has become increasingly fragmented and diffuse. From labour–market and family transitions being strongly linked, as in Western Europe in the post-war period, they are now de-coupled. Instead there is an increasing diversity of styles of life and living arrangements with people moving in and out of different stages of life rather than making standardized and regular transitions. In post-communist Europe, the standardized age transitions which were regulated by the official youth organizations have disappeared along with those organizations as youth is no longer as strongly constructed or controlled as a group. However, we do not wish to argue that youth has disappeared. Rather, young people face new problems of identity and social support in this more chaotic situation. Changes in education and the labour market mean that they are more than ever a marginalized and vulnerable group, having to depend increasingly upon families or state institutional structures. The universal inclusiveness which is implied by the ubiquity of mass media and subcultural communications conceals the fact that young people are very differently located in terms of access to leisure facilities, jobs and independent incomes. Their inclusion or exclusion from social goods depends upon their gender, their ethnicity, their religion, their social origin and educational advantages and these are in turn exaggerated by the different regions of Europe. Increasing problems of homelessness, crime and unemployment affect young people more than other groups. What is needed is a conception of 'youth' which does not allow it to disappear but rather considers the significance of age in determining exclusion or inclusion in different regions. In this way more humane forms of intervention can be devised to tackle the real and growing problems of the new generation. The lack of any consensus on social policy amongst European states and the collapse of social intervention for youth in post-communist Europe reveal a gaping hole in the ways of thinking about generational relations and the social construction of age and in dealing with it in concrete policies.

In developing the themes in this book we drew upon a number of theoretical sources. For example, we did find some evidence for the 'juventicization' thesis of the Romanian sociologist Fred Mahler as societies are regenerated through the ideas and activities of young people in politics and in youth culture. In times of rapid social change and increasing use of information technology, young people are often ahead of adults, so this thesis seems particularly apposite. However, we also found evidence for the 'generational' thesis of Karl Mannheim as different generations of young people grow to maturity bearing with them the ideas or experiences which impressed them in their youth. However, it applies to a greater or lesser extent in different historical epochs.

We do not wish to argue that modernization or the collapse of communism have led to any kind of convergence in European experiences. Rather, the divergences between different styles of marketization and between different parts of Europe are becoming more readily apparent. Increased communication does not necessarily lead to increased uniformity. However, the same trends within modernity can be experienced in very different ways in different places. Social policies for young people will have to recognize this as well and to leave space for the 'solutions' which young people already found for themselves.

Many youth policies are now initiated at a pan-European level through the European Union or the Council of Europe. There is therefore a growing need for comparative materials to document the lives of young people. Insufficient systematically comparative data exist, something which was a handicap to us in writing this book. The experience of writing this book has shown us in a very stark way how important it is to be able to compare the experiences of young people in different parts of Europe and also how necessary it is for policies to be formulated which are sensitive to the national differences which we have described but also to the real problems of young people in contemporary Europe. Here, we have provided some ways of conceptualizing this. What is needed now is more comparative research on a systematic basis.

In this book we have struggled to develop concepts which can explain developments in life-course transitions among youth in different parts of Europe. In doing so, we have not been able to cover all parts of Europe as comprehensively as we would have liked. We lack the appropriate materials and detailed experience. We confined ourselves to Europe because youth as a product of welfare states and state intervention is mostly a European phenomenon and we are confined by our own 'Eurocentric' experiences. Youth studies generally have been Eurocentric and in this respect we follow a trend of which we are also critical. However, we have tried to go beyond the technique of simply juxtaposing different countries in different chapters. This has proved an immensely challenging experience and it therefore took us a long time to write this book. We hope that others will be able to take this challenge further in explaining and understanding contemporary Europe as well as other parts of the world.

References

P. Abbott and C. Wallace, *The New Right and the Family* (London: Pluto Press, 1992)

P. Abbott and C. Wallace, *An Introduction to Sociology. Feminist Perspectives* 2nd Edition (London: Routledge, 1997)

M. Abrams, *The Teenage Consumer* (London: London Press Exchange, 1961)

W. Adamski and P. Grootings (eds) *Youth, Education and Work in Europe* (London: Routledge, 1989)

L. Adkins, *Gendered Work: Sexuality, Family and the Labour Market* (Buckingham: Open University Press, 1995)

P. Aggleton, *Rebels with a Cause* (Basingstoke: Falmer, 1987)

P. Ainly, *Young People Leaving Home* (London: Cassell, 1991)

P. Ainly, *Class and Skill. Changing Divisions of Knowledge and Labour* (London: Cassell, 1993)

P. Ainly, *Degrees of Difference. Higher Education in the 1990s* (London: Lawrence and Wishart, 1994)

Albermarle Report, *The Youth Service in England and Wales* (London: HMSO, 1960)

P. Allatt and S. Yeandle, *Youth Unemployment and the Family. Voices of Disordered Times* (London: Routledge, 1992)

S. Allen, 'Some Theoretical Problems in the Study of Youth' in Williams, W.M. (ed.) *Occupational Choice* (London: Allen and Unwin, 1974) First appeared as an article in Sociological Review in 1968

S. Allen and C. Walkowitz, *Homeworking. Myths and Realities* (London: Macmillan, 1987)

K. Allerbeck, *Demokratisierung und Sozialer Wandel in der Bundesrepublik Deutschland. Sekundaranalyse von Umfragedaten 1953–1974* (Opladen, 1976)

A. Amin, (ed.) *Post-Fordism* (Oxford: Blackwells, 1994)

V. Amit-Talai and H. Wulff (eds) *Youth Cultures. A Cross-cultural Perspective* (London and New York: Routledge, 1995)

R. Andorka, 'Half a Century of Trends in Social Mobility in Hungary' in J.L. Peschar (ed.) *Social Reproduction in Eastern and Western Europe* (University of Groningen, Department of Sociology, 1990)

F. Anthias and N. Yuval-Davis, *Racialised Boundaries: Race, Nation, Gender, Colour, Class and the Anti-racist Struggle* (London: Routledge, 1993)

S.L. Archer (ed.) *Interventions for Adolescent Identity Development* (London, California, New Delhi: Sage, 1994)

D.N. Ashton and D. Field, *Young Workers* (London: Hutchinson, 1976)

D. Ashton and M. Maguire, *Young Adults in the Labour Market*, Department of Employment, Research Paper No.55 (London: HMSO, 1986)

T. Babushkina, 'Some Problems of the Transition of Young People from School to Work in the Soviet Union' in P. Grootings and M. Stefanov (eds) *Transition from School to Work* (Sofia: Institute of Youth Studies, 1985)

L. Back, *New Ethnicities and Urban Culture. Racisms and multiculture in young lives* (London: UCL Press, 1996)

L. Balbo, 'Crazy Quilts: Re-Thinking the Welfare Debate from a Woman's Point of View', in A. Sassoon, *Women and the State* (London: Hutchinson, 1987)

P. Balkanski, 'The Structure of Groups According to Interests', *Proceedings*, 1: 191–211 (Sofia: Institute for Youth Studies, 1981)

M. Banks, I. Bates, G. Breakwell, J. Bynner, N. Emler L. Jamieson, and K. Roberts, *Careers and Identities* (Basingstoke: Open University Press, 1992)

S. Banks, 'Contemporary Issues in Youth Work' *Youth and Policy* 46: 1–4 (1994)

S. Banks, 'Youth Work, Informal Education and Professionalisation' *Youth and Policy* 54: 13–25 (1996)

M. Barry, 'The Empowering Process: Leading from Behind?' *Youth and Policy* 54: 1–12 (1996)

M. Basanez, R. Inglehart and A. Moreno, *Human Values and Beliefs: A Cross-cultural Sourcebook. Findings from the 1990–1993 World Values Survey* (Ann Arbor: University of Michigan Press, 1997)

I. Bates and G. Riseborough (eds), *Youth and Inequality* (Buckingham: Open University Press, 1993)

Z. Bauman, *Modernity and the Holocaust* (Cornell: Cornell University Press, 1989)

Z. Bauman, *Intimations of Postmodernity* (London: Routledge, 1992)

Z. Bauman, *Life in Fragments. Essays in Postmodern Morality* (Oxford: Blackwells, 1995)

U. Beck, *Risikogesellschaft: Auf dem Weg in eine andere Moderne* (Frankfurt: Suhrkamp, 1986)

U. Beck and E. Beck-Gernsheim, *The Normal Chaos of Love* (Oxford: Polity, 1995)

U. Beck, A. Giddens and S. Lash, *Reflexive Modernization. Politics, Tradition and Aesthetics in the Modern Social Order* (Oxford: Polity, 1994)

H. Becker, *German Youth: Bond or Free* (London: Kegan Paul, Trench, Trubner and Co. Ltd, 1946)

D. Bell, *The Coming of Post-Industrial Society* (New York: Basic Books, 1973)

M. Beltcheva and P. Bozhikov, 'Internal Migration of the Youth in the People's Republic of Bulgaria /1965–1975/', *Proceedings*, (Sofia: Institute of Youth Studies, 1981), pp. 155–75

R. Bendit, 'Bestimmungfacktoren von Lebenslagen Ausländischer Jugendlicher in der Bundes Republic Deutschland oder gesellschaftlicher Reproduktion einer marginilisierten Untershicht' in *Lebenslage Jugend* (München: DJI Materialen, 1985)

R. Bendit, W. Gaiser and U. Nissen, 'Growing up in the Federal Republic of Germany: Chance and Risk in a Modern Sozialstaat' in L. Chisholm, E. Liebau (eds) *Youth, Social Change and Education: Issues, Problems and Policies in Post-1992 Europe. Journal of Education Policy* Special Issue 8 (1)(1993)

D. Bertaux, 'Oral History Approaches to an International Social Movement' in E. Oyen *Comparative Methodology* (London and Beverley Hills: Sage, 1990)

H. Bertram, 'Youth Findings and Critique of Youth Research on the Occasion of the International Youth Year' (Muenchen: DJI mimeo, 1985)

B. Bertram, 'Aufbrauch in Umbruch. Beruflicher Orientierung von Jugendlichen in den neuen Bundesdänder' *Diskurs* 2/91 (1992) pp. 40–41

B. Bertram, 'Nich Züruck an den Kochtopf. Aus und Weiterbildung in Ost Deutschland' in G. Helwig and M. Hildegard (eds) *Frauen in Deutschland* (Bonn, 1993)

R. Biorcio, A. Cavalli and P. Segatti, 'Cultural Change and Political Orientations among European Youth' in CYRCE (ed.) *The Puzzle of Integration* (Berlin and New York: De Gruyter, 1995)

G. Bhattacharyya and J. Gabriel, 'Racial Formations of Youth in Late Twentieth Century England' in J. Roche and S. Tucker (eds) *Youth in Society* (California, London, New Delhi: Sage, 1997)

M. Blanch, 'Imperialism, Nationalism and Organised Youth' in J. Clarke, C. Critcher and R. Johnson *Working Class Culture* (London: Hutchinson, 1979)

S. Bobchev, *Bulgarian Patriarchal Community (Family Clan) and Its Legal (Juristic) Character*, a report on the first congress of Bulgarian lawyers (Sofia, 1906)

L. Böhnisch and W. Schefeld, 'Jugendarbeit' in W. Gaiser, S. Huebner-Funk, W. Krueger and R. Rathgeber *Immer Diese Jugend!* (Muenchen: Koesel-verlag, 1985)

M. du Bois-Reymond, R. Diekstra, K. Hurrelmann and E. Peters (eds) *Childhood and Youth in Germany and the Netherlands. Transitions and Coping Strategies of Adolescents* (New York and Berlin: Walter de Gruyter, 1995)

D. Bok, *Universities in Transition: Observations and Recommendations for Hungary and Czechoslovakia* A CDC Report, 1991

P. Bourdieu and J.C. Passeron, *Reproduction in Education, Society and Culture* (London and Beverley Hills: Sage, 1977)

P. Bourdieu, *Distinction. A Social Critique of the Judgement of Taste* (London: Routledge, 1986)

S. Bowles and H. Gintis, *Schooling in Capitalist America: Educational Reform and the Contradictions of Economic Life* (London: Routledge and Kegan Paul, 1976)

A. Brah, 'Unemployment and Racism: Asian Youth on the Dole' in S. Allen, A. Waton, K. Purcell and S. Wood (eds) *The Experience of Unemployment* (London: Macmillan, 1996)

M. Brake, *The Sociology of Youth Culture and Youth Subculture* (London: Routledge and Kegan Paul, 1980)

M. Brake, *Comparative Youth Culture,* (London and New York: Routledge, 1990)

J. Brannen, K. Dodd, A. Oakley and P. Storey, *Young People, Health and Family Life* (Buckingham: Open University Press, 1994)

R. G. Braungart and M. M. Braungart, Europaische Jugendbewengungen in den 1980er Jahren *Diskurs* 0/90: 45–53, 1990

S. Bridger, 'Rural Youth' in J. Riordan (ed.) *Soviet Youth Culture* (Bloomington and Indiana: Indiana University Press, 1989)

S. Bridger and R. Kay, 'Gender and Generation in the New Russian Labour Market' in H. Pilkington (ed.) *Gender, Generation and Identity in Contemporary Russia* (London and New York: Routledge, 1996)

P. Brown, *Schooling Ordinary Kids. Inequality, unemployment and the new vocationalism* (London: Tavistock, 1987)

C. Bryant and E. Mockrzycki (eds) *The New Great Transformation?* (London: Routledge, 1994)

P. Büchner, 'Growing Up in the Eighties: Changes in the Social Biography of childhood in the FRG' in L. Chisholm, P. Büchner, H-H. Krüger and P. Brown *Childhood, Youth and Social Change* (Basingstoke: Falmer, 1990)

Bundesministier für Jugend, Familie, Frauen und Gesundheit. Fuenfter Jugendbericht (Bonn, 1980)

Bundesministier für Jugend, Familie, Frauen und Gesundheit. Sechster Jugendbericht (Bonn, 1984)

Bundesministier für Jugend, Familie, Frauen und Gesundheit. Siebter Jugendbericht (Bonn, 1986)

Bundesministier für Jugend, Familie, Frauen und Gesundheit. Achter Jugendbericht (Bonn, 1990)

Bundesministier für Bildung und Wissenschaft. *Grund und Struktur Daten* (Bonn, 1993)

R. Burrows and B. Loader (eds) *Towards a Post-Fordist Welfare State?* (London: Routledge, 1994)

P. Burton et al. *Urban Environment: Accommodation, Social Cohesion. The Implications for Young People. Consolidated Report* European Foundation for the Improvement of Living and Working Conditions, Shankill, Co. Dublin, Ireland (1989)

Butler, *Gender Trouble. Feminism and the Subversion of Identity.* (New York and London: Routledge, 1990)

J. Bynner and K. Roberts (eds) *Youth and Work: Transition to Employment in England and Germany* (London: Anglo-German Foundation, 1991)

M. Cain, *Growing up Good: Policing the Behaviour of Girls in Europe* (London and California: Sage, 1989)

A. Campbell, *The Girls in the Gang: a Report from New York City* (Oxford: Blackwells, 1984)

B. Campbell, *Wigan Pier Re-Visited* (London: Virago, 1984)

P. Carlen, *A Political Criminology of Youth Homelessness* (Buckingham: Open University Press, Taylor and Francis, 1996)

E.E. Cashmore, *Rastaman* (London: Allen and Unwin, 1987)

N. Chakarov (ed.) *History of Education and Educational Ideas in Bulgaria*, vol. I (Sofia: Public Education Press, 1975).

I. Chambers, *Urban Rhythms. Pop Music and Popular Culture* (London: Macmillan, 1985)

L. Chisholm and J.M. Bergeret, *Young People in the European Community: towards an agenda for research and policy* (Commission of the European Community. Youth Task Force Report, 1991)

L. Chisholm, P. Büchner, H-H. Krüger and M. du Bois-Reymond (eds) (1995) *Growing Up in Europe. Contemporary Horizons in Childhood and Youth Studies* (Berlin and New York: Walter de Gruyter)

F. Churenev, 'Social Setting and Religious Transmission in the Rhodopi', *Proceedings of the Museums of Southern Bulgaria*, vol. 10 (Plovdiv, 1984) pp. 209–16

J. Clark (ed.) *James S. Coleman* (London, Washington: Falmer Press, 1996)

R. Cochrane and M. Bilig, 'Youth Politics in the Eighties' *Youth and Policy* 2 (1982) pp. 31–4

C. Cockburn, *Two Track Training. Sex Inequalities and the YTS* (London: Macmillan, 1987)

F. Coffield, C. Borrill and S. Marshall, *Growing up at the Margins* (Milton Keynes: Open University Press, 1986)

P. Cohen, *Rethinking the Youth Question. Education, Labour and Cultural Studies* (London: Macmillan, (1997)

S. Cohen, *Folk Devils and Moral Panics. The Creation of Mods and Rockers* (London: MacGibbon and Kee, 1972)

J.C. Coleman and L.B. Hendry, *The Nature of Adolescence* (London and New York: Methuen, 1990)

J.C. Coleman and C. Warren-Adamson, *Youth Policy in the 1990s. The Way Forward* (London: Routledge, 1992)

J.S. Coleman, *The Adolescent Society* (Glencoe IL: The Free Press, 1961)

J.S. Coleman, *Foundations of Social Theory* (Cambridge Mass, London: Harvard University Press, 1990)

J.S. Coleman and T. Husen, *Becoming and Adult in a Changing Society* (Paris: OECD, 1985)

B. Coles, *Youth and Social Policy. Youth, Citizenship and Young Careers* (London: UCL Press, 1995)

R.W. Connell, *Which Way Is Up? Essays on Class, Sex and Culture* (Allen and Unwin, 1983)

H. Corr, L. Jamieson, and N. Tomes, 'Parents and Talking Politics' ESRC 16–19 Initiative Occasional Papers No. 29. SSRU, City University, London, 1990

P. Corrigan, *Schooling the Smash Street Kids* (London: Macmillan, 1979)

C. Corrin (ed.) *Superwomen and the Double Burden* (London: Scarlet Press, 1992)

J. Cote and A.L. Allahar, *Generation on Hold. Coming of Age in the Late Twentieth Century* (New York: New York Free Press, 1996)

A. Cranston, *A Study of Active Employment Policy in Czechoslovakia* (Study commissioned by the Ministry of Labour and Social Policy, Czech Republic, 1992)

G. Csepeli and A. Orkeny, *Ideology and Political Beliefs in Hungary* (London and New York: Pinter Publishers, 1992)

CYRCE (ed.) *The Puzzle of Integration. European Yearbook on Youth Policy and Research* Vol. 1 (Berlin and New York: Walter de Gruyter, 1995)

D. Dahlerup, *Unfinished Democracy*. Paper to the UNESCO conference Culture and Democracy, Prague, 4–6 September 1991

D. Damm, 'Freizeit – ein Hauch von Freiheit' in W. Gaiser et al. *Immer Diese Jugend!* (Muenchen: Koesel-Verlag, 1985)

R. Daskalov, *Essays about Totalitarianism and Post-Totalitarianism* (Sofia: St Kliment Ohridski Sofia University Press, 1991)

L. Davidoff, L'Esperance and H. Newby 'Landscape with Figures: Home and Community in English Society' in J. Mitchell and A. Oakley (eds) *The Rights and Wrongs of Women* (Harmondsworth: Penguin, 1976)

B. Davies, *Threatening Youth. Towards a National Youth Policy* (Milton Keynes: Open University Press, 1986)

D. Davin, 'Population policy and Reform: the Soviet Union, Eastern Europe and China' in S. Rai, H. Pilkington and A. Phizacklea (eds) *Women in the Face of Change* (London: Routledge, 1992)

R. Deem, *Women and Schooling* (London: Routledge and Kegan Paul, 1978)

R. Deem (ed.) *Schooling for Women's Work* (London: Routledge and Kegan Paul, 1980)

K. Delyannis-Kouimtzi and R. Ziogou, 'Gendered Youth Transitions in Northern Greece: between Tradition and Modernity through Education' in L. Chisholm et al. *Growing Up in Europe* (Berlin and New York: Walter de Gruyter, 1995)

M. Demcak, 'Social and Psychological Self-Aid Sources of Temporary Unemployed Youth' in L. Machacek *Youth and State CSFR* (Slovak Academy of Sciences, Bratislava, 1991)

M. Dennis, 'Youth in the German Democratic Republic' in E. Kolinsky (ed.) *Youth in East and West Germany* (University of Aston: Modern German Studies, 1985)

Department of Environment, *Single and Homeless* (London: HMSO, 1981)

E. Dimitrieva, 'Orientations, Re-orientations and Dis-orientations? Expectations of the future among Russian school leavers' in H. Pilkington (ed.) *Gender, Generation and Identity in Contemporary Russia* (London and New York: Routledge, 1996)

G. Dimitrov, *Conscious Being as a Problem of the Empirical Sociology* (Sofia: St Kliment Ohridski University Press, 1991)

G. Dimitrov, *Bulgaria in the Orbit of Modernization.* (Sofia: Sofia University St Kliment Ohridski Press, 1995)

K. Dimitrov (ed.) *Socio-Class Structure of Contemporary Bulgarian Society* (Sofia: Science and Arts, 1986)

R. Dimitrov, 'The New Generations and the Old Institutions', *Philosophical Thought*, vol. 1: 3–12 (Sofia, 1989)

R. Dimitrov, *Nomenculturata* (Sofia: St. Kliment Ohridski University Press, 1991)

M. Dinkova, Z. Serafimova, M. Beltcheva, A. Kutev, L. Zagorova, D. Kjulanov and M. Popova, 'Children in Particularly Difficult Circumstances', *Youth and Society*, vol. 2: 65–160 (Sofia: Institute of Youth Studies, 1991)

J. Donald and A. Rattansi (eds) *'Race' Culture and Difference* (London, California and New Delhi: Sage, 1992)

C. Dyhouse, *Girls Growing Up in Victorian and Edwardian England* (London: Routledge and Kegan Paul, 1981)

P. Easton, 'The Rock Music Community' in J. Riordan (ed.) *Soviet Youth Culture* (Bloomington and Indiana: Indiana University Press, 1989)

B. Einhorn, *Cinderella Goes to Market* (1993)

S.N. Eisenstadt, 'From Generation to Generation' (1956) reprinted in H. Silverstein (ed.) The *Sociology of Youth: Evolution and Revolution* (New York: Macmillan, 1973)

N. Elias (1976) *Über den Prozeß der Zivilation. Soziogenetische un psychogenetische Untersuchung.* Bd. 2.: Wandlungen der Gesellschaft. Entwurf zu einer Theorie der Zivilisation (Frankfurt/Main)

E.H. Erikson, *Identity, Youth and Crisis* (New York: Norton, 1968)

K. Evans and W. Heinz, *Youth, Identity and Transition* (London: Anglo-German Foundation, 1994)

EUROSTAT (1992) *Basic Statistics of the Community*, Luxembourg

EUROSTAT (1993a) *Basic Statistics of the Community*, Luxembourg

EUROSTAT (1993b) *Europe in Figures*, Luxembourg

EUROSTAT (1995) *Basic Statistics of the Community*, Luxembourg

EUROSTAT (1997) *Economic Statistics of the European Community* 6/97

D. Fabian, 'Programmes of Unemployed Youth Participation' in L. Mechacek (ed.) *Youth and State, CSFR* (Slovak Academy of Sciences, Bratislava, 1991)

L. Fagin and M. Little, *Forsaken Families* (Harmondsworth: Penguin, 1984)

M. Featherstone, *Consumer Culture and Postmodernism* (London, California and New Delhi: Sage, 1991)

Z. Ferge in Deacon, B. and J. Szalai (eds) *Social Policy in the New Eastern Europe* (Aldershot: Avebury, 1990)

J. Finch, *Family Obligations and Social Change* (Cambridge: Polity Press, 1989)

D. Finn, *Training without Jobs. New Deals and Broken Promises* (London: Macmillan, 1987)

R. Flynn, 'Quasi-welfare, Associationalism and the Social Division of Citizenship', *Citizenship Studies* 1 (3) (forthcoming)

J. Fornäs and G. Bolin (eds) (1995) *Youth Culture in Late Modernity* (California, London, New Delhi: Sage)

M. Foucault, *Discipline and Punish* (Harmondsworth: Penguin, 1975)

S. Frith, *The Sociology of Rock* (London: Cassell, 1978)

M. Fuller, 'Black Girls in a London Comprehensive School' in R. Deem (ed.) *Schooling for Women's Work* (London: Routledge and Kegan Paul, 1980)

A. Furlong and F. Cartmel, *Young People and Social Change. Individualization and Risk in Late Modernity* (Buckingham: Open University Press, 1997)

W. Gaiser and H-U. Müller, 'Wohnungsmarkt – Engpässe für junge Nachfrager' in W. Gaiser et al. *Immer Diese Jugend!* (München: Koesel Verlag, 1985)

W. Gaiser and R. Munchmeier 'Problems, Perspectives and Projects in Youth Services in Germany', *Youth and Policy*, 44, pp. 48–61 (1994)

E. Gellner, *Nations and Nationalism* (Ithace New York: Cornell University Press, 1983)

E. Gellner, *Encounters with Nationalism* (Oxford: Blackwells, 1994)

E. Gellner, *Postmoderism, Reason and Religion* (Chicago: Kazi Publications, 1996)

P. Georgiev, 'The Young Person of Gypsy Origin', In P-E. Mitev, *Youth Studies. Theory, Methodology, Practice* (Sofia: People's Youth Press, 1978)

Z. Georgiev and S. Zhelev, 'Privatization through the Lens of Mass Consciousness', part II, *24 Hours*, July 1st, Sofia (1992)

A. Giddens, *Capitalism and Modern Social Theory* (Cambridge: Cambridge University Press, 1971)

A. Giddens, *Modernity and Self-Identity* (Cambridge: Polity Press, 1991)

J.R. Gillis, *Youth and History. Tradition and Change in Age Relations 1770–present* (New York: Academic Press, 1981)

B. Gjoshev and B. Ruchkin (eds) *Komsomol Building*, part I (Sofia: People Youth's Press, 1985)

D. Gleeson, *TVEI and Secondary Education: a Critical Appraisal* (Milton Keynes: Open University Press, 1987)

S. Gomulka and A. Polonski (eds) *Polish Paradoxes* (London and New York: Routledge, 1990)

D. Gorham, *The Victorian Girl and the Feminine Ideal* (London: Croom Helm, 1982)

K. Gospodinov, 'Introduction to Juventology', *Proceedings*, pp. 85–110 (Sofia: Institute of Youth Studies, 1981)

M. Grekova, *From Custom to Law. Bulgarian Man in the Spheres of Strangeness* (Sofia: Sofia University St. Kliment Ohridski Press, 1991)

C. Griffin, *Typical Girls?* (London: Routledge and Kegan Paul, 1985)

C. Griffin, *Representations of Youth. The Study of Youth and Adolescence in Britain and America* (Cambridge: Polity, 1993)

J. Habermas, *Toward a Rational Society* (Cambridge: Polity Press, 1969)

C. Haerpfer, 'Postmoderne Demokratie in Österreich. Die Zukunft des politischen Systems und des Partiensystems', in Vranitsky, F. (ed.) *Themen der Zeit* (Wien: Passagen Verlag, 1994)

J. Hajnal, 'European Marriage Patterns in Perspective', in D.V. Glass and D.V.C. Eversley (eds) *Population in History* (London: 1965)

S. Hall and T. Jefferson (eds) *Resistance Through Ritual* (London: Hutchinson, 1976)

A.H. Halsey et al. *British Social Trends since 1900. A Guide to the Changing Social Structure of Britain* (London: Macmillan, 1988)

Halson, 'Young Women, Sexual Harassment and Heterosexuality: Violence, Power Relations and Mixed-Sex Schooling' in Abbott, P. and Wallace, C. *Gender, Power and Sexuality* (London: Macmillan, 1991)

A. Harchev and M. Mazkovskij, *The Contemporary Family and Its Problems* (Moscow: Statistics, 1978)

J. Hartmann, *Youth in the Welfare Society* (Department of Sociology, University of Uppsala, Sweden, 1985)

J. Hartmann, 'The Impact of New Technologies on Youth–Parent Relations in Contemporary Societies: the Trend for Individualisation' Paper presented at the CFR/CYR International Seminar Young People and their Families, Freising, Munich 1987

D. Harvey, *The Condition of Postmodernity* (Oxford: Blackwells, 1989)

V. Hasko, 'Youth Unemployment Programmes' in L. Machacek, *Youth and State CSFR* (Slovak Academy of Sciences, Bratislava, 1991)

H. Havelkova, 'A Few Prefeminist Thoughts' in N. Funk and M. Mueller (eds) *Gender, Politics and Post-Communism* (London and New York: Routledge, 1993)

P.C.L. Heaven, *Contemporary Adolescence. A Social Psychological Approach* (Australia: Macmillan, 1994)

D. Hebdidge, *Subculture: the Meaning of Style* (London: Methuen, 1979)

D. Hebdidge, *Hiding in the Light. On Images and Things* (London: Routledge, 1988)

W. Heinz (ed.) *The Life Course and Social Change: Comparative Perspectives* (Wienheim: Deutscher Studien Verlag, 1991)

P. Hockenos, *Free to Hate. The Rise of the Right in Post-Communist Eastern Europe* (London: Routledge, 1993)

U. Hoffman-Lange and C. Eilders, 'Die Rechtradicale Potential under Jugendlichen in der Bundesrepublic', *Diskurs* 0/90: 24–30, 1990

R. Hoggart, *The Uses of Literacy* (Harmondsworth: Penguin, 1958)

R. Hollands, *The Long Transition: Class, Culture and Youth Training* (London: Macmillan, 1990)

B. Hudson, 'Feminity and Adolescence' in McRobbie, A. and Nava, M. (eds) *Gender and Generation* (London: Macmillan, 1984)

S. Humphries, *Hooligans or Rebels? An Oral History of Working Class Childhood and Youth 1889–1939* (Oxford: Blackwells, 1981)

K. Hurrelmann (ed.) *International Handbook of Adolescence* (Westport Connecticut, London: Greenwood Press, 1994)

S. Hutson and R. Jenkins, *Taking the Strain. Families, Unemployment and the Transition to Adulthood* (Milton Keynes: Open University Press, 1989)

S. Hutson and M. Liddiard, *Youth Homelessness: the Construction of a Social Issue* (London: Macmillan, 1994)

I. Ilynsky, 'Trends in the Development of Soviet Youth' in J. Riordan (ed.) *Soviet Social Reality in the Mirror of Glasnost* (London and Basingstoke: St. Martins Press, 1992)

U. Imam, T. Khan, H. Lashley and A. Montgomery, 'Black Perspectives on Young People and Youth Work', *Youth and Policy*, 49 editors of Special Edition: 1–91, 1995

R. Inglehart, *Culture Shift in Advanced Industrial Societies* (Princeton: Princeton University Press, 1990)

R. Inglehart, *Modernization and Postmodernization. Cultural, Economic and Political Change in 43 Societies* (Princeton: Princeton University Press, 1997)

S. Irwin, *Rights of Passage. Social Change and Transition from Youth to Adulthood* (London: UCL Press, 1995)

A. Ivanov, 'Principles for Dealing with Komsomol Cadres', in K. Kitanov (ed.) *The Komsomol Cadres* (Sofia: People's Youth Press, 1981)

F. Jameson, *Postmodernism and the Cultural Logic of Late Capitalism* (London: Verso, 1991)

S. Jeffreys, *The Spinster and Her Enemies. Feminism and Sexuality 1880–1930* (London: Pandora Press, 1985)

T. Jeffs and M. Smith (eds) *Youth Work* (London: Macmillan, 1987)

T. Jeffs and M. Smith, *Young People, Inequality and Youth Work* (London: Macmillan, 1990)

T. Jeffs and M. Smith, 'Young People, Youth Work and the New Authoritarianism', *Youth and Policy* 46: 17–32 (1994)

T. Jeffs and M. Smith, 'Getting the Dirtbags off the Streets. Curfews and other Solutions to Juvenile Crime', *Youth and Policy* 53:1–14 (1996)

R. Jenkins, *Lads, Citizens and Ordinary Kids. Working Class Youth Life-*

Styles in Belfast (London: Routledge and Kegan Paul, 1983)

R. Jenkins and B. Troyna, 'Educational Myths, Labour Market Realities' in B. Troyna and D. Smith (eds) *Racism, Schools and the Labour Market* (Leicester: National Youth Bureau, 1983)

P. Jephcott, *Time of One's Own. Leisure and Young People* (Edinburgh: Oliver and Boyd, 1967)

L. Johnson, *The Modern Girl: Girlhood and Growing up* (Buckingham and Philadelphia: Open University Press, 1993)

R. Johnson, 'Notes on the Schooling of the English Working Class, 1780–1850' in R. Dale, G. Esland and M. MacDonald *Schooling and Capitalism*. Open University Reader (London: Routledge and Kegan Paul, 1976)

G. Jones, 'Young Workers in the Class Structure', *Work, Employment and Society* 1 (4)(1987a), pp. 487–508

G. Jones, 'Leaving the Parental Home: an Analysis of Early Housing Careers', *Journal of Social Policy* 16 (1), 49–74, (1987b)

G. Jones, 'The Cost of Living in the Parental Home', *Youth and Policy* 32, (1990) 19–29

G. Jones, 'Short term reciprocity in parent–child economic exchange', in C. Marsh and S. Arber (eds) *Household and Family: Divisions and Change* (London: Macmillan, 1992)

G. Jones, *Leaving Home* (Buckingham: Open University Press, 1995)

G. Jones and C. Wallace, 'Beyond Individualisation: What Sort of Social Change?', in L. Chisholm, P. Büchner, H-H. Krüger and P. Brown (eds) *Childhood, Youth and Social Change. A Comparative Perspective* (London and New York: Falmer, 1990)

G. Jones and C. Wallace, *Youth, Family and Citizenship* (Basingstoke: Open University Press, 1992)

S. Jones, *Black Culture, White Youth. The Reggae Tradition from JA to UK* (London: Macmillan, 1988)

B. Jung, 'Changing Patterns of Leisure and Consumption in Poland', Warsaw School of Economics, mimeo, 1994

P.H. Juviler, 'No End of a Problem: perestroika for the family' in A. Jones, W.D. Connor and D.E. Powell, *Soviet Social Problems* (Boulder Colorado: Westview Press, 1992)

A. Kabátek, 'The Youth – A Social Factor in Revolutionary Changes in Czechoslovakia', in L. Machacek (ed.) *Sociology of Youth CSFR* Slovak Academy of Sciences, Bratislava, 1990

L. Karavelov, 'About Female (Women's) Education', *Knowledge*, year II, vol. 2–3 (1876)

K. Keniston, 'Youth – a "New" Stage in Life', *The American Scholar* Vol. 39 (4): 631–54 (1970)

P. Kenkmann, 'Changes in the Conceptual Bases of Studying Youth's Development in Soviet Sociology', unpublished paper, no date

J. Kett, *Adolescence in America. 1770-present* (New York: Basic Books, 1977)

I. Khadzijski, *Optimistic Theory about Our People* (Sofia: Bulgarian Writer's Press, 1974)

T. Khinova, 'Problems of the Development of the Socialist Punitive Legislation Dealing with Criminal and Anti-Social Behaviour of Minors', in L. Vassilev (ed.) *The Role of Socialist Legislation in the Twenty Five Years of Socialist Construction in the People's Republic of Bulgaria* (Sofia: Bulgarian Academy of Sciences, 1969)

K. Kitanov (ed.) *The Komsomol Cadres* (Sofia: People's Youth Press, 1981)

D. Kjulanov, P. Balkanski, L. Zagorova, and M. Popova, 'Children in a Time of Crisis: A Crisis of Childhood', *Youth and Society*, vol. 2: 9–60 (Sofia: Institute of Youth Studies, 1991)

C. Kjuranov (ed.) *The Bulgarian Family of Today* (Sofia: Science and Arts, 1987)

H. Klein, 'Adolescence, Youth and Young Adulthood', *Youth and Society* vol. 21 (4) : 446–71 (1990)

H.W. Koch, *The Hitler Youth. Origins and Development 1922–1944* (London: MacDonald and James, 1975)

V. Koditz, 'The German Federal Republic: How the State Copes with Crisis – a Guide through the Tangle of Schemes' in R. Fiddy, *Youth Unemployment and Training. A Collection of National Perspectives* (Lewes: Falmer, 1985)

L. Koklyagina, 'Urban Youth: A Sociological View' in J. Riordan (ed.) *Soviet Social Reality in the Mirror of Glasnost* (London: St. Martins Press, 1992)

E. Kosha, 'The Characteristics of the Young Family in Hungary', *Youth Problems*, vol. 43 (Sofia: Institute of Youth Studies, 1985)

S. Kovatcheva, 'Student Political Culture in Transition: the Case of Bulgaria' in CYRCE (ed.) The *Puzzle of Integration. European Yearbook on Youth Policy and Research* Vol. 1 (Berlin and New York: Walter de Gruyter, 1995)

S. Kovacheva and C. Wallace, 'Why Do Youth Revolt?', *Youth and Policy* 44:7–20 (1994)

M. Kozakevitch, 'Spontaneous Youth Groups', *Youth problems (Russian)*, vol. 47: 125–7 (Sofia, 1985)

H. Krüger, 'Gesellschaft also Strukturkategorie im Bildungssystem: alter und neue Konturen geschlechtspezifischer Diskrimminierung', *Arbeitskries Sozialwissenschaftliche Arbeitsmarktforschung* (Paderborn: SAMF, 1989)

H. Krüger, 'The Shifting Sands of the Social Contract: young people in the transition from school to work', in L. Chisholm, L. Büchner, H-H. Krüger and P. Brown (eds) *Childhood Youth and Social Change: a comparative perspective* (London and New York: Falmer, 1990)

Kumar, *From Post-Industrial to Post-Modern Society* (Oxford: Blackwells, 1995)

A. Kurzynowski, *Social Changes in Poland in the years 1944–1990: selected problems* (Warsaw: Warsaw School of Economics, 1990)

A. Kutev, *Professional Training – A Way to Effective Realization* (Sofia: People's Youth Press, 1983)

D. Laing, *One Chord Wonders. Popular Music in Britain* (Milton Keynes: Open University Press, 1985)

D. Langazova, 'Young People as Parents', in M. Dinkova (ed.) *The Young Family* (Sofia: People's Youth Press, 1985)

S. Lash and J. Urry, *The End of Organised Capitalism* (Oxford: Polity Press, 1987)

S. Lash and J. Urry, *Economies of Signs and Space* (California, London and New Delhi: Sage 1994)

S. Lash, *The Sociology of Post-Modernism* (London: Routledge, 1990)

C. Leccardi, 'Growing up in Southern Italy: between Tradition and Modernity', in L. Chisholm et al. *Growing Up in Europe* (Berlin and New York: Walter de Gruyter, 1995)

J. Le Grand and W. Bartlett, Quasi-Markets and Social Policy (London: Macmillan, 1993)

D. Lee, D. Marsden, P. Rickman and J. Duncombe, *Scheming for Youth. A Study of YTS and the Enterprise Culture* (Milton Keynes: Open University Press, 1990)

S. Lees, *Losing Out. Sexuality and Adolescent Girls* (London: Hutchinson, 1986)

M. Leichty, 'Media, markets and modernization: youth identities and the experience of modernity in Kathmandu, Nepal', in V. Amit-Talai and H. Wulff (eds) *Youth Cultures. A Cross-Cultural Perspective* (London and New York: Routledge, 1995)

D. Leonard, *Sex and Generation: a Study of Courtship and Weddings* (London: Tavistock, 1980)

R. Lindner, 'Jugendkultur', in W. Gaiser et al. *Immer Diese Jugend!* (Muenchen: Koesel-Verlag, 1985)

D.S. Linton, *Who Has Youth Has a Future* (Cambridge: Cambridge University Press, 1991)

V. Lisovskij, 'Spontaneous Youth Groups', *Youth Problems (Russian)*, vol. 47: 82–90 (Sofia, 1985)

C. Lury, *Consumer Culture* (Cambridge: Polity Press, 1996)

J. Lyotard, *The Postmodern Condition: a Report on Knowledge* (Minneapolis: University of Minnesota Press, 1984)

M. Mac an Ghaill, *The Making of Men: Masculinities, Sexuality and Schooling* (Buckingham: Open University Press, 1994)

L. Machacek, *State and Youth in CSFR* (Slovak Academy of Sciences, Bratislava, 1991)

M. Malysheva, 'Some Thoughts on the Soviet Family' in J. Riordan (ed.) *Soviet Social Reality in the Mirror of Glasnost* (Basingstoke and London: St. Martin's Press, 1992)

K. Mannheim, 'The problem of generations', in P. Kecskemeti (ed. and trans) *Essays on the Sociology of Knowledge* (London, 1952, first published, 1927)

H. Marcuse, *One-Dimensional Man* (London: Sage, 1968)

D. Marsland, *Education and Youth* (Lewes: Falmer, 1987)

D. Marsland, *Understanding Youth. Issues and Methods in Social Education* (St Albans: Claridge Press, 1993)

B. Martin, *The Sociology of Contemporary Cultural Change* (Oxford: Blackwells, 1983)

M. Marody, 'The Political Attitudes of Polish Society in the Period of Systematic Transitions', *Praxis International*, vol. II, #2, July, 1991

P. Mateju, 'Early effects on educational attainment in Czechoslovakia, Netherlands and Hungary', in J.L. Peschar (ed.) *Social Reproduction in Eastern and Western Europe* (Department of Sociology, University of Groningen, 1990)

P. Mateju, 'Determinants of Economic Success in the First Stage of the Post-communist Transformation in the Czech Republic 1989–1992' (Working Paper, Institute of Sociology, Prague, 1993)

P. Mateju and B. Rehakova, 'Revolution for Whom? Analysis of Selected Patterns of Inter-generational Mobility in the Czech Republic, 1989–1992' (Working Paper, Institute of Sociology, Prague, 1993)

C. Mayer, H. Krüger, U. Rabe-Kleberg and U. Schütte (eds) *Mädchen und Frauen. Beruf und Biographie* (München: DJI Materialen-verlag, 1983)

M. Mazkovskij, 'Man's Role in the Family Today', in M. Minkov, *The Family and Socio-Demographic Development* (Sofia: BAN, 1982)

A. McRobbie and J. Garber, 'Girls and Subcultures: an Exploration', in S. Hall and T. Jefferson *Resistance Through Ritual* (London: Hutchinson, 1976)

A. McRobbie, 'Working Class Youth Subcultures and the Culture of Feminity', in Women's Studies Group, Centre for Contemporary Cultural Studies, *Women Take Issue* (London: Hutchinson, 1978)

A. McRobbie, *Feminism and Youth Culture* (London: Macmillan, 1991)

M. Mead, *The Coming of Age in Samoa: a Study of Adolescence and Sex in Primitive Society* (Harmondsworth: Penguin, 1943)

U. Meier, B. Schmid and G. Winzen, 'Junge Frauen in Ost und West. Emanzipation im Spannungsfeld von Beruf und Familie', *Diskurs* 2/91 pp. 33–9 (1992)

N. Mejnert, 'As Rock Wills', *Sociological Studies*, vol. 4: 88–93 (Moscow, 1987)

S. Mestrovic, *The Balkanisation of the West. Confluence of Postmodernism and Postcommunism* (London: Routledge, 1994)

C. Michajlov, 'The Beginning of Revolutionary Changes', *Social Work*, vol. 8: 8–9 (Sofia, 1984)

S. Michajlov, *The Optimal Functioning of Social Governance* (Sofia: Party Press, 1986)

D. Mitchev (ed.) *History of Youth Revolutionary Movement in Bulgaria* (Sofia: People's Youth Press, 1987)

P-E. Mitev, *Youth and the Book* (Sofia: People's Youth Press, 1979)

P-E. Mitev, 'Sociology Facing Youth Problems', *Youth Problems* (Russian) vol. 34: 90–93, pp. 1–274 (Sofia, 1982)

P-E. Mitev, 'Youth Groups Formed Spontaneously', *Express Information*, 12: 3–33 (Sofia, 1984)

P-E. Mitev (ed.) *Youth – Problems and Studies* (Sofia: People's Youth Press, 1985a)

P-E. Mitev, 'Spontaneous Youth Groups', *Youth Problems*, vol. 47 (Sofia, 1985b)

P-E. Mitev, *Youth and Social Change* (Sofia: People's Youth Press, 1988)

P-E Mitev (ed.) *Bulgarian Youth under the Conditions of Transition.* (Committee on Youth and Children in the Council of Ministers, Sofia, 1996)

M. Mitterauer, *Socialgeschichte der Jugend* (Frankfurt: Suhrkamp-verlag, 1986) English version A *History of Youth* (Oxford: Blackwells, 1992)

P. Molnár, 'Youth and Socio-Cultural Changes', Paper presented at the Conference 'Social Responses to Political and Economic Transformation in East-Central Europe' CEU, Prague (1992)

D. Moore, *The Lads in Action. Social Process in Urban Youth Culture* (Aldershot: Arena, 1994)

L. Morely, 'Empowerment and the New Right. Culture of Change' *Youth and Policy* 51:1–10 (1995)

I. Mozny, 'The Czech Family in the Transition from Social to Economic Capital', in S. Ringen and C. Wallace (eds) *Social Reform in the Czech Republic. Prague Papers in Social Transition Volume 11* (Prague: Central European University, 1994)

M. Mueller and N. Funk (eds) *Gender Politics and Post-Communism* (New York: Routledge, 1993)

W. Müller and W. Karle, 'Social Selection in Educational Systems in Europe', *European Sociological Review* Vol 9 (1) : 1–20 (1993)

J. Muncie, *The Trouble with Kids Today. Youth, Crime and Post-War Britain* (London: Hutchinson, 1984)

G. Mungham and G. Pearson (eds) *Working Class Youth Culture* (London: Routledge and Kegan Paul, 1976)

M. Murdock and R. McCron, 'Youth and Class: the Career of a Confusion', in G. Mungham and G. Pearson (eds) *Working Class Youth Cultures* (London: Routledge and Kegan Paul, 1976)

C. Murray, *Losing Ground: American Social Policy 1950–1980* (New York: Basic Books, 1986)

C. Murray, *The Emerging British Underclass* (London: Institute of Economic Affairs, 1990)

F. Musgrove, *Youth and the Social Order* (London: Routledge and Kegan Paul, 1964)

M. Nava, 'Young Women and the Youth Service' in A. McRobbie and M. Nava (eds) *Gender and Generation* (London: Macmillan, 1984)

M. Nava, *Changing Cultures. Feminism, Youth and Consumerism* (London and Beverley Hills: Sage, 1992)

H.M. Nickel 'Frauen in der DDR' Aus Politik und Zeitgeschechte, Beilage zur Wochenzeitung das Parlament B-16-17 13th April 1990

M. O'Donnel, *Age and Generation* (London: Tavistock, 1985)

G. Okeanov-Dimitrov, 'Are the "Alternative Groups" Alternative?', *Youth and Society*, vol. 7/8: 16–29 (Sofia: 1989)

T. Olk, 'Gesellschafttheoretische Ansaetze in der Jugendforschung' in H.H. Krueger (ed.) *Handbuch der Jugendforshung* (Opladen: Leske and Budrich, 1988)

V. Ovchinskij, 'Criminal Behaviour in Youth Settings', *Sociological Studies*, vol. 4:85–8 (Moscow, 1987)

J.M. Pais, 'Growing Up on the EU-Periphery: Portugal', in L. Chisholm *et al.*, *Growing Up in Europe* (New York and Berlin: Walter de Gruyter, 1995)

H. Parker, 'Boys will be Men: Brief Adolescence in a Down Town Neighbourhood', in G. Mungham and G. Pearson (eds.) *Working Class Youth Cultures* (London: Routledge and Kegan Paul, 1976)

T. Parsons and R.F. Bales, *Family: Socialization and Interaction Processes* (London: Routledge and Kegan Paul, 1956)

T. Parsons, 'Youth in the Context of American Society', in H. Silverstein (ed.) *The Sociology of Youth: Evolution and Revolution* (New York: Macmillan, 1973)

J. Pataki, 'Hungarian Youth Party Comes of Age', *RFE/RL Research Report* 2 (21) pp. 42–5 (1993)

S. Pateva, 'The Leisure Time of Student Youth', *Proceedings*: 73–126 (Sofia: Institute for Youth Studies, 1982)

F. Pavelka and M. Stefanov, *Rural Youth Yesterday, Today, Tomorrow* (Sofia: Institute of Youth Studies, 1985)

G. Pearson, *Hooligans. A History of Respectable Fears* (London: Macmillan, 1983)

A. Peneva, 'Problems of the Formation and Social Realization of the Komsomol Worker', *Proceedings*: 127–50 (Sofia: Institute of Youth Studies, 1982)

S. Penna and M. O'Brien, 'Postmodernism and social policy: a small step forwards?', *Journal of Social Policy* 25 (1): 39–61

J.L. Peschar, *Social Reproduction in Eastern and Western Europe* (University of Groningen, Department of Sociology, 1990)

A. Phoenix, *Young Mothers?* (Cambridge: Polity, 1991)

J. Pilcher, *Age and Generation in Modern Britain* (Oxford: Oxford University Press, 1995)

H. Pilkington, 'Whose Space is it Anyway? Youth, Gender and Civil Society in the Soviet Union', in S. Rai, H. Pilkington and A. Phizaklea (eds) *Women in the Face of Change* (London: Routledge, 1992a)

H. Pilkington, 'Going out in Style: Girls in Youth Cultural Activity', in M. Buckley (ed.) *Perestroika and Soviet Women* (Cambridge: Cambridge University Press, 1992b)

H. Pilkingon, *Russia's Youth and its Culture. A Nation's Constructors and Constructed* (London and New York: Routledge, 1994)

H. Pilkington (ed.) *Gender, Generation and Identity in Contemporary Russia* (London and New York: Routledge, 1996)

J. Planas, 'The Transition from School to Work in Spain', in P. Grootings and M. Stefanov *Transition from School to Work* (Sofia: Institute of Youth Studies, 1985)

B. Polster (Hg.) *Swing Heil. Jazz im Nationalsozialismus* (Berlin: Transit, 1989)

N. Postman, *The Disappearance of Childhood* (London: Allen and Unwin, 1983)

M. Presdee, 'Creating Poverty and Creating Crime: Australian Youth Policies in the Eighties', in C. Wallace and M. Cross, *Youth in Transition: the Sociology of Youth and Youth Policy* (Lewes: Falmer Press, 1990)

U. Preuss-Lausitz, *Kriegskinder, Konsumskinder, Krisenkinder* (Weinheim und Basel: Beltz, 1983)

K. Pryce, *Endless Pressure* (Harmondsworth: Penguin, 1979)

L. Radulov (ed.) *Public Funds and Youth Needs* (Sofia: Committee on Youth and Sports, 1973)

D. Raffe (ed.) *Education and Youth Labour Markets* (Lewes: Falmer, 1988)

A. Raychev, *The Young Personality and the 'Little Justice'* (Sofia: People's Youth Press, 1985)

A. Raychev, 'Instead of Ten Words', *Youth and Society* vol. 7/8: 3–5 (Sofia, 1989)

S. Redhead, *The End of the Century Party. Youth and Pop towards 2000* (Manchester and New York: Manchester University Press, 1990)

S. Redhead (ed.) *Rave Off. Politics and Deviance in Contemporary Youth Culture* (Aldershot: Avebury, 1993)

T.L. Rees and G. Rees, 'Juvenile Employment and the State between the Wars', in T.L. Rees and P. Atkinson (eds) *Youth Unemployment and State Intervention* (London: Routledge and Kegan Paul, 1982)

F. F. Ridley, 'View from a Disaster Area: Unemployed Youth in Merseyside', *Political Quarterly* 52 (1981), pp. 16–27

J. Riordan, 'The Komsomol', in J. Riordan (ed.) *Soviet Youth Culture* (Bloomington and Indiana: Indiana University Press, 1989a)

J. Riordan, 'Teenage Gangs, 'Afgantsy' and Neofascists', in J. Riordan (ed.), *Soviet Youth Culture* (Bloomington and Indiana: Indiana University Press, 1989b)

K. Roberts and G. Parsell, 'The Political Orientations, Interests and Activities of Britain's 16–18 Year Olds in the Late 1980s', ESRC Initiative Occasional Papers No. 26, SSRU, City University, London (1990)

K. Roberts, R. Campbell and A. Furlong, 'Class and Gender Divisions amongst Young Adults at Leisure', in C. Wallace and M. Cross *Youth in Transition* (Lewes: Falmer, 1990)

K. Roberts, G. Duggan and M. Noble, 'Youth Unemployment: an Old Problem or a New Lifestyle?', *Leisure Studies* 1 (2) pp. 71–182 (1982)

K. Roberts, *School Leavers and their Prospects. Youth and the Labour Market in the 1980s* (Milton Keynes: Open University Press, 1984)

K. Roberts, *Youth and Employment in Modern Britain* (Oxford: Oxford University Press, 1995)

K. Roberts and B. Jung with S. Clark, A. Kurzynowski, T. Szumlicz and C. Wallace, *Poland's First Post-Communist Generation* (Avebury: Gower, 1995)

J. Roche and S. Tucker (eds.) *Youth in Society* (California, London, New Delhi: Sage, 1997)

J. Roll, *Young People at the Crossroads. Education, Jobs, Social Security and Training* (London: Family Policy Studies Centre, 1988)

J. Roll, *Young People. Growing up in the Welfare State* Occasional Paper no. 10 (London: Family Policy Studies Centre, 1990)

C. Rootes, 'Student Radicalism. The Politics of Moral Protest and Legitimation Problems of the Modern Capitalist State', *Theory and Society* 9 pp. 473–502 (1980)

C. Rootes, 'Student Movements in Advanced Capitalist Societies', *Associations Transnationales* 4 (1990)

R. Rose, *What is Europe?* (New York: Harper Collins, 1996)

R. Rose and G. Wignanek, *Training without Trainers?* (London: Anglo-German Foundation, 1990)

R. Rose and E. Carnaghan, 'Generational Effects on Attitudes to Communist Regimes. A Comparative Analysis', *Centre for the Study of Public Policy*, Working Paper no. 234. University of Strathclyde, Scotland, 1994

L. Rosenmayr, *Die Schnüre vom Himmel. Forschung und Theorie zum Kulturellen Wandel* (Wien, Köln, Wiemar: Böhlau Verlag, 1992)

A. Ross and T. Rose, *Microphone Friends. Youth Music and Youth Culture* (London and New York: Routledge, 1994)

D. Rushkoff (ed.) *The GenX Reader* (New York: Ballantine Books, 1994)

SAPIO Research Centre, 'Human Resources, Employment and Unemployment in Bulgaria' (Sofia, 1992)

N. Sarkitov, 'From "Hard-Rock" to "Heavy Metal": The Effect of Stupidity', *Sociological Studies*, vol. 4: 93–4 (Moscow, 1987)

J. Sarsby, *Romantic Love and Society* (Harmondsworth: Penguin, 1983)

S. Sassen, *The Global City* (Princeton: Princeton University Press, 1991)

M. Schade-Poulson, 'The Power of Love: Rai Music and Youth in Algeria' in V. Amit-Talai and H. Wulff *Youth Cultures. A Cross-cultural Perspective* (London and New York: Routledge, 1995)

C. Schenk, 'Lesbians and their Emancipation in the Former German Democratic Republic: Past and Future', in N. Funk and M. Mueller (eds.) *Gender Politics and Post-Communism* (London and New York: Routledge, 1993)

H. Schneider, 'Jugendlicher Rechtsextremismus in der Bundesrepublik nach 1945', *Diskurs* 0/90 (1990), pp. 62–9

M. Schofield, *The Sexual Behaviour of Young Adults* (London: Allen Lane, 1973)

G. Schöpflin, 'Post-Communism: Constructing New Democracies in Central Europe', *International Affairs*, 67 (2) (1991)

G. Schöpflin, 'The Political Traditions in Eastern Europe', *East-East*, vol. 6, (Sofia, 1992)

A. Scull, *Decarceration. Community Treatment and the Deviant. A Radical View.* (Cambridge: Polity Press, 1977)

J. Seabrook, *Unemployment* (London: Quartet Books, 1982)

M. Semov, *The Changes in Youth* (Sofia: Centre for Sociological Studies of Youth, 1972)

M. Semov, P.-E. Mitev, P. Balkanski and P. Bozhikov (eds.), *Three 'April' Decades* (Sofia: People's Youth Press, 1986)

L. Shacklady Smith, 'Sexist Assumptions and Female Delinquency', in C. Smart and B. Smart (eds) *Women, Crime and Criminology* (London: Routledge and Kegan Paul, 1978)

S. Sharpe, *Just Like a Girl* (Harmondsworth: Penguin, 1976)

S. Sharpe, *Falling for Love. Teenage Mothers Talk* (London: Virago Upstarts, 1987)

D. Smith, *Unemployment and Racial Minorities* (London: Policy Studies Institute, 1981)

D. Smith, 'New Movements in the Sociology of Youth: a critique', *British Journal of Sociology* 32 (2) (1981), pp. 239–51

E. Smollet, 'Jar Economy. Kinship relations in Bulgaria.' *Sociologicheski Problemi*, vol. 6: 96–108 Sofia (1986)

Social Trends 16 (London: HMSO, 1986)

Social Trends 19 (London: HMSO, 1989)

Social Trends 22 (London: HMSO, 1992)

Social Trends 26 (London: HMSO, 1996)

J. Solomos, *Black Youth, Racism and the State. The Politics of Ideology and Policy* (Cambridge: Cambridge University Press, 1988)

L. Spasovska, *Generations and Family: Sociological Aspects* (Sofia: Fatherland Front Press, 1985)

J. Spence, 'Feminism in Work with Girls and Women', *Youth and Policy* 52: 1–11 (1996)

Der Spiegel 49/1992
Der Spiegel 53/1992
J. Springhall, *Youth, Empire and Society. British Youth Movements 1883–1940* (London: Croom Helm, 1977)
J. Stacey, *Brave New Families* (New York: Basic Books, 1990)
A. Stafford, *Trying Work. Gender, youth and work experience* (Edinburgh: Edinburgh University Press, 1991)
O. Stafseng, *Youth and Youth Movements towards Year 2000* (UNGforsk Rapport nr 22, Oslo 1992)
O. Stafseng, *Associated Youth in Europe* (UNGforsk Rapport No 9/94, Oslo, 1994)
G. Stanley Hall, *Adolescence. Its Psychology and Its Relation to Physiology, Anthropology, Sociology, Sex, Crime and Religion* (New York and London: D. Appleton and Company, 1907)
J. Stastna, 'Youth Cultures in the Czech Republic', unpublished reports, Prognostics Institute, Prague (1988)
Statistical Yearbook of Republic Bulgaria (Sofia: National Institute of Statistics, 1991)
Statistical Yearbook of Republic Bulgaria (Sofia: National Institute of Statistics, 1997)
G. Stedman Jones, *Outcast London. A Study in the Relationships between Classes in Victorian Society* (Oxford: Oxford University Press, 1971)
I. Stefanov (ed.) *Youth in the Orbit of Arts: Sociological Coordinates* (Sofia: Centre for Youth Studies, 1975)
I. Stefanov, 'Young People Facing Mass Communications and Arts', in P-E. Mitev, *Youth Studies. Theory, Methodology, Practice* (Sofia: People's Youth Press, 1978)
M. Stefanov, *The Student – Life Plans and Realization* (Sofia: People's Youth Press, 1983)
M. Stein and K. Carey, *Leaving Care* (Oxford: Blackwells, 1986)
K. Stojchev, 'Why are They Chasing Us?', *Youth and Society*, vol. 7/8: 30–37 (Sofia, 1989)
L. Stojkov, 'The Poles of Youth Fashion', *Youth Problems*, vol 4: 40–52 (Sofia, 1987)
R. Sviridon, 'Youth Work in Russia and Great Britain Compared', *Youth and Policy* 44 (1994), pp. 70–109
J. Svitek, 'Comment on Civic Society, the Youth and Punk in the Czechoslovakia of the 1980s', in L. Machacek (ed.) *Sociology of Youth CSFR* Slovak Academy of Sciences, Bratislava, 1990
J. Szalai', 'The Crisis of Social Policy for Youth in Hungary', *Critical Social Policy* (1983), pp. 55–64
M. Titma, 'Life Careers in a Society that is being Transformed: a Longitudinal Study of the Former Soviet Union', unpublished paper, no date 1991
V. Tonchev and L. Jordanova, *Elections 1991. Public Opinion in Bulgaria* (Sofia: LOGIS, 1991)
V. Tonchev and Z. Tamar, 'HIV/AIDS: Knowledge, Attitudes and Beliefs', *Express Information*, vol. 32 (Sofia: Institute of Youth Studies, 1989)
S. Tucker (1994) 'Changing Times, Changing Roles?', An Examination of Contemporary Youth and Community Work Practice, *Youth and Policy* 46: 5–16, 1994

UNESCO, *Statistical Yearbook*, 1992

O. Voronina, Zenschina v Muzskom Obshtestve, *Sociologicheskie Issledovania*, vol. 2:104–10 Moscow (1988)

J. Walkowitz, *Prostitution and Victorian Society. Women, Class and the State* (Cambridge: Cambridge University Press, 1980)

R. Wall, 'Leaving Home and the Process of Household Formation in Pre-Industrial England', *Continuity and Change* 2 (1) (1987) pp. 77–101

C. Wallace, 'From Generation to Generation: the Effects of Unemployment upon the Transition to Adulthood', in P. Brown and D.N. Ashton *Education and Economic Life* (Lewes: Falmer, 1986)

C. Wallace, *For Richer, For Poorer. Growing Up in and out of Work* (London: Routledge, 1987a)

C. Wallace, 'Between the Family and the State', in M. White (ed.) *The Social World of the Young Unemployed* (London: Policy Studies Institute, 1987b)

C. Wallace, 'Young People and Youth Policies in Germany', *Youth and Policy* 32, pp. 20–9 (1991)

C. Wallace, 'Young People in Rural South-west England', *Youth and Policy* 33, pp. 10–17, 1992

C. Wallace, 'Young Women', in K. Evans and W. Heinz (eds.) *Youth, Identity and Transition* (London: Anglo-German Foundation, 1994)

C. Wallace, 'Eine Westfeministin geht in den Osten', *Transit* 9: 129–45, 1995a

C. Wallace, 'Young people and families in Poland: changing times, changing dependencies?', *Journal of European Social Policy* 5 (2) : 97–109 (1995b)

C. Wallace, 'Who is for Capitalism, Who is for Communism? Attitudes towards Economic Change in Post-Communist Eastern Europe: a 10 nation comparison', Institute for Advanced Studies, Vienna. East European Series No. 44, 1997

C. Wallace, 'Crossing Borders: Mobility of Goods, Capital and People in the Central European Region', in A. Brah, M. Hickman and M. Mac an Ghaill (eds) *Future Worlds: migration and globalisation* (London: Macmillan, 1998)

C. Wallace and A. Palyanitsya, 'East-West Migration in the Czech Republic', Journal of Public *Policy*: 89–109 (1995)

C. Wallace and S. Kovacheva (1996) 'Youth Cultures and Consumption in Eastern and Western Europe', *Youth and Society* 28, (2): 189–214 (1996)

P. Watson, 'Eastern Europe's Silent Revolution: Gender' *Sociology* 27 (3) (1993), pp. 471–88

W.F. Whyte, *Street Corner Society: the Social Structure of an Italian Slum* (Chicago: University of Chicago Press, 1943)

H. Wilkinson and G. Mulgan, *Freedom's Children. Work, Relationships and Politics for 18–34 Year Olds in Britain Today* (London: Demos, 1995)

P. Willis, *Learning to Labour* (Farnborough: Saxon House, 1977)

P. Willis, 'Youth Unemployment 2. Ways of Living', *New Society* 5th April (1984), pp. 13–15.

P. Willis, *Common Culture* (Milton Keynes: Open University Press, 1990)

D. Wilson, 'Sexual Codes and Conduct', in B. Smart and C. Smart (eds) *Women, Sexuality and Social Control* (London: Routledge and Kegan Paul, 1978)

J. Wood, 'Groping Towards Sexism: Boys' Sex-Talk', in A. McRobbie and M. Nava (eds) *Gender and Generation* (London: Macmillan, 1984)

World Bank, *Bulgaria. Crisis and Transition to a Market Economy* (Vol. 11, Washington, DC, 1991)

K. Worotynska, 'Transition from School to Work in Poland', in P. Grootings and M. Stefanov (eds) *Transition from School to Work* (Sofia: Institute for Youth Studies, 1985)

J. Wrench, M. Cross and S. Barrett, 'Ethnic Minorities and the Careers Service: an Assessment of Placements', Department of Employment (1989)

J. Wrench and G. Lee, 'Young Black People and the Labour Market', in D. Smith and B. Troyna *Education, Race and the Labour Market* (Leicester: National Youth Bureau, 1983)

H. Wulff, 'Introducing Young Culture in its Own Right: the State of the Art and New Possibilities', in V. Amit-Talai and H. Wulff (eds) *Youth Cultures. A Cross-Cultural Perspective* (London and New York: Routledge, 1995)

J. Wyn and R. White, *Rethinking Youth* (London, California, New Delhi: Sage, 1997)

C.M. Young, *People Leaving Home in Australia: the Trend towards Independence* (Australian Family Formation Project Monograph No. 9. Canberra, 1987)

V.T. Yoncheva, 'Growing Village Generation', *Problems of Agriculture*, vol. 4: 12–19 (Sofia, 1943)

V. Zhechev and B. Borisov, 'The National Conflict and Its Development', *Express Information*, vol. 35:3–55 (Sofia: Institute of Youth Studies, 1990)

J. Zinnecker and L. Fuchs, *Jugend '81. Lebenswuerfe, Alltagskulturen, Zukunftsbilder* (Hamburg: Shell, 1981)

J. Zinnecker, 'What Does the Future Hold? Youth and Socio-cultural Change in the FRG', in L. Chisholm, P. Büchner, HH Krüger and P. Brown *Childhood, Youth and Social Change* (Basingstoke: Falmer, 1990)

S. Znepolski, 'Higher Education in People's Republic of Bulgaria', in *Fifteen Years of People's Education* (Sofia: Public Education, 1959), pp. 122–41

Index